Undergraduate Research in the Sciences

Engaging Students in Real Science

**Sandra Laursen
Anne-Barrie Hunter
Elaine Seymour
Heather Thiry
Ginger Melton**

Foreword by
Jim Swartz, Jim Gentile,
Mary Allen, Sheldon Wettack

JOSSEY-BASS
A Wiley Imprint
www.josseybass.com

Published by Jossey-Bass

A Wiley Imprint

989 Market Street, San Francisco, CA 94103-1741—www.josseybass.com

Jossey-Bass books and products are available through most bookstores. To contact Jossey-Bass directly call our Customer Care Department within the U.S. at 800-956-7739, outside the U.S. at 317-572-3986, or fax 317-572-4002.

Jossey-Bass also publishes its books in a variety of electronic formats. Some content that appears in print may not be available in electronic books.

Library of Congress Cataloging-in-Publication Data

Undergraduate research in the sciences : engaging students in real science / Sandra Laursen . . . [et al.] ; foreword by Jim Swartz . . . [et al].
   p. cm.
 Includes bibliographical references and index.
 ISBN 978-0-470-22757-2 (pbk.)
1. Research—Study and teaching (Higher) I. Laursen, Sandra.

  Q180.A1U48 2010
  507.1′1—dc22

                                       2010008094

Printed in the United States of America

FIRST EDITION

PB Printing   10 9 8 7 6 5 4 3 2 1

Undergraduate Research in the Sciences

The Jossey-Bass
Higher and Adult Education Series

Contents

The Authors

ETHNOGRAPHY & EVALUATION RESEARCH (E&ER) is an independent research and evaluation unit at the University of Colorado at Boulder. Our interdisciplinary team specializes in qualitative studies of education, career paths, and diversity in science, technology, engineering, and mathematics, most often at the undergraduate, graduate, and professional levels. Founded by Elaine Seymour and Nancy Hewitt, the group is currently led by Anne-Barrie Hunter and Sandra Laursen. At the university, E&ER has been affiliated with the Center to Advance Research and Teaching in the Social Sciences.

• • •

Anne-Barrie Hunter, codirector and senior professional researcher with E&ER, served as lead researcher and analyst of this eight-year study to establish and explore the benefits and costs of undergraduate research (UR). Since 1991, she has collaborated with group members to conduct qualitative research and evaluations on science, technology, engineering, and mathematics (STEM) initiatives to improve college science education, including the research study that produced *Talking About Leaving: Why Undergraduates Leave the Sciences* (Seymour & Hewitt, 1997). She has played a major role in evaluations for ChemConnections, the College Board, Project Kaleidoscope, and the Los Alamos National Laboratory internship program. More recently, she has collaborated on evaluations of several UR programs: Louisiana State University's LA-STEM Scholars program, Carleton College's off-campus Marine Biology Seminar, the University of Colorado's Biological Sciences Initiative, the Significant Opportunities in Atmospheric Research and Science program (SOARS) sponsored by the University Corporation for Atmospheric Research, and the Society of Physics Students internship program. She is also coauthor (with Seymour) of *Talking About Disability: The Education and Work Experiences of Graduates and Undergraduates with Disabilities in Science, Mathematics and Engineering* (1998), the first study of STEM students with disabilities. Current research interests include issues for women and underrepresented groups in STEM education and career pathways, faculty professional development, and organizational change and development in higher education.

· · ·

Sandra Laursen works in both research and practice in science education. As codirector and research associate with E&ER, her research interests include underrepresentation of women and minorities in the sciences, professional socialization and career development of scientists, teacher professional development, and science education reform. In addition to UR, her recent publications have addressed scientists' participation in education and outreach, STEM graduate education, and gender issues in academe. In her work as curriculum developer and outreach scientist with the Cooperative Institute for Research in Environmental Sciences, she has developed inquiry-based teaching materials and led professional development for educators and scientists on a wide range of topics in earth and physical science and inquiry-based teaching and learning. As an undergraduate at Grinnell College, her summer research efforts yielded brown gunk of high molecular weight, leading her to abandon synthetic inorganic chemistry and pursue instead a Ph.D. in physical chemistry from the University of California at Berkeley. She later taught and conducted chemistry research with undergraduates at Kalamazoo College. She has published chemistry curriculum modules and journal articles in chemistry, education, gender studies, and the *Journal of Irreproducible Results*; codirected a documentary film on scientific inquiry; and recorded a CD with Resonance Women's Chorus.

· · ·

Ginger Melton was a research associate with E&ER for several years. She worked for fourteen years as an electrical engineer before obtaining her Ph.D. in sociology from the University of Colorado at Boulder. Her area of special interest is the experiences of racial minorities and women in the sciences, mathematics, and engineering. As a researcher with E&ER, she was the lead interviewer and analyst for the evaluation of SOARS and studied the professional development of teaching assistants and of scientists involved in science education. She is currently working as a project manager for implementations of geographic information system software.

. . .

Elaine Seymour was cofounder and, for seventeen years, director of E&ER. Her best-known work, coauthored with Nancy M. Hewitt, is *Talking About Leaving: Why Undergraduates Leave the Sciences* (1997). In 2005 she and E&ER members published *Partners in Innovation: Teaching Assistants in College Science Courses*, a work drawing on several of the group's science education studies. She has been an evaluator for many initiatives focused on improving quality and access to science education and careers. In response to the learning assessment needs of classroom innovators, she designed two online resources for undergraduate faculty: the Field-Tested Learning Assessment Guide and the widely used online instrument, the Student Assessment of their Learning Gains. In 2002, in recognition of her work on women in science, she was awarded the Betty Vetter Award for Research. In retirement, she is helping to organize a national endeavor, Mobilizing STEM Education for a Sustainable Future. She is a sociologist and a British American whose education and career have been conducted on both sides of the Atlantic.

. . .

Heather Thiry is a research associate with E&ER. She has a Ph.D. in education and a background in women's studies. She has worked with E&ER since 2003 on research and evaluation studies on undergraduate research, STEM education reform and assessment, professional development, teacher education, career pathways in the sciences, and graduate education. She specializes in qualitative research and analysis, and her current research interests include gender and science and the professional socialization of doctoral students in the sciences. Her recent publications examine the needs and motivations of scientists involved with educational outreach and nontraditional career paths of doctoral students in the life sciences.

Foreword

ALL FOUR OF us had experiences as undergraduates that substantively involved us in scientific research. Those experiences made significant differences in our professional lives. We all have spent our careers at institutions that have strong traditions of undergraduate research (UR) in the sciences and believe that such experiences have positive educational value. Reviews of the literature, however, yielded scant scholarly work about what kinds of learning occur in undergraduate research. The literature revealed studies correlating undergraduate research with pursuing graduate study or careers in science and plenty of anecdotal testimonials, but it was essentially devoid of studies of learning. Based on our experiences as students, faculty members, and administrators, we believed that undergraduate research results in high-quality student learning, but we did not know that with confidence since no careful assessment had been done.

Grinnell College decided to look at this issue using funding from its National Science Foundation (NSF) Award for Integration of Research and Education (AIRE). At an AIRE project directors meeting, Jim Swartz, professor of chemistry, vice president for academic affairs, and dean of the college, and David Lopatto, professor of psychology, discussed this project and invited others to participate. Mary Allen, professor of biological sciences at Wellesley College, Jim Gentile, professor of biology and dean of the natural sciences at Hope College, and Sheldon Wettack, professor of chemistry and vice president and dean of the faculty at Harvey Mudd College, all expressed enthusiasm, and their institutions agreed to engage in a pilot project in the summer of 1999. Elaine Seymour, a sociologist from the University of Colorado at Boulder, attended that project meeting, expressed a real interest, and joined in the pilot project. Elaine and her research group, Ethnography & Evaluation Research (E&ER), had done seminal work in science education using ethnographic techniques to shed light on the issue of why excellent students leave the study of science and had helped to assess a major pedagogical development project in which one of us (J.S.) was a principal. Thus we were thrilled to partner with a group with experience and credentials to help in the assessment of student learning and whose members could offer a complement to the quantitative research that David Lopatto was starting.

That first summer, our AIRE funds were used to pay for surveys and interviews with participants in summer research projects on our campuses. During the time when we were working on the pilot project, David and Elaine submitted a proposal to the NSF in the first round of funding of the Research on Learning and Education program. The focus of the project was to address the question of what learning gains are achieved by students who engage in undergraduate research. Specifically, the grant proposal requested support to:

- Clarify the nature of authentic undergraduate research experiences—and their variations—in a sample of science disciplines from the viewpoints of participating and nonparticipating undergraduates (both as seniors and one year from graduation), faculty, and their institutions
- Identify and categorize the essential elements of good UR experiences, the learning gains (cognitive, behavioral, affective, social, and professional) that they produce over time, the conditions and processes by which these occur, and their relative significance in the achievement of outcomes that students and faculty value.

Ultimately a grant was awarded, and the project took off. Since this was a research project, we decided to start with a relatively homogeneous set of subjects—like chemists trying to use the purest reagents to study a chemical reaction. The study would examine students at liberal arts colleges who were engaged in full-time, ten-week summer research projects supervised by the faculty members at those same colleges. Our colleges were certainly not the only sites where these questions could be explored, but we knew there was much to learn on our campuses that would be of interest to us and to others—and importantly, we and our colleagues were willing to host the study. Furthermore, we were interested in the possibility that the results would help our institutions seek support from foundations and individuals to expand and enhance our UR programs. The colleges also brought the study some diversity: Wellesley is an eastern women's college; Harvey Mudd in the West focuses on science, engineering, and mathematics; and Grinnell and Hope are midwestern colleges, with Grinnell having a more national and Hope a more regional student body.

David and Elaine regularly gathered the four of us to talk about their findings, coordinate surveys and interviews, and suggest directions and questions for the project. Three of the four of us have changed jobs since this project started, but we remained committed to the project. The work described here and in Lopatto's forthcoming book, *Science in Solution*, gives the findings of this important project. The E&ER team and David Lopatto accomplished much more than we had imagined in those first informal conversations.

The results mirror much of what we, as practitioners, intuitively thought were the benefits of UR. There are, however, some surprising findings, in particular about the impact on student career choices and faculty concerns about the costs and benefits of UR. We not only learned about what students learned but also about faculty views of their work with students. Although the work started with summer research in science, engineering, and mathematics at liberal arts colleges, we believe that much of what was learned can be extrapolated to other institutional types and disciplines. There is much to learn from it about how to create fertile environments for both students and faculty members to engage in what George Kuh calls a "high-impact" educational practice. We are very happy to see this product of the work.

Jim Swartz, Grinnell College, Grinnell, Iowa
Jim Gentile, Research Corporation for the Advancement of Science, Tucson, Arizona (formerly at Hope College)
Mary Allen, Wellesley College, Wellesley, Massachusetts
Sheldon Wettack, Hope College, Holland, Michigan (formerly at Harvey Mudd College)
March 2009

Preface

EACH YEAR IN the summer and during academic terms, thousands of undergraduate science, mathematics, and engineering students participate in research in U.S. university, college, and government laboratories. Some students attend organized programs that involve them with a cohort of peers and a planned curriculum of academic, career, and social activities to support the research experience; others simply join a laboratory group at the invitation of an individual faculty member. Millions of public and private dollars are spent to provide these opportunities. Faculty and institutional leaders affirm undergraduate research as a powerful form of experiential education, and departments track the entrance of their research students into graduate programs. Many scientists recall their own undergraduate research project as a formative experience that launched them on a path to a scientific career.

Undergraduate research (UR) experiences in the sciences are thus a common practice in U.S. higher education, and their benefits to students are nearly a matter of faith. Yet until quite recently, little evidence from educational research underlay this belief. In this book, we report on evidence gathered from a decade of research on the nature and outcomes of UR as practiced in the sciences—using the latter term broadly to include the natural sciences but also mathematics, engineering, computer science, and psychology, all represented in our research. Our findings identify the benefits to students in the short and longer terms and address the extent to which these benefits are uniquely derived from research experiences. We also describe the practices of research advisors who supervise students' work and guide their development, and the inherent tensions that frame that work as faculty balance their own scholarly goals with students' educational needs. Together with recent work from other scholars and evaluators who have examined undergraduate research as an educational and scholarly practice, our studies yield a body of evidence that elucidates and supports many practitioners' long-held beliefs, challenges others, and provides a research basis to ground the development of future innovations.

While current interest in inquiry-based science education has led to broadened use of the term *undergraduate research* to include research-like activities and projects included in formal course work, this book focuses on the traditional and most intensive model of undergraduate research, where students are immersed in a multiweek, open-ended scientific project, often part of a larger, scientist-led research effort. Summer is the time when this intensive immersion is most readily, though not exclusively, accomplished. One crucial component is the relationship of the novice researcher as apprentice to an experienced scientist. As the novice learns the intellectual craft and social practice of science by doing it, she is guided by advice, help, and moral support from a more experienced colleague. Also crucial is the authentic nature of the scientific problem under study, which motivates and gives intellectual significance to the investigation, but also offers a limitless supply of teachable moments that research advisors exploit for their deep educational value. As we shall argue, the participation of a faculty research advisor as both a scholar and a teacher is a key aspect that distinguishes this apprentice model of undergraduate research from course-based forms of inquiry.

This book is aimed at all those who are interested in undergraduate research in the sciences:

- STEM faculty and other scientists, engineers, and mathematicians who work with student researchers, are considering it, or seek similar outcomes from their classroom work
- Faculty in other fields where UR is less common but who seek to understand the fundamental nature of UR so that they can adapt it to the forms of scholarly and creative work practiced in their own disciplines
- Academic administrators interested in the value added by UR to their institution's programs, the costs incurred, and the choices to be made about whether, and in what form, UR can be supported and sustained
- Program developers and facilitators who coordinate UR efforts on campuses or run UR programs for universities and laboratories
- Policymakers and program officers whose organizations promote and support UR or are interested in the broad educational and workforce issues that UR is thought to address

- Researchers and evaluators who seek to improve science education through studying or evaluating UR program outcomes or by collaborating with UR practitioners.

We have sought to elucidate the outcomes and processes of undergraduate research as practiced by science students and faculty. Most of our data come from two studies, each of which examines UR in a best-case scenario of a particular type. The four-college study examines apprentice-model UR as practiced at four liberal arts colleges with long experience of UR. The Significant Opportunities in Atmospheric Research and Science program, known as SOARS, serves as an exemplar of structured UR programs designed to recruit, retain, and support students from groups underrepresented in the science, technology, engineering, and mathematics (STEM) fields. These sites are not unique in providing the student benefits and elucidating the practices of research advisors that we document here, but as excellent examples of both faculty-led and structured UR programs, each offered an opportunity to study a well-defined and relatively homogeneous phenomenon. This research thus addresses the question, "What outcomes are possible from well-designed and well-implemented apprentice-model UR experiences, and by what means do these arise?" This is distinct from the separate, and also important, question of what outcomes actually result from the broader set of practices encompassed by all the forms of UR that have arisen in diverse institutions and settings. Given the lack of research on UR in nonscience disciplines and on all the varieties of UR and similar experiences available to students, the latter question cannot be generally answered at this time.

Chapter One establishes our definition of undergraduate research and its crucial components of authenticity and apprenticeship. It traces the history of UR in the United States and its apparent, though ill-documented, growth in recent decades. The national context for the interest in UR now is described, and the design of our research studies is outlined to illuminate the source and nature of the evidence offered throughout the book.

Chapter Two summarizes the literature that provides evidence about the outcomes of undergraduate research, in both faculty-led research efforts and structured programs, particularly those targeted to students from groups underrepresented in the STEM fields. Relatively few well-designed research and evaluation studies have been published, and most of these have appeared within the past few years. To date, the outcomes of these studies align well with each other and with our own findings.

Chapter Three describes the benefits to students of conducting research as undergraduates, based on the evidence from interviews with

UR students, alumni, and research advisors in our four-college study. These benefits are grouped into six main categories and identified in reports from students, alumni, and advisors.

Chapter Four addresses whether these benefits of UR can also be gained from other sources, including courses, based on data from interviews with a group of comparison students who did not undertake summer UR. Because these students participated in a variety of other educational experiences, we can discern alternative sources of the same benefits gained by the UR students and discuss the efficacy of these alternative sources, relative to UR, in providing the benefits.

Chapter Five discusses the longer-term outcomes of UR that are seen in longitudinal data from both UR and comparison students when interviewed as alumni, two to three years after they finished college. These outcomes emphasize the influences of UR on early career paths for alumni, and they reveal gains that were enhanced with the perspective of time as students recognized additional gains and came to value others more fully.

Chapter Six examines the use of UR in programs seeking to recruit and retain students from groups that are underrepresented in STEM fields. Because certain benefits of UR directly address the challenges minority students face, UR is often a centerpiece of such programs. Through a case study of one such program, we examine critical elements and how they build on, amplify, and augment general features of undergraduate research to address minority students' needs.

Chapter Seven discusses how UR advisors work with students, based primarily on data from interviews with faculty who were active or former UR advisors, and with program administrators. Advisors clearly identify aspects of their UR work as teaching, while also emphasizing the importance of working on unsolved problems of genuine interest in their field. Their use of authentic projects and methods with students gives rise to several distinct pedagogical strategies that are individually adjusted to foster individual students' development. This chapter emphasizes the strategies that advisors use in their everyday work with research students.

Chapter Eight examines research advisors' mentoring and career advising work. By the use of distinctive markers, they monitor and assess students' progress toward their learning objectives for students. These more global functions of advisors arise from their close daily work and observation of their research students but extend beyond it.

Chapter Nine discusses the costs and benefits to UR advisors of conducting UR as part of their faculty work. It explores what motivates and sustains faculty's UR work, what they need to sustain it, how they balance the costs and benefits of undertaking UR, and how these shape individual decisions to participate. Central to this discussion is the dual role of UR as an educational experience for students and a scholarly activity for faculty. Faculty report benefits that are largely intrinsic, but their costs are more concrete. Some difficulties are inherent in conducting research with short-term, novice assistants, while other strains arise from unresolved considerations of the place of UR in the institutional mission.

Chapter Ten summarizes key findings and makes arguments about the implications of these findings for faculty, campus leaders, funders, and researchers, including those working in diverse institutional settings. Some emergent issues and issues for future study are also highlighted.

In order to keep the main narrative readable and engaging for those who do not have prior experience with social science research methods, we have documented in a set of appendixes the methodological details for the four-college study that provides the bulk of the evidence discussed. Appendix A describes the interview samples in detail, providing break-outs by discipline, gender, and other key variables. Appendix B elaborates on the methods of the study. Appendix C summarizes the interview protocols. Appendix D provides a detailed table that includes the frequency counts for each student benefits category for all five main interview groups. These counts underlie the discussion of quantitative evidence in the student-focused chapters.

This book is not a how-to manual for those starting new UR programs or labs. For such resources, we recommend that readers consult the extensive publication list of the Council on Undergraduate Research. This research aims instead to identify the good outcomes of UR for students, elucidate how and why these outcomes arise, and clarify what factors support or constrain UR. It can thus work in tandem with the wisdom of experienced UR practitioners to guide program designers and faculty in identifying trade-offs and making choices among approaches or in creating new types of programs that aim to secure similar benefits for students. Which strategies best protect the fundamental importance of authenticity in achieving the benefits of UR for students? What methods might begin to foster the same benefits in younger students or in more constrained circumstances? How should institutions recognize and reward UR as part of faculty work? Our research does not answer these questions, but it does provide a platform of evidence on which possible answers can be devised and tried by individual advisors, programs, and institutions.

If our findings come as no surprise to readers who are personally familiar with undergraduate research as students or advisors, then that is validation that we have gotten something right. The details of how research advisors work—and, to a lesser extent, how students respond—will necessarily vary from place to place. But we are persuaded that many of the UR outcomes and processes documented here can be achieved in other institutions and through other models of UR when those settings adhere to fundamental principles that are apparent in the accounts of research advisors and research students that we share in this book.

Acknowledgments

WE HAVE MANY people to thank for their many contributions to this book. We are especially grateful to the faculty and students who shared their experiences and ideas at the four colleges that hosted this study and to the faculty, staff, and leaders who made arrangements and facilitated our work. We have valued the insights and assistance of our collaborators at these colleges: Jim Swartz and David Lopatto at Grinnell College, Jim Gentile at Hope College, Sheldon Wettack at Harvey Mudd College, and Mary Allen and Adele Wolfson at Wellesley College. From the Significant Opportunities in Atmospheric Research and Science (SOARS) program, we thank the protégés, mentors, and other study participants for their welcome and for their candid observations. Thomas Windham and Rajul Pandya were gracious, astute, and interested supporters of our SOARS work. We also thank Tom and Raj for their input into Chapter Six. We award a special gold star to Joanne Stewart for her rapid reading, critical commentary, and long-time encouragement to "get it out." S.L. thanks her former research students for their good work, scientific insights, and companionship: Luke, Stew, Jamie, Becky, Hannah, John, Mike, Jenny-Meade, Craig, James, Alice, Kwasi, and Heather.

A variety of funding agencies provided essential support for our work across its life span of nearly a decade. Initiated under a National Science Foundation (NSF) award to Grinnell College for Integration of Research and Education, the four-college study was supported by the NSF's Research on Learning and Education program under grant 0087611 and by a grant from the Howard Hughes Medical Institute. Additional data analysis and dissemination were made possible by a grant from the Spencer Foundation. The SOARS evaluation study was supported by the NSF's Division of Atmospheric Sciences, Geoscience Directorate, under grant

0401704, and by the University Corporation for Atmospheric Research. Funds for the preparation of this book were contributed by the Alfred P. Sloan Foundation, the Noyce Foundation, and Research Corporation for Science Advancement, with additional assistance from the National Science Foundation under grant 0548488, jointly supported by the Division of Chemistry, the Division of Undergraduate Education, the Biological Sciences Directorate, and the Office of Multidisciplinary Affairs.

The late John J. Coppers, Elaine's long-time partner, was a great cheerleader for our work: he stood ready to brag about E&ER's accomplishments to anyone who would listen. John was not an academic but had the knack of getting to central issues quickly. When he attended one of our early brown bag sessions on this work, he listened carefully to everything we had to say and then asked, "Why would these good people put themselves through that every summer?" We have been trying to answer his question ever since. John was particularly supportive of the UR book project during a period when funding was elusive. After several setbacks, he encouraged Elaine to persist until she put together the collaborative sponsorship that made it possible to write this book. John was often right about things that matter. We miss him.

This book truly represents a group effort. From conceiving the project and writing proposals (and still more proposals), to conducting the many interviews, transcribing them, coding, parenting, and analyzing them, every author has taken responsibility for particular tasks and done a lot of heavy lifting. At various stages, each has provided significant professional contributions in carrying out this research. A qualitative study as large as this indeed depended on a team effort. Close collaboration and cooperation throughout was essential. We thank others in our group whose efforts also helped this research: Tracee DeAntoni, Catherine Riegle-Crumb, Kris De Welde, Rebecca Crane, Liane Pedersen-Gallegos, Richard Donohue, Becky Gallegos, and our many student transcribers. Susan Lynds was our punctilious and speedy technical editor and spreadsheet wrangler; her expertise and calm were invaluable. Special thanks go to Sandra Laursen, who took charge, organized our unwieldy group, put us on a schedule, coordinated this volume, and ultimately sewed our individual ragged bits and pieces together into (we hope) a strong, coherent whole. The collegiality and friendship experienced throughout this project are in themselves immeasurable rewards. To Elaine Seymour, our fearless, indefatigable leader, we offer our deep gratitude and best wishes for her retirement.

Undergraduate Research in the Sciences

Chapter 1

What Is Undergraduate Research, and Why Does It Matter?

CONDUCTING RESEARCH IS an important culminating experience in the education of many undergraduate science students in the United States. This book describes the outcomes of undergraduate research (UR) experiences, the processes by which these outcomes are achieved, and the meaning of these outcomes for both students and the mentors who work with them on scientific research projects, based on our findings from a multi-year study of undergraduate research and its role in science education. An overarching theme in these findings is the notion of "real science," which recurs throughout the comments of undergraduate research students and their advisors. Their work together on scientific research projects provides the experiences and observations that form the backbone of this book. The importance of "real science" for students' educational and professional growth is evident in their own words:

> It's kind of scary, especially at the beginning. I was like, "How can someone like me be doing this?" [But now] I'm coming up with valuable information and it's great. I mean, actually producing data and actually doing it, I felt like a scientist. But you really feel more like a scientist when you have something good! (female UR student, biology)

. . .

> Once your superiors—whom you admire and look up to as scientists— start asking your opinion on a scientific matter. . . . Personally, it made me feel like I was actually a real physicist. (male UR alumnus, physics)

. . .

Presenting at a conference made me feel like I was a part of the scientific community. . . . I have been able to talk about my work and feel like an equal [with my advisor], and do it with other people [at my school]—but being able to do that with a total stranger was a really, really neat experience. It gave me a lot of confidence and made me feel like I was a real chemist! (female UR alumnus, chemistry)

• • •

A lot of things you do in school, like you do homework or whatever, and you never feel like you're really doing something real. And this was one of the first things that I did that, like, really encompassed everything and really brought things together. It was one of the first times I really felt like I was really doing something. (male UR student, engineering)

Clearly, being "real" is important to students. So what makes a research project "real"? As we will show, real research is an investigation whose questions, methods, and everyday ways of working are authentic to the field. The research questions are well defined so that they can be systematically investigated, but, importantly—and unlike most questions in a classroom—their answers are unknown. Research results may not be quickly forthcoming, but they constitute a genuine contribution to the field if and when they do emerge. The research methods are ones used in the discipline and seen as valid by disciplinary experts. As in any other research project, the choice of methods may be constrained by intellectual, technical, or financial resources. For an undergraduate research project, such constraints may arise from the involvement of novices and the educational mission of their institution—but the term *undergraduate research* does not inherently rule out particular approaches to the research question. Perhaps most important, as we shall see throughout this book, students and faculty work together in ways that are typical of their field and authentic to the profession. Thus, students learn the intellectual and social practices of science by doing it. By engaging deeply themselves in a particular question, they begin to understand more generally how scientists engage questions and construct knowledge, and that this is a human activity in which they too could participate.

As Merkel (2001) points out, the use of the term *undergraduate research* has not always been clear—indeed, the term *research* itself has different meanings in different disciplines and settings. The Council on Undergraduate Research (CUR, n.d) offers a broad-based definition: "An inquiry or investigation conducted by an undergraduate student that makes an original intellectual or creative contribution to the discipline" (see also

Wenzel, 2003). This language is inclusive of CUR's multidisciplinary audience, but in its lack of mention of faculty guidance or mentoring, it does not fully describe UR as typically practiced in the sciences. As we shall describe, the research advisor's role is critical in guiding students' work and inducting them into the intellectual and social ways of the profession. The way that UR advisors work with students parallels the master-apprentice relationship that is traditional in many professions, including graduate education in science.

A note is in order to clarify our choice of language. Throughout this book, we commonly use the terms *science, scientist*, and *scientific* with the intent to include psychology, mathematics, and engineering, at least with respect to UR in these fields. The acronym STEM, standing for science, technology, engineering, and mathematics, is also used, but this acronym is sometimes inelegant and comes with neither a corresponding adjective nor a term for the individuals who practice it. The studies that we discuss in the bulk of the book involve mainly students and faculty in the natural sciences, but they also include mathematicians, engineers, computer scientists, and psychologists. Our intent is to be fully inclusive while avoiding unwieldy language.

In this book, we restrict our discussion to intensive, multiweek research experiences in the sciences, mathematics, and engineering that involve student collaboration with faculty or other experienced scientists, and we refer to this as the *apprenticeship model*. Moreover, we argue that the goals and practices of apprentice-model UR are shaped and sustained by its value as both an educational activity for students and a scholarly activity for their research advisors. Because course-based inquiry is generally driven by educational concerns only, we intentionally exclude it from our definition of undergraduate research. Although course-based inquiry is important and still too uncommon in undergraduate STEM education, it should not be conflated with the apprenticeship model of undergraduate research, for reasons that we hope become apparent in this book.

Undergraduate research is widely conducted in the sciences, led by faculty at primarily undergraduate institutions (PUIs) across the United States. At research universities too, faculty whose laboratories include graduate students, postdoctoral researchers, and technicians often also host undergraduate researchers. We use the term *faculty-led UR* to refer to all such research experiences that are largely initiated and directed by faculty themselves and hosted by individual research groups, with modest or no coordination at the departmental or institutional level.

More recently, universities and government laboratories have sponsored structured research programs, sometimes with the goal of recruiting students from groups that are nationally underrepresented in fields. We call these *structured UR programs* because they often include UR along with organized training, presentation and professional development activities, and other kinds of academic and financial support. Many involve a particular cohort of students who enter the program together and participate for longer than just one summer. While some practices differ in these varied contexts and, to a lesser extent, by discipline, UR experiences in the United States appear to have in common several features:

- A well-defined research project designated to the student or a student team, connected in some way to an ongoing effort in the research group or to an area of scholarly interest of the supervising researcher
- Multiweek immersion—often full time for ten weeks during the summer, though UR may also be carried out through the academic year
- Individualized guidance from an experienced scientist

There is growing interest in earlier entry to UR, but at this time, most students participate in UR as college juniors, seniors, or rising seniors in the summer between the junior and senior years (American Society for Biochemistry and Molecular Biology, 2008; Russell, 2006).

History of Undergraduate Research

The idea that undergraduates should conduct real investigations is not new. The California Institute of Technology traces the origins of its undergraduate research program to Arthur Noyes's tenure as chemistry department chair beginning in 1920, touting an early publication by two students who later became Nobel laureates (McMillan & Pauling, 1927; Merkel, 2001). A century ago, Drinker (1912) surveyed the practice of UR at undergraduate medical colleges, one of which dated its own UR efforts to 1895. A proponent of UR, Drinker argued that medical students "have a right to gain some notion of what investigation entails," but "the doing of fixed experiments in fixed hours does not entail the exercise of investigative faculties other than those of the most mechanical nature" (p. 730).

Drinker and his survey respondents postulated outcomes of UR little different from those claimed by practitioners today: in doing research, students must bring to bear both "imagination" and "high scientific accuracy" (p. 730). Students learn "the difficulty of putting a problem on a working basis" (p. 730) and experience "an intellectual awakening" (p. 736) that is as valuable to the "practical man" as to the "laboratory man" (p. 732). Respondents presumed that doing research helped to recruit students into the profession of research, but also argued that research-derived critical thinking skills transferred to other fields. "All of us believe in its value," wrote one dean, "otherwise we would discourage it—not, I fancy, for the value of the scientific results obtained, but for its educational value on the picked men and the belief that the group of the serious workers in medical science will be recruited from this body of students" (p. 736). A follow-up report (Starr, Stokes, & West, 1919) indicated that opportunities for undergraduate research had "increased greatly since 1912" (p. 311).

In her review of the history of UR, Merkel (2001, 2003) traces the beginnings of organized UR activities at research universities to MIT's program, started in 1969 (Massachusetts Institute of Technology, 2000, n.d.). At liberal arts colleges, undergraduate research was under way, at least in chemistry departments, by the postwar science boom of the 1940s and 1950s, further spurred in the 1960s by post-*Sputnik* concerns about American competitiveness in science and technology (Bunnett, 1984; Craig, 1999; Neckers, 2000; Trzupek & Knight, 2000; see also Crampton, 2001; Hansch & Smith, 1984; Pladziewicz, 1984). Participants in a 1959 conference on teaching and research debated whether scientific research was an appropriate activity for undergraduate colleges, or instead a cost- and time-intensive distraction from faculty's main work of teaching (Spencer & Yoder, 1981). In the mid-1980s, college presidents met at Oberlin College to draw attention to the success of liberal arts colleges in producing large numbers of science majors who went on to science careers and science Ph.D.s. Prompted by findings such as Spencer and Yoder's (1981) analysis of research activity in chemistry departments at liberal arts colleges and the number of their graduates who earned Ph.D.s in chemistry, the Oberlin report lauded student-faculty collaborative research as a major contributor to strong science education at these schools (Crampton, 2001; Gavin, 2000;). Accounts of UR in this era are consistent in portraying UR as a form of faculty scholarship particular to PUIs, initiated and sustained by individual determination, scrappy grantsmanship, and grassroots networks (in addition to sources cited above, see Doyle, 2000; Mohrig & Wubbels, 1984; Pladziewicz, 1984). Faculty valued research as a means to stay scientifically up to date and connected to their discipline, and thus fresh in the classroom; obtain equipment useful in laboratory courses; and build a positive reputation for their department. They recognized UR's positive side effects for students, but had not claimed them in public until withdrawal of National Science Foundation (NSF) funding for undergraduate science education in 1981 forced them to reconsider how they might finance faculty development, course improvement, and student research activity (Mohrig & Wubbels, 1984; National Science Foundation, n.d.).

As the arguments caught on that UR was not only important as scholarship for faculty at PUIs but also high-quality science education for students, the profile of UR rose among funding agencies and professional organizations. In the mid-1980s, the NSF initiated the Research at Undergraduate Institutions program to support UR through single-investigator grants from the research directorates (Council on Undergraduate Research, 2006). This was followed by the Research Experiences for Undergraduates (REU) program, now in its third decade, which supplies site grants to support undergraduates to work on research (National Science Foundation, n.d.). (Both programs were predated by NSF's Undergraduate Research Program, which made awards between 1971 and 1981.) The Howard Hughes Medical Institute began to award undergraduate science education grants that often supported UR programs, and the American Chemical Society's Petroleum Research Fund, the Camille and Henry Dreyfus Foundation, and Research Corporation all offered research grant programs with tracks targeted to faculty working primarily with undergraduates. CUR was founded by chemists in 1978 as an organization to promote and support student research in PUIs. The National Conference on Undergraduate Research began in 1987 to provide an opportunity for student researchers to present their work, and disciplinary professional societies began to include poster sessions for undergraduate research student presenters as part of their conference programs.

In the 1990s, national reports such as the Boyer Commission report (1998) cited UR as a practice that could contribute to improving undergraduate science education, move students from didactic to inquiry-based learning experiences, and reduce the dichotomy between teaching and research (see Katkin, 2003; Merkel, 2001, 2003). The 1990s also marked the accelerated development of programs to recruit and retain students from underrepresented groups, which often incorporated undergraduate research. If the early decades were the years for grassroots growth of UR, the 1980s the decade of its professionalization among faculty, and the 1990s the decade of recognition by policymakers of UR as an educational practice, then the 2000s appear to begin the era of evaluation and research. After "decades of blind faith" in the benefits of UR (Mervis, 2001a), researchers and evaluators have begun to identify its outcomes, assess their prevalence, and examine how they come about. We review these studies in detail in Chapter Two.

Current National Context for Undergraduate Research

In this book, we examine UR at the local level as an educational experience for students and as an educational and scholarly activity of faculty and departments. However, this local practice takes place in a national context of high interest in UR as an educational strategy, influenced by the traditional role of the research apprenticeship in scientists' education and by growing interest in students' development of thinking skills important for public science literacy.

Scientists, educators, and government and industry leaders have raised concerns over the supply and quality of STEM-trained workers needed to maintain American technological and economic leadership in a globally competitive economy (for a recent high-profile report, see National Research Council, 2007; for a summary of such reports, see Project Kaleidoscope, 2006). Since 1980, the number of nonacademic science and engineering jobs has grown at more than four times the rate of the U.S. labor force as a whole (National Science Board, 2008). Increasing the diversity of the science workforce is another "urgent need," given changing demographics, decreasing numbers of foreign citizens entering the U.S. STEM workforce, and growing international competition for scientific and engineering talent (Committee on Equal Opportunities, 2004). Equally important, concerns for equity and justice demand that all Americans have equal opportunities to enter the high-status, well-paid positions typically offered by science and engineering careers. Economic competitiveness too depends on a diverse workforce, because diversity fosters greater innovation and problem solving (Chubin & Malcom, 2008; Page, 2007). However, at higher levels of STEM education in many fields, the proportion of both women and people of color declines sharply—the so-called leaky pipeline—and progress in bringing their representation up to match the general population has been slow (National Science Foundation, 2007b). Thus, availability and access to high-quality STEM education remain critical for meeting U.S. workforce needs and providing equal opportunity for all citizens.

While multiple solutions to these pressing problems lie throughout the spectrum of K–12 and higher education, many calls for reform have focused on making undergraduate STEM education more practical, relevant, engaging, and grounded in research on how people learn (Bransford,

Brown, & Cocking, 1999; Handelsman et al., 2004; Project Kaleidoscope, 2006; Seymour, 2002; Wieman, 2007). For example, the American Association of Colleges and Universities has called for higher education institutions to foster more "empowered, informed, and responsible learners" (Greater Expectations National Panel, 2002). The Boyer Commission (1998) urged that research-based learning become the standard in undergraduate education, particularly at research universities. National bodies have called for increased opportunities for student-centered, inquiry-based learning, including undergraduate research, in the STEM disciplines (Kuh, 2008; National Research Council, 1999; National Science Foundation, 1996). Many faculty and institutions are exploring the addition of "research-like" components to regular courses and labs (see DeHaan, 2005). Although different wording is often used, these efforts in undergraduate STEM education parallel efforts in K–12 education to incorporate scientific inquiry as both a strategy for teaching scientific concepts and an element of the curriculum. The aim is for students to develop not only conceptual understanding of the big ideas of science, but also the abilities to conduct an investigation and the understandings of science as a human process of constructing scientific knowledge (National Research Council, 1996; see also Laursen, 2006).

Undergraduate research is relevant to these national concerns because it is commonly believed to be "invaluable" for "engaging, training and inspiring undergraduates (many from underrepresented groups) to pursue higher . . . degrees" (National Science Foundation, 2007a, p. 10) and to have "central importance" in "preparing scientists" (American Society for Biochemistry and Molecular Biology, 2008, p. 19). UR may be seen as one end of a spectrum of educational strategies that engage students, both a model for and a culmination of classroom-based inquiry (see, for example, Healey & Jenkins, 2009; Karukstis & Elgren, 2007). But there are substantial barriers to pedagogical change in undergraduate teaching, including the high autonomy of college instructors, their primary allegiance to their discipline, student and collegial resistance, and institutional barriers to research-based pedagogical reforms (Boyer Commission, 2002; DeHaan, 2005; Henderson, 2005; Henderson & Dancy, 2008; Kuh, 2008; Seymour, 2007; Walczyk, Ramsay, & Zha, 2007; Wieman, 2007). Thus, UR may be seen by funders, institutional leaders, and faculty developers as a path of lesser resistance to change in undergraduate STEM education than is classroom-focused reform. Indeed, a recent survey of members of a discipline-based scientific society, the American Society for Biochemistry and Molecular Biology (2008), highlights the seeming paradox that although faculty placed high value on "undergraduate research and integrative thinking" (p. 3), their classroom pedagogy was "not reflective of research on student learning" (p. 5)—fully 80 percent of their classes, at all levels, emphasized lecture. Thus, for all these reasons, undergraduate research is often viewed as a solution to national STEM education problems.

Scope of Undergraduate Research

If UR is in fact to aid in solving any of these problems, the numbers of students who participate will have to be substantial. However, that number is difficult to determine. In a survey by SRI International of thirty-four hundred students who received STEM bachelor's degrees between 1998 and 2003, just over half of respondents said they had participated in UR (Russell, 2005). The Boyer Commission (2002) offers the lower estimate that one-fifth of science and engineering students at research universities engage in UR. Results of the National Survey of Student Engagement indicate that 19 percent of all undergraduates participate in research with faculty (Kuh, 2008), including 39 percent of those with majors in the biological and physical sciences (American Council of Learned Societies, 2007). While Kuh's (2008) averages across broad institutional types and student characteristics vary surprisingly little, the participation rate is in fact quite variable from one school to another—higher at many smaller schools where faculty lead UR for their own students and lower where no on-campus opportunities are available. Wood (2003) cites 45 percent participation in UR for his biology department at the University of Colorado, while Merkel (2001) cites figures for student participation in UR of 80 percent at MIT, 60 percent at CalTech, and 22 percent for the University of Washington. Figures like these illustrate how departmental and institutional differences affect students' access to UR, even at schools that have established or are moving toward a "culture of undergraduate research," in Merkel's words. Most institutions do not systematically gather these data for themselves (Katkin, 2003). Participation also varies strongly by discipline; STEM graduates in the SRI survey reported participation rates near 30 percent for mathematics and computer science and up to over 70 percent for chemistry and environmental sciences (Russell, 2005).

These variable participation rates are one reason that it is difficult to tally the total numbers of UR participants. Russell (2006) has estimated that the NSF may support some fourteen thousand students per year, but Merkel (2001) reported thirty-two thousand students supported by NSF REU programs alone in fiscal year 2001. (We requested data from NSF on undergraduate research participation but were unable to obtain either agency-wide or individual division data from those contacted.) Whatever the numbers, it is likely that the number of UR opportunities is not enough to accommodate all students who seek the opportunity. A 2004 study reported that the NSF REU program in chemistry, which then supported about 650 students each year, could accommodate fewer than one in four students who apply (Henry, 2005).

Financial investment in UR by public and private foundations is substantial and supports students through both targeted UR programs and grants to individual investigators at PUIs. Again, numbers indicating the magnitude of this investment are difficult to come by. Academic Excellence, a study of undergraduate research at 136 PUIs, reported a ten-year total (1991–2000) of $682 million in funding for research and research instrumentation at these colleges, with 74 percent coming from federal and state government sources (Research Corporation, 2001). From the cost side, and taking the perspective that the faculty is an institution's primary investment, Gentile (2001) has estimated the projected investment in a faculty member over a thirty-year academic lifetime to be $4 million, including both research- and teaching-related costs. His worksheet enables this figure to be computed for a particular local setting. From a student perspective, funding for NSF REU awards in chemistry for 2009 averaged $10,000 per summer UR student, covering both direct student support and associated program costs (Colon, 2009).

Without good data about the participation level of students and faculty, the resources committed, or their cumulative impact, it is difficult to state whether the prevalence of UR is growing, shrinking, or staying the same. However, most sources agree that UR is on a rising trajectory. The SRI study (Russell, 2005) noted that participation rates in UR had increased from 48 percent among 1988–1992 STEM graduates to 56 percent for 1998–2003 graduates; concurrently, the proportion of respondents who said it had not occurred to them to participate in research declined from 24 percent to 15 percent. The Academic Excellence study found that the number of students engaged in summer research at the 136 PUIs in this study increased by 65 percent in the decade 1991 to 2000 (Research Corporation, 2001). In a follow-up study to the Boyer Report, Katkin (2003) reported that research universities had taken many steps to expand UR opportunities and raise the visibility of UR, often establishing centralized offices to support UR and advertise it to students, promote it in departments, and raise funds. Katkin's data also showed increases in the number and percentage of participating students and the number of faculty UR supervisors. However, the lack of systematic data collection by institutions is a problem: as Kenny (2003) points out, "A lot may be happening, but no one is charged with keeping score" (p. 105).

Several indicators reflect growing interest in UR by funding agencies. For example, NSF's Division of Chemistry has experimented with undergraduate research centers to explore novel forms of UR that might engage students at an earlier stage or from previously untapped populations, including UR at two-year colleges and curricular forms of research activity (*Exploring the Concept*, 2003). The National Aeronautics and Space Administration and NSF have supported "extreme research" opportunities for students, such as the chance to conduct engineering experiments in the weightless environment of the "Vomit Comet" research aircraft, use international telescopes at distant observatories, or make geoscience field observations from oceangoing research vessels, Iceland, or the South Pole (Service, 2002). Several private foundations that support undergraduate research signaled their interest in UR by commissioning the *Academic Excellence* study to address their concerns about declining research proposal pressure from these PUIs (Lichter, 2000; Mervis, 2001b; Research Corporation, 2001). Despite the foundations' observations, the study found that overall, the sciences were healthy at these schools, which educate a disproportionate share of the nation's scientific workforce. Research-related grant dollars awarded to these schools had increased, as had colleges' investment in faculty start-up funds and capital facilities for science (Abraham, 2001).

Another indicator of growing interest in UR is a proliferation of how-to resources that seek to help those initiating UR at an ever-widening group of institutions. The *CUR Quarterly* and the *Journal of Chemical Education* offer long-running article series. Books by Merkel and Baker (2002) and by Handelsman and colleagues (2005) offer advice on mentoring UR students (see also Pfund, Pribbenow, Branchaw, Lauffer, & Handelsman, 2006), while Hakim (2000) discusses the institutional development and implementation of UR programs. CUR recently compiled a compendium of practices to develop and sustain a "research-supportive curriculum" (Karukstis & Elgren, 2007). Kinkead (2003) has reviewed resources on UR programs and inquiry-based teaching approaches that support them. Gaglione (2005) and Brown (2006) offer advice to two-year college faculty on starting a UR program, and Ball and coauthors (2004) do the same for those at comprehensive institutions (see also Husic, 2003). While interest is growing in UR and other forms of scholarly and creative activity in disciplines beyond STEM (Karukstis & Elgren, 2007; Katkin, 2003; Merkel, 2003), most non-STEM fields do not yet have well-established UR traditions. Similarly, international interest in UR is growing in countries that do not currently have a UR tradition.

The niche of how-to resources for students is also increasingly occupied. WebGURU is an online clearinghouse for students with practical information on how to seek an undergraduate research position and what to do once they get one. At its Web site, CUR maintains a list of the growing number of online undergraduate research journals, which provide opportunities for students to publish their work and learn the skills of professional writing and peer review (Netwatch, 1998).

Finally, there is grassroots evidence that UR is gaining popularity among students. Some campuses document rising participation in UR by their own students (see, for example, Bhushan, 2007; Biggs, 2006; Singngam, 2007). Katkin (2003) observes an increase in the number and visibility of centralized UR offices on campuses to serve growing student demand. These offices typically advertise research opportunities to enrolled students and facilitate students' matchup with advisors, projects, and funding. As part of its much-publicized annual college rankings used by prospective students and families planning for college, *U.S. News and World Report* spotlights schools with strong undergraduate research programs. The growing popularity of UR is even captured in pop culture. As of early 2010, over fifteen hundred YouTube videos bore the tag "undergraduate research." These online videos enable students to share their UR experiences and institutions to market UR to prospective students as a distinctive educational experience.

Together these indicators suggest that interest in UR is increasing among many stakeholders. This trend is positive insofar as it leads to opportunities to provide the educational and professional benefits of UR to larger numbers of more diverse students and encourages faculty to integrate their teaching and research work, as some have argued (see Prince, Felder, & Brent, 2007, for a thorough review of this literature). However, this trend can also have negative impacts, introducing new political and financial pressures for institutions that have not considered research part of their educational mission (Husic, 2003) and placing additional strain on individual faculty who may already be stretched to their limits with teaching, service, and other scholarly work (Tobochnik, 2001), as we discuss in Chapter Nine.

Studying UR: The Nature of the Evidence Presented

The high participation and investment in UR signify widespread belief in the value of UR for students' educational and career development. However, only recently have researchers and evaluators begun to establish an evidence-based understanding of the character and range of benefits to students, faculty, or institutions that are generated by different types of UR experiences. Traditional institutional outcome measures, such as the fraction of UR students who later pursue a Ph.D. in science, do not reflect the potential value of UR as an educational and personal growth experience for students. Although such data are widely cited, few data exist to justify any causal connection between UR and career outcomes. This lack of knowledge about the educational outcomes of UR, and their meaning for students, faculty, and institutions, was the impetus for our work.

The findings presented in this book are based on two studies that together involved nearly six hundred interviews, conducted over five years, with students, their research advisors, other mentors, UR program directors, administrators, and staff. Most of the chapters are based on data from a large interview study, comprising over 360 interviews, of faculty-led summer UR as conducted at four colleges (thus, "the four-college study"). That study was developed to examine fundamental research questions about the nature of UR and its role in undergraduate science education:

- What are the benefits to students of conducting UR—both immediate and longer term, and as viewed by both students and their research advisors?
- What, if anything, is lost by students who do not participate in UR?
- What are the processes by which gains to students are generated?
- What are the benefits and costs to faculty from their own engagement as UR advisors?

In addition to the four-college study, we draw on findings from a program evaluation of a structured summer UR program that was conducted at a research laboratory for students from groups underrepresented in the sciences. Although that study evaluated a particular program to provide feedback to its developers, it serves here as a case exemplar of structured programs targeted to minority students. That study, based on over two hundred interviews, is the focus of Chapter Six. We also draw on findings from evaluation studies of structured UR programs at two research universities (Hunter, Thiry, & Crane, 2009; Thiry & Laursen, 2009).

In this section, we describe the design of the four-college study and the process by which data were gathered and analyzed, so that readers will understand the nature of the evidence presented. Further details of the study methods and interview samples are given in Appendixes A, B, and C. Our group's other studies that are mentioned were also interview studies that followed similar methods to those described.

Selecting a Model of UR: The Study Sites

We chose to study UR in a best-case scenario represented by the summer apprenticeship model. Our sites were four undergraduate liberal arts colleges: Grinnell College (Iowa), Harvey Mudd College (California), Hope College (Michigan), and Wellesley College (Massachusetts). Because these schools do not have graduate programs in the sciences, their faculty have uniformly committed to teaching and mentoring undergraduates. Many departments had a long tradition of summer UR and hired science faculty with the expectation that they would involve students in scholarly work. Full-time summer UR work was the model chosen for study because it is a common and widely practiced model, less variable in structure and implementation than academic-year UR activities, and because this intensive form was expected to provide the strongest and most distinctive benefits to students that might most easily be attributed to UR or other educational experiences. These choices do not mean that our findings apply only to these settings; on the contrary, we have evidence that well-implemented UR in other forms can achieve the same results. However, the relatively homogeneous model of summer UR at these colleges enabled us to define with clarity the phenomenon under study and to attribute student outcomes to that phenomenon. Thus, this study addresses the question of what is possible from well-designed, well-implemented, apprentice-model UR. Studies examining other research questions—including the outcomes of other UR models, comparison of outcomes across different UR models, and characterization of the wide range of activities that have been labeled "undergraduate research"—are still needed.

Our four-college interview samples included essentially all rising seniors who were participating in UR in summer 2000 and their faculty research advisors; a few were visiting students from other campuses. Comparison samples were developed of nonparticipating faculty and of nonparticipating student majors from the same class year as the UR students. As we discovered, colleges did not often track UR participation, and departments often did not know that students they had identified as not participating in UR had in fact pursued UR opportunities off campus.

Although the number and organization of departments varied across these campuses, all STEM departments that had summer UR students were included. The study thus spans the natural sciences and includes psychology, mathematics, computer science, and engineering in schools where these majors were offered and faculty in these disciplines also conducted UR. We make no claims about the applicability of specific findings beyond these fields, although we believe that our general emphasis on authenticity offers lessons relevant to other disciplines. The largest numbers of interviewees came from biology and chemistry, and smaller numbers from physics, mathematics, computer science, psychology, and engineering.

Gathering Multiple Perspectives on UR: The Study Samples

The four-college study examined UR from the distinctive perspectives of several groups: students who conducted research and students who did not, faculty advisors of UR and faculty who did not participate, and some administrators whose roles included institutional oversight of UR. The seventy-six UR students were science majors who as rising seniors—about to enter their senior year—participated in summer research in their discipline. Students from this group were interviewed three times: near the end or soon after the summer UR experience, at the end of their senior year, and about two years after graduation. These interim interviews with UR students did not produce notably different findings from the first interviews and are not discussed in any detail in this book.

A group of sixty-two comparison students was interviewed to investigate whether the gains from UR were unique or could be achieved through other educational experiences. This group came from the same departments and the same graduating class as the UR student sample, but included students who were not participating in UR in summer 2000 for a variety of reasons: some chose not to pursue UR, some applied but did not get a summer UR position on their campus, and some undertook other forms of UR as seniors during the regular academic year. These students were interviewed twice: at the end of their senior year, in order to allow for gains, if any, to emerge from their entire undergraduate experience; and again about two years later. These students pursued a variety of internships, work, senior theses, and off-campus UR, in addition to the classroom and campus experiences they shared with the UR students. Thus they cannot be viewed as an idealized control group—which is seldom available in any educational research. Rather, they serve as a comparison group whose range of experiences realistically reflects the rich array of undergraduate experiences that science students may undertake and to which UR may be compared. As we discuss in the chapters, we can detect but not control for incoming differences in these students' goals and interests, as well as in their outcomes. For both UR students and comparison students, the numbers of interviewees in the later rounds declined, as not all alumni could be reached or chose to participate.

To hear the faculty perspective, we interviewed a group of fifty-five faculty who were the research advisors of the UR students we interviewed. Their comments collectively reflect their many years of research experience with students. In addition, we interviewed thirteen faculty who had previously led UR but had temporarily or permanently discontinued their work with student researchers. Like the UR-active faculty, they provided an experienced perspective on UR and offered additional commentary on their reasons for discontinuing UR work. Interviews with twelve administrators—department chairs, deans, provosts, and UR program directors, all of whom also were or had been active UR advisors—provided information on UR in a broader institutional context.

In each chapter, we note the interview groups that offered the evidence we present. We consistently use the following terminology: *UR student* refers to a participant in the first interviews with student researchers and *comparison student* to a participant in the first interviews with the comparison group. Where relevant, observations made by comparison students are also identified according to their other educational experiences, such as internships or courses. *UR alumni* and *comparison alumni* refer to individuals from the two student samples interviewed again two to three years after their college graduation. *Research advisors* are all faculty and administrators, active or inactive, who had supervised UR students. We use this term when referring to their UR role, and the term *faculty* when discussing their other functions within their colleges, such as teaching and collegial interactions. Our choice of the term *advisor* is deliberately inclusive: at these four colleges, research advisors were faculty, but UR conducted at universities may involve advisors who are graduate students and postdoctoral researchers; at nonacademic laboratories, advisors may be working research scientists. The term thus emphasizes the functions of UR advisors, not their job title. Full details of the four-college interview samples and their makeup by gender, discipline, and other variables are provided in Appendix A.

Working with Evidence from Interviews: The Study Methods

To address our major research question about the benefits of UR to students, we began by gathering published studies and descriptive accounts of UR and built from these a checklist of possible benefits to students. These covered a range of possible changes in knowledge, skills, behaviors, and attitudes: scientific knowledge in and beyond their discipline; understanding of the process of science; growth in practical, intellectual, and teamwork skills; changes in confidence and attitude; career preparation; career choice; and others. An earlier report (Seymour, Hunter, Laursen, & DeAntoni, 2004) includes our analysis of this literature.

We then used this checklist (Appendix C) in our interviews, querying students about these possible gains as areas where "faculty think students may gain from doing undergraduate research." Interviews with UR students tended to focus on the UR experience itself, but we checked with students about whether the gains they described came from UR or other sources. Similar language, without reference to research, was used to probe the same gains among comparison students, whose accounts of the sources of particular gains are discerning and informative (Chapter Four).

In responding to the gains checklist—or in spontaneous narratives elsewhere in the interview—students described benefits they made, did not make, or made to some extent. Beginning with the UR student interviews, we coded the interview transcripts for these gains (and for other concepts) in detail, including gains that matched the checklist as well as additional gains that students raised. Coding interview data is a painstaking process: the coder reads the written transcript, tagging each separate idea raised with a code. When the same idea is raised again in a later comment or by another person, the same tag is reused; as new ideas are raised, each is given a distinct code. Each code may tag one or several distinct observations. Codes also record whether the gain was positive, negative, or mixed: gained, not gained, or partially gained. When the coding is complete, the set of codes or tags—known as the codebook—reflects the overall content of the data set. The codes are then sorted and categorized under broader labels, called *parent codes*, and the analyst searches for patterns in these parent codes, the frequency with which they are used, and linkages between codes and speakers, such as by gender or role. Some patterns may be noticed and explained by interviewees themselves, while others emerge from the data and are discerned by the analyst without interviewees' explicit awareness.

We sometimes liken the analysis process to disassembling necklaces and organizing the loose beads. In this analogy, each interview is a necklace, a string of many individual observations by a speaker. Coding labels each bead in detail: a round red plastic bead, a shiny yellow oblong bead. Analysis thus resembles sorting beads into jars: red or yellow, shiny or not; beads from short necklaces or long ones. Using powerful text analysis software packages to stand in for jars, codes can be sorted simultaneously across multiple dimensions.

We can then describe the jars—the codes, parents, and broader domains that together constitute the qualitative content of the interviews. We can also count the beads in each jar or set of jars. Counting observations is one way to estimate the relative weight of opinion about a set of topics or identify differences in the weight of opinion among different interview groups. We count conservatively to avoid overrepresenting any views, such as when a single speaker makes the same point several times. Most often, we report the number of observations, which far exceeds the number of people, as each person may make multiple comments on any given topic. Sometimes we report the number of speakers to indicate the occurrence of a particular phenomenon or view. These frequency counts are often informative, but interview data cannot be treated by statistical techniques as can responses to standardized survey items. Throughout this book, we refer to frequency counts in discussing the relative importance of ideas, but we remain mindful of the advice apocryphally posted on Einstein's office wall: "Not everything that can be counted counts, and not everything that counts can be counted." (We thank Richard Donohue for pointing out the appropriateness of this quotation to our work.) Appendix B includes a detailed discussion of our coding and analysis methods, including treatment of the frequency counts.

Trusting the Evidence: Validity and Reliability

We are often asked how we know that our data can be "trusted." In interview studies, as in all good scientific work, this depends on both gathering good evidence and interpreting it with an open and skeptical mind. First, our interviewees had little reason to dissemble to us as external researchers. Indeed, we were often struck by the candor and emotion with which they spoke, discussing failures or conflicts as well as successes and rewards. Speakers participated voluntarily and gave informed consent; their anonymity and confidentiality were protected by the ethical and professional standards of our field and formalized by human subjects research review. Thus, speakers could know that personal information would not be shared. We were careful to phrase questions neutrally so as not to lead respondents to an answer, for example, asking about "what gains you did or did not make." By conducting interviews with essentially all summer student researchers, their advisors, and nearly all nonparticipants we could identify in the same departments, we avoided biasing our samples.

We also built checks and balances into our data analysis. That the same ideas emerged over and over from so many separate interviews, where collusion was impossible, is one powerful indicator of their validity. Research team members continually discussed the work, reviewing the coding to define and refine categories and ensure that we agreed in how we coded similar information, and arguing about the meaning of our observations. Triangulation, or comparing different sources of information, such as from students and advisors, helped to refine the analytical themes and detect similarities and differences in perspective. When interviewing alumni, we conducted "member checks" to validate our findings by sharing them with alumni who could then agree, disagree, or offer commentary. Our multidisciplinary research team brought a variety of personal and professional perspectives to the project, including for one of us (Laursen) experiences as both a UR student and a faculty advisor of UR. While we distinguish evidence from interpretation as we do the work itself, for readability we have presented our findings in a form that does not sharply distinguish them.

Drawing Conclusions: Limitations and Strengths of the Four-College Study

The study examines UR as practiced at four highly ranked liberal arts colleges. These colleges attract a very capable student body that is largely middle class, white, and academically well prepared. The faculty are teaching oriented; they conduct research with students as a primary scholarly and educational activity, not as a satellite of graduate-level research. These choices allowed us to define a particular model of UR whose outcomes could be investigated and examine some local variations of that model. However, they also place some constraints on the extent to which the findings may be generalized to other forms of UR and other settings, and they leave some questions unanswered.

However, this choice does not mean that the findings are idiosyncratic. This study is very large for a qualitative study; the data were gathered from many research groups in several departments on four campuses. While some features of the organizational and cultural context of these sites are likely particular to liberal arts colleges, we shall argue that many of our findings are not particular to these settings. We offer evidence that both student outcomes and research advisors' strategies for working with UR students are not unique to these settings, and we have seen both in research universities and national labs. We also see little evidence of significant variations in student outcomes or advisor strategies by discipline. In several chapters, we discuss the extent to which the findings presented may be generalizable, and we return to this point in the concluding chapter.

Overview of This Book

This book is aimed at all those who are interested in UR in the sciences, including faculty who lead research groups with undergraduates, faculty and program developers interested in adapting the lessons learned from UR in science to other fields, academic administrators, policymakers, program officers, researchers, and evaluators. Research findings like these establish a knowledge base and begin to define effective practices from which variations and innovations can be created to achieve the same good outcomes in other ways.

Chapter Two provides a review of the literature on UR, comparing findings from published research and evaluation studies that provide evidence about the outcomes of both faculty-led research and structured UR programs. The body of the book is organized into two large sections: Chapters Three through Six focus on the student outcomes of UR, and Chapters Seven through Nine offer insight into the processes by which these outcomes are achieved and sustained, largely from a faculty perspective.

Chapter Three is the linchpin of the student section, as it defines the benefits to students of conducting research and provides a student perspective on how these gains arise. This discussion is extended in Chapter Four to consider how and whether these same benefits can also be gained from other college experiences, and in Chapter Five to elucidate the longer-lasting impacts of UR on students' postcollege work and educational paths. Chapter Six addresses the case of structured UR programs targeted to the recruitment and retention of students underrepresented in the sciences.

The perspective of research advisors is critical for understanding how student outcomes come about. Chapter Seven describes research advisors' everyday work with students as they make use of authentic problems to achieve the student outcomes that they desire. Chapter Eight takes a more global look at how advisors mentor students and assess their progress. And Chapter Nine examines research advisors' work within their institutional context, identifying the costs and benefits of their UR work and examining how advisors balance these in pursuing their own scholarly work while also attending to students' educational growth and professional development.

The concluding chapter revisits key findings and reflects on their implications for practitioners, leaders, and funders. The appendixes set out methodological details that provide transparency about the evidence we discuss without weighing down the narrative, and that may be useful to other researchers. Appendix A describes the interview samples in detail, Appendix B elaborates on the methods of the study, and Appendix C summarizes the interview protocols. The detailed table in Appendix D includes the frequency counts for each student benefits category, for all five main interview groups, to provide supporting detail for the quantitative evidence presented in each chapter.

Chapter 2

What Is Known About the Student Outcomes of Undergraduate Research?

A NUMBER OF research and evaluation studies document student outcomes from undergraduate research (UR) experiences. Following a comprehensive, initial literature review (Seymour, Hunter, Laursen, & DeAntoni, 2004), we provide a summary and update on what is known about the benefits of this experience for students. We assess reported gains to students across the set of studies and survey the outcomes of programs targeting the recruitment and retention in science, technology, engineering, and mathematics (STEM) of students from underrepresented groups. Many other aspects of UR discussed in this book are not documented elsewhere in the literature.

We identify three major strands of literature relevant to student outcomes of UR: one focusing on general types of UR programs and how these contribute to students' education; one focusing on structured programs targeting students from underrepresented groups; and one investigating ties between theory and practice and offering explanations for documented outcomes. Following a brief overview of the literature, we discuss each of these strands and their contributions.

Overview of the Literature on UR

Until recently, the empirical bases of the literature on UR claiming benefits were largely lacking (Seymour et al., 2004). Most commonly, descriptive articles have detailed particular faculty-developed, institutional, or multi-institution programs in which accounts of evaluation methods were missing, incomplete, or problematic. Promotional and discussion pieces described the perceived merits of undergraduate research, either in general or for particular models of activity, but offered no supporting evidence. Reviews and histories of UR often contained limited or no reference to evaluation. Of the few available program evaluations, some used methods that were incompletely documented, problematic, or lacking comparison groups. In the end, we found only a handful of research and evaluation studies that met accepted methodological standards, provided complete descriptions of research methods and design, and supported their claims for benefits.

Although belief is widespread in the value of undergraduate research for students' education and career development, only recently have research and evaluation studies produced empirical evidence that begins to throw light on the benefits to students, faculty, or institutions generated by UR opportunities. Other recent studies have begun to document the effects of UR experiences on retention, persistence, and promotion of science career pathways, particularly for students from racial and ethnic groups that are underrepresented in the pool of STEM students relative to their representation in the general U.S. population. These include primarily African Americans, Hispanic Americans, Native Americans, first-generation college students, and, in some fields, white and Asian American women.

The evidence on the benefits of UR comes from two sources: research studies and evaluations. Research studies on UR seek to answer general questions about its effects and may explore links between theory and practice. Evaluations assess specific program outcomes and how these align with the program's stated objectives. Often the two are combined, when some program-specific questions are also of general interest, and this is the case with several of the studies reviewed here. These different perspectives offer an array of findings on the benefits of UR and some insight into how these are achieved.

Table 2.1 itemizes all the gains documented in well-designed, well-supported research and evaluation studies of UR and synthesizes what researchers collectively have found as benefits of UR. The benefits categories follow our qualitative findings on student benefits (Hunter, Laursen & Seymour, 2007; Seymour et al., 2004), which are fully described in Chapter Three. These categories reflect six major types of benefits from UR experience: personal/professional gains, intellectual gains, gains in professional socialization, gains in skills, enhanced preparation for graduate school and work, and career clarification and confirmation.

Undergraduate research takes place in a variety of contexts, with students who vary in age, developmental stage, and background. While the research and evaluation studies reviewed here investigate UR based on

TABLE 2.1

Comparison of Findings on Student Benefits from UR from Published Research and Evaluation Studies

Type of student gain	British University	Studies Conducted at Research Institutions															Multi-Institution Studies								Laboratory	Totals
	1	2	3	4	5	6	7	8	9	10	11	12	13	14	15	16	17	18	19	20	21	22	23	24	25	
Includes findings on students from under-represented groups				*	*	*	*		*		*					*							*	*	*	
Personal/ professional gains																										
Increased confidence			S,F	S		S	S		S	S	S,F	S−	S					S	S	S+,F		S			U	14
Establishing collegial relationships with advisors			S,F		S	S					S	S	S	F		S			S	S,F			U		U	13
Establishing collegial relationships with peers			S,F		S	S					S							S	S	S,F					U+	8
Seeing that scientists are real people	S				S															S,F						3
Feeling like a scientist																					S,F				U	2
Thinking and working like a scientist																										
Deepened knowledge in field; making conceptual connections			S	S+,F−	S			S+,F−			F		S+				S,F−	S	S	S,F			U			10

(Continued)

TABLE 2.1 (Continued)

Type of student gain	British University	Studies Conducted at Research Institutions														Multi-Institution Studies									Laboratory	Totals
	1	2	3	4	5	6	7	8	9	10	11	12	13	14	15	16	17	18	19	20	21	22	23	24	25	
Appreciating relevance of course work					S						S								S	S,F−					U	5
Improved critical thinking and problem solving; ability to analyze and interpret results					S			S+,F+					S+	F+	S+		S	S		S,F					U	9
Understanding research through hands-on experience	S		S,F		S			S+,F+			S				S+		S,F	S+	S+	S+,F+		S	U		U	13
Understanding how to pose and investigate research questions		S						S−,F−												S,F−		S				4
Understanding how knowledge is constructed	S									S		S−						S	S	S,F		S				7
Becoming a scientist																										
Working independently			S					S+,F+				S	S	F	S+		S,F	S	S	S,F						10
Approaching problems creatively, thinking synthetically												S		F				S	S	S,F						5

Outcome								
Increased understanding of the nature of research work	S		S			S,F	S	U	6
Demonstrated gains: increased tolerance and perseverance	S		S	S	S	S,F	S	U	6
Understanding professional practice: working collaboratively	S	F			S	S,F	S	U+	6
Understanding professional practice: presenting and publishing; importance of communication skills, including writing	S		S			S,F		U	4
Increased intrinsic interest in learning, intellectual curiosity	S	F+	S+	S	S	S,F	S		5

Skills

Technical skills	S	S+	S+	S+	S,F	S	U		8
Communication skills: presenting, argument	S+, F+	S	S-	S	S,F	S-	S	U	10
Communications skills: writing	S-, F-	S	S+	S+	S,F	S-	S	U	7
Computer skills	S	S+			S,F		U		3
Reading and critiquing literature	S,F-	S	S	S	S,F	S	S	U	6

(Continued)

TABLE 2.1 (Continued)

Type of student gain	British University 1	Studies Conducted at Research Institutions 2	3	4	5	6	7	8	9	10	11	12	13	14	15	Multi-Institution Studies 16	17	18	19	20	21	22	23	24	Laboratory 25	Totals
Information searching and retrieval													S+		S+					S,F						3
Collaborative work																				S,F					U	2
Time management, organization																				S,F					U	2
Enhanced career preparation																										
UR provides good preparation for work or graduate school						S									S					S,F		S			U	5
Provides opportunity to network with peers, faculty, scientists																					S+,F		U		U	3
Career clarification																										
Clarified, confirmed, refined career interests and goals (including graduate school)				S	S					S			S	F	S		S	S−	S−	S,F		U				13
Gained insight into profession or graduate school; assessment of fit			S,F	S	S							S					S			S,F		S	U		U	9

Increased likelihood of postgraduate education	S	S	S	S,U	S	S	S	S	S	S,F	S	U	16
Increased interest in science	S	S	S			S		S,F+				U	6
Introduced new field of study	S	S						S,F					3
Research is not for me	S		S		S	S	S	S,F					6
UR experience prompted choice, is a causal factor in decision to enroll in graduate school	U	U	U	U		S	S	U	U			U	10
Career outcomes													
Retention to graduation	S,U	U	S,U	U		U			U			U	9
High rates of students going to graduate school	S,U	U	S,U	U	S	U	S	S		U	U	U	13
High rates of students earning advanced degrees in STEM fields or medicine	U		S	U		S			U	U	U	U	6

Note: The numbers across the top of the table identify particular studies and correspond to the references listed in Exhibit 2.1. U.S. research institutions are all classified as "high" or "very high" research institutions by the 2007 Carnegie Classification (Carnegie Foundation for the Advancement of Teaching, 2007).

S = Student gain reported (by students or alumni); **S+** = Highest student-rated gain; **S** = Lowest student-rated gain; **F** = Faculty-rated student gain; **F+** = Highest faculty-rated student gains; **F–** = Lowest faculty-rated student gains; **U** = Gain for students from underrepresented groups.

EXHIBIT 2.1

Index to Research and Evaluation Studies Referenced in Table 2.1 and the Text

	Author and Date	Study Location
1	Ryder, Leach, & Driver, 1999	University of Leeds, Great Britain
2	Kremer & Bringle, 1990	Indiana University
3	Alexander, Lyons, Pasch, & Patterson, 1996	University of Wisconsin-Madison
4	Foertsch, Alexander, & Penberthy, 1997	University of Wisconsin-Madison
5	Alexander, Foertsch, & Daffinrud, 1998	Rice University
6	Nagda, Gregerman, Jonides, von Hippel, & Lerner, 1998	University of Michigan
7	Hathaway, Nagda, & Gregerman, 2002	University of Michigan
8	Kardash, 2000	Midwestern, Carnegie Research University
9	Maton, Hrabowski, & Schmitt, 2000	University of Maryland, Baltimore County
10	Rauckhorst, Czaja, & Baxter Magolda, 2001	Miami University
11	Adhikari, Givant, & Nolan, 2002	University of California, Berkeley
12	Ward, Bennett, & Bauer, 2002	University of Delaware
13	Zydney, Bennett, Shahid, & Bauer, 2002b	University of Delaware
14	Zydney, Bennett, Shahid, & Bauer, 2002a	University of Delaware
15	Bauer & Bennett, 2003	University of Delaware
16	Barlow & Villarejo, 2004	University of California, Davis
17	Fitzsimmons, Carlson, Kerpelman, & Stoner, 1990	Multi-institution
18	Lopatto, 2004	Multi-institution
19	Lopatto, 2007	Multi-institution
20	Hunter, Laursen, & Seymour, 2007; see also Seymour, Hunter, Laursen, & DeAntoni, 2004	Multi-institution
21	This book (four-college study)	Multi-institution
22	Russell, 2005; see also Russell, Hancock, & McCullough, 2007	Multi-institution
23	National Research Council, 2005	Multi-institution
24	Clewell, de Cohen, Deterding, & Tsui, 2006	Multi-institution
25	This book (SOARS case study); see also Pandya, Henderson, Anthes, & Johnson, 2007	National Center for Atmospheric Research

the apprenticeship model, how this operates in practice may vary significantly among campuses or programs. Thus, we caution readers to recognize this variability in interpreting the literature, especially whether students participate in a structured UR program that incorporates other formal elements or in informal, faculty-led UR. As shown in Table 2.1, most studies were conducted at large research universities. Some are evaluations of small programs run within a single department or college. Others are large evaluations of long-established, well-developed institutional programs detailed in multiple and longitudinal reports. Studies investigating student recruitment, retention, and persistence were most commonly done at these large research universities. Studies involving multiple institutions included both large research studies and large, funder-driven evaluations of multisite programs. The participating students did UR at an array of universities and colleges where UR may be more formally organized and operating through multiple programs but is rarely centralized. In primarily undergraduate institutions, where faculty-led UR has developed more organically over time, programs may be loosely organized, if at all. Given this continuum of practice, it is interesting to see what has been learned. For easy cross-referencing, the following discussion cites particular studies by number, corresponding to the numbers in Table 2.1.

Studies Establishing the Benefits of UR

Most evaluation and research studies focus on the benefits of UR, documenting ways in which UR enhances students' education and influences their thinking about graduate school and careers in STEM fields. As noted, there is a good deal of variability in how UR is implemented place to place. For example, most student researchers in these studies were apparently required to present their work, but may or may not have participated in extra professional and career development seminars or organized social activities, though these are commonly reported elements.

Researchers at the University of Delaware surveyed nearly a thousand alumni to evaluate the contributions of a long-standing, institution-wide UR program to students' educational experience [12–15]. Following publication of their first findings on a subset of UR alumni in engineering [13], the researchers reported other analyses of the alumni data, including a comparison of gains reported by alumni who had participated in UR with those reported by the rest of the alumni sample [15] and a content analysis of open-ended evaluation letters written by students in the Science and Engineering Scholars program [12]. They also surveyed engineering faculty perceptions [14].

Several cross- and multi-institutional studies have also investigated the benefits of UR. Fitzsimmons and collaborators [17] conducted an early evaluation of NSF's Research Experiences for Undergraduates program, analyzing survey responses from nearly two thousand participating students. Building on our research study, Lopatto developed a survey based on our qualitative results and administered it at the same four liberal arts colleges to test our findings using quantitative methods. From this, Lopatto developed the online Survey of Undergraduate Research Experiences (SURE) to investigate the benefits of UR among a broader student population at an array of universities, colleges, and master's-level institutions; 1,135 students from forty-one institutions responded [18]. A follow-up study replicated and validated previous SURE results, this time with 2,021 students responding from sixty-one institutions [19]. More recently, SRI International carried out an evaluation of NSF-supported undergraduate research [22]. Using four Web-based surveys involving nearly fifteen thousand respondents, this very large national study sought to better understand the effects of UR experiences on students. Research and evaluation studies focusing on recruitment, retention, and persistence of underrepresented groups have also documented certain learning gains, which are discussed in detail later in this chapter.

Alignment of Findings on Student Gains Across Studies

Table 2.1 shows the most commonly reported student gains from a majority of research and evaluation studies:

- Increased confidence (fourteen studies)
- Establishing collegial relationships with advisors (thirteen studies)
- Understanding research through hands-on experience (thirteen studies).

    Up to half of studies reported the following benefits to students:

- Improved ability to work independently (ten studies)
- Deepened knowledge in the field and improved understanding of conceptual connections (ten studies)
- Improved communication skills through presentation of research (ten studies)
- Improved critical thinking and problem-solving skills, including analyzing and interpreting results (nine studies)
- Familiarity and comfort with laboratory techniques and instrumentation (eight studies)
- Establishing collegial relationships with peers (eight studies)

- Understanding how knowledge is constructed (seven studies)
- Improved writing skills (seven studies).

About one-quarter of studies found these gains to students:

- Improved ability to comprehend and critique literature (six studies)
- Increased interest in science (six studies)
- Increased understanding of the nature of research work (six studies)
- Increased tolerance and perseverance (six studies)
- Understanding collaboration as a professional work norm (six studies)
- Increased intrinsic interest in learning (five studies)
- Thinking creatively (five studies)
- Understanding how to pose and investigate research questions (four studies).

In looking across the studies at outcomes related to graduate school entry and career choices, UR was found to contribute to students' decision making in several ways. Participating in research:

- Increased the existing likelihood that students would go on to graduate school (sixteen studies)
- Clarified, confirmed, and refined existing career interests through hands-on experience with research or in the field (thirteen studies)
- Offered insight into the profession and ability to assess the fit of research with students' own interests and temperament (nine studies)
- Showed some students that "research is not for me" (six studies).

For underrepresented groups, particular career influence and longitudinal outcomes were documented in these studies, showing:

- High proportions of students who went to graduate school (thirteen studies)
- Retention to graduation (nine studies)
- High proportions of students who earned advanced degrees in STEM fields or other professional degrees, largely M.D.s (six studies).

While several of these studies admit a strong bias in students' predisposal toward graduate school on entering college [19–23], the finding that UR experience was a causal factor in students' decisions to enroll in graduate school was reported primarily for members of underrepresented groups [4, 5, 7, 9, 11, 16, 18–25].

In sum, the literature converges on a broad set of benefits as arising from students' engagement in authentic research. Notably congruent are gains in confidence and establishing collegial working relationships with faculty and peers; increases in students' intellectual and practical understanding of how science research is done; students' greater ability to work and think independently from faculty; and the role of UR in helping students to assess the fit of research as a career and clarify career and graduate school plans. Across the studies, these results underscore UR experience as offering a constellation of gains that collectively reflect students' personal, intellectual, and professional growth.

While our own findings align broadly with those of other scholars, no other single study addresses all the categories of gain that were identified by research students and advisors in our own four-college study. No other study has reported gains that we did not identify, and our study is unique in reporting some gains, most notably student gains in "feeling like a scientist." Thus the student benefits that we discuss in Chapter Three add significantly in both content and nuance to the literature on the student outcomes of UR.

Missing thus far in the literature is any account of what may be lost by those who do not participate in research and how gains from other educational experiences compare to UR, in both the short and longer terms (Chapters Four and Five). Also missing are any detailed descriptions of how these gains are generated (Chapters Seven and Eight) and of what it costs faculty to mentor students in UR (Chapter Nine). Findings on these issues begin to fill out our understanding of all the outcomes arising from undergraduate research as a component of undergraduate science education that is linked with faculty scholarship.

Studies of Programs Aimed at Undergraduate Retention and Recruitment to Graduate School

In addition to studies establishing the benefits of UR experience, a number of research and evaluation studies have examined programs specifically developed to address undergraduate retention and recruitment to graduate school, especially for students from groups whose representation still lags behind white majority students at all stages of the STEM pipeline. This literature includes several studies of UR programs targeting undergraduate retention in STEM majors and recruitment to graduate STEM degrees and careers [4–7, 9, 11, 16, 23, 24, 25]. Because these programs are formally organized, they often include additional elements aimed at addressing program objectives. Some of these studies reference theoretical work that offers explanations for the outcomes achieved, and we discuss this work in a later section. Again, Table 2.1 itemizes the gains to students that these studies document; a few other salient results are noted in the narrative.

Foertsch, Alexander, and Penberthy [4] used interviews and surveys to evaluate the University of Wisconsin-Madison's Summer Undergraduate Research Program (SURP), which sought to increase recruitment of minority students to the university's Ph.D. programs. A visiting research program, SURP brought minority undergraduate students and students from schools with limited research facilities to the university for eight weeks of research. Students presented their research to a group at the end of the summer.

Alexander, Foertsch, and Daffinrud [5] evaluated the Spend a Summer with a Scientist program at Rice University. They examined student outcomes and essential program elements using interviews and surveys of past and current participants, as well as data on students' academic outcomes. This program used summer research as a tool for recruiting minority undergraduates into graduate school and retaining minority graduate students. In helping students to feel part of a community, it aimed to counteract isolation often experienced by minority and female students.

Adhikari, Givant, and Nolan [11] present some results of their evaluation of the Summer Institute in the Mathematical Sciences (SIMS) program for women undergraduates at the University of California, Berkeley. They surveyed two cohorts of women who had participated in this six-week summer research intensive in mathematics. Developed to prepare and encourage women's entry to graduate school and careers in mathematics, this program was directly modeled on an early experiment to retain students of color in mathematics, the Summer Mathematics Institute for Minorities implemented by Treisman and Henkin at Berkeley the year before. In the SIMS program, women did independent research, read journal articles, reported project results to a group, and attended professional development activities.

Barlow and Villarejo [16] conducted a comprehensive quantitative evaluation of the Biology Undergraduate Scholars Program (BUSP) at the University of California, Davis. This educational enrichment program was designed to reduce attrition of minority students from the biological sciences and borrowed from early successes of Treisman's (1992; Fullilove & Treisman, 1990) calculus workshops and from Xavier University's SOAR (Stress On Analytic Reasoning) program (Carmichael, Labat, Huter, Privett, & Sevenair, 1993). Following the SOAR model, BUSP provided academic, financial, and advising support through the freshman and sophomore years. It also worked to develop strong peer networks through the small size of the program, intensive enrichment instruction, and facilitated study groups as a means to integrate students academically and socially. Though it was not required, students commonly engaged in research experiences. Barlow and Villarejo tracked institutional and program data for four hundred students, a larger study than the above case studies, which had small sample sizes of thirty-seven to sixty-eight participants.

Larger research and evaluation studies from two research universities with institutionalized UR efforts also targeted retention of students from underrepresented groups. Researchers at the University of Michigan conducted an ongoing series of studies on the university's Undergraduate Research Opportunities Program (UROP) program. Originally instituted to improve the retention and academic performance of minority students, UROP was later opened to all students. Summer and academic-year research experiences were offered institution-wide, across the sciences, social sciences, and humanities, to first- and second-year students. Peer advising, peer research interest groups, and end-of summer presentations were among the elements of this program. Nagda and coauthors [6] reported the effects of UR experiences on student retention and persistence to graduation. They examined institutional retention and academic performance data for 613 students who had participated in UROP and 667 who did not. The improvement in retention rates was greatest for African American students who had low incoming grades and for sophomore over first-year participants. Later, Hathaway, Nagda, and Gregerman [7] examined the relationship of UR participation to pursuit of graduate and professional education. Research participants were significantly more likely to pursue graduate education and additional research activity than were those without research experience, based on survey responses from over 290 alumni. Faculty-student interaction appeared to play a strong role in academic achievement, undergraduate retention, and students' decisions to pursue further education. UROP's design was not explicitly based on other models, but these authors [6, 7] drew on theoretical work on the importance of students' early academic and social integration into college life in analyzing their findings.

Maton, Hrabowski, and Schmitt [9] report findings from a longitudinal evaluation of the Meyerhoff Scholars Program, established at the University of Maryland, Baltimore County, to increase the number of underrepresented minorities who pursue graduate and professional degrees in science and engineering. The program evaluation sought to identify longitudinal academic outcomes and factors contributing to program effectiveness from institutional retention and academic data on three cohorts of program participants and matched comparison samples, plus interview and survey data. The Meyerhoff Scholars Program has offered comprehensive support to students, including financial support, a high school-to-college summer bridge program, research experience and faculty mentoring, tutoring, program staff advising, study groups, and social activities. Participants graduated in STEM majors at higher rates and went to graduate school at higher rates than comparison groups. A process evaluation, using surveys and interviews, identified key program elements. Maton, Hrabowski, and Schmitt [9] frame their findings in terms of theoretical work on minority academic achievement and retention.

Two evaluations examined federally funded, multi-institution programs directed at the retention and recruitment of underrepresented minorities in STEM fields: the National Institutes of Health (NIH) Minority Research and Training Programs [23] and the NSF's Louis Stokes Alliances for Minority Participation (LSAMP) [24]. For the NIH program, outcomes for participants at forty-seven sites documented increased likelihood of graduating, going to graduate school, and earning advanced degrees. Important elements included research, mentoring, travel to conferences, financial support, skills development, and networking with peers, faculty, and other scientists [23]. LSAMP programs offered multiple structured elements too: financial support, summer bridge, research, academic enrichment curricula and resources, peer study groups, and academic advising. Through interview and survey data, as well as longitudinal data comparing nationally representative samples, Clewell and associates [24] found that LSAMP participation increased students' likelihood of graduating in STEM majors and of going to graduate school, and increased the numbers of students earning STEM Ph.D.s to rates above the national average. Research experience, a summer bridge program, and mentoring were important factors in promoting positive student outcomes.

Melton, Pedersen-Gallegos, and Donohue [25] conducted an evaluation study of the SOARS program (Significant Opportunities in Atmospheric Research and Science), a multiyear summer research program for underrepresented groups hosted by the National Center for Atmospheric Research. Their interviews with SOARS students, alumni, mentors, and staff documented student outcomes and key program elements, and the program has tracked students' undergraduate degree completion, graduate school entry, and career choices over time. SOARS is discussed in detail as a case study in Chapter Six.

These results across multiple studies on the outcomes for underrepresented students are encouraging. They document success in retaining students and promoting their entrance into graduate school and provide empirical evidence about the efficacy of common program elements (for reviews, see Gándara, 1999, and Tsui, 2007). They also bolster the validity of theoretical work on student engagement and development in college, the third strand of the literature that ties theory to effective practice.

Ties Between Theory and Practice: Explaining Documented Outcomes

The studies discussed so far describe the educational benefits of participating in UR and document the effectiveness of programs using UR as a way to improve undergraduate retention and recruitment to graduate school. They also offer empirical evidence to support theoretical work that relates retention in college to students' engagement on campus and its impacts on learning and personal and professional development. Here we discuss a few of the most salient of these theoretical contributions.

Tinto (1975, 1987, 1993) has investigated the links between persistence in college and students' social and academic integration into campus life. *Leaving College* (Tinto, 1987) presented a longitudinal model connecting the institution's academic and social systems, the people involved in those systems—largely faculty and peers—and success in student retention. The patterns of interaction between the student and other members of the institution were especially important in the critical first year of college, when most leaving occurs. Astin (1977, 1982, 1992) and Astin and Astin (1992) also explored the relationships between students' persistence, personal and intellectual growth, and the nature, degree, and quality of their engagement in campus activities where these interactions occurred. Pascarella and Terenzini (1991, 2005) have also researched the impact of college on students. These bodies of work originally highlighted the importance of positive faculty-student and peer group interactions in influencing students' growth and retaining them to graduation.

While student engagement had been identified as important in itself, this did not help practitioners determine how to do it. Thus, Treisman's calculus workshops and the SOAR program at Xavier University were particularly important as models that pointed the way. The demonstrated success of these programs in retaining students indicated effective ways to engage students in the academic and social life of the institution. The calculus workshops used structured peer group learning to support underprepared minority students in mathematics (Fullilove & Treisman, 1990). SOAR developed an enriched curriculum supported by tutoring and advising (Carmichael et al., 1993). Findings from both of these programs emphasized the need to support students who came to college academically underprepared and addressed other factors that affected persistence for students of color—among others, campus racial climate, social isolation, and financial stresses. For such students, strategies that provided academic resources and enrichment, built positive peer networks, and linked students to program staff and faculty research mentors were particularly effective.

Several of the programs in Table 2.1 have drawn on this foundational work on persistence and academic achievement of minority undergraduates. For instance, because most leaving occurs during the first years of college, efforts to reduce attrition have targeted first- and second-year students [6, 7, 9, 16]. Shared experiences such as research, plus study groups and social activities, are used to build a strong community among program participants. The successes of these programs provide additional practical models for others who share the same goals [4, 5, 6, 7, 9, 11, 16, 25]. In addition, these theoretical models based on empirical research have now begun to show why these educational strategies, including UR, are effective.

Conclusion

This growing body of evidence on the outcomes of UR for students is large enough to make it possible to draw broader conclusions. In addition to the synthesis offered here, several recent efforts have examined what works for intervention programs for underrepresented groups. Tsui (2007) has reviewed the research evidence behind ten intervention strategies commonly adopted by programs striving to increase diversity in STEM fields. Building Engineering and Science Talent (2004) gathered experts together to assess successful program practices supporting minority recruitment and retention in STEM, and the National Research Council (Olson & Fagen, 2007) hosted a workshop where researchers and practitioners explored the efficacy of programs to support students from underrepresented groups. Both committees sought to distill from exemplary programs a set of principles on which similar interventions might be successfully founded. Matching recommendations based on theoretical models, these reports also advised further building to achieve a campus climate that appreciates and represents diversity, community among peers, and opportunities for meaningful faculty-student interaction.

Most recently, drawing on research on student engagement, Kuh (2008) has defined a set of "high-impact educational practices" that are demonstrated to improve student success for all students. Kuh describes this set of educational practices as "unusually effective" because they typically:

- Demand a high level of student involvement
- Promote substantial and meaningful interaction among the student, faculty, and peers over a period of time
- Increase the likelihood of students' experiences with diverse people, situations, and cultures
- Provide immediate feedback to students about their performance
- Allow students to apply, integrate, and synthesize their learning within a coherent context.

Key among Kuh's findings is that these educational practices benefit underserved students even more than they do their advantaged peers. Unfortunately, the students who may benefit most are also less likely to experience these practices.

Each of these recent reports identifies UR as an effective way to engage students in their learning and in the academic and social communities of the college. This in turn increases undergraduate retention in their majors, persistence to graduation, and the likelihood of entry to advanced study. The broad agreement in these sources is encouraging because it enables practitioners to begin to build programs of their own, based on sound empirical and theoretical foundations. However, there is much yet to learn. These digests largely concur about what works for students and what "working" means, but the literature does not yet tell us enough about how it works and why—critical information for those who seek to develop specific programs in specific places for specific student audiences. Many questions remain about the circumstances under which UR provides these benefits and the processes by which benefits do or do not accrue. Moreover, little attention has yet been paid to the personal, financial, and opportunity costs to faculty and institutions of providing these benefits, and whether and in what circumstances the positive educational outcomes outweigh these costs. We begin to examine many of these issues in the chapters that follow.

Chapter 3

What Do Students Gain from Conducting Research?

WHAT BENEFITS DO students derive from undergraduate research (UR)? To answer this question, we asked student research participants directly and compared their self-reported gains with those observed by their research advisors. We also sought to learn whether these gains could also be achieved through other undergraduate learning experiences—courses, internships, work, or off-campus forms of UR—undertaken by students who do not conduct summer research on their campuses.

In this chapter, we discuss our findings on the student benefits from UR. Chapter Four focuses on whether these benefits are unique; Chapter Five addresses outcomes recognized in the longer term, after students graduated; and Chapter Six examines the special case of UR programs targeted to minority students. In discussing student benefits, this chapter incorporates students' observations on how these benefits emerged from their UR experience; Chapter Seven details research advisors' perspective on how they work to achieve these gains.

Probing Student Gains from Research

Using the coding and sorting procedures described in Chapter One, we identified over twelve hundred coded statements, or observations, about gains from research in the transcribed interviews with the main UR student sample. We grouped these into five major categories, each with several subcategories: personal/professional gains, gains in thinking and working like a scientist, specific skills, enhanced career and graduate school preparation, and clarification and confirmation of career plans (Seymour, Hunter, Laursen, & DeAntoni, 2004).

This initial analysis of student data then guided our coding of interviews with research advisors. The original student-derived categories applied to many observations made by advisors of how their research students benefited from UR. However, analysis of the advisor data also yielded a sixth major category, becoming a scientist, that was distinctive in advisors' accounts. From their vantage point of deep experience in their discipline and seeing over time how their students proceeded from UR experiences to careers and graduate education, advisors could characterize how students adopted the practices, attitudes, and behaviors of science as a profession. Thus, "becoming a scientist" describes gains in students' professional socialization.

With this category defined from faculty observations, we could then recognize, in retrospect, comparable gains within student accounts. This difference between student and faculty perspectives makes sense: students fresh from summer research—often their first research experience—did not yet have enough experience in science to recognize such gains as related to the profession. They thus framed this growth largely in terms of their personal confidence and ability to apply science in practice, while faculty, as experienced scientists, could recognize these changes as growth toward the behaviors and understandings of a young professional. We reanalyzed the UR student data in light of research advisors' perspective on "becoming a scientist" (Hunter, Laursen, & Seymour, 2007). This is a good example of why ethnographic researchers examine phenomena from multiple perspectives, seeking to triangulate their findings (Bowden & Marton, 1998; Strauss, 1987).

Analyses of additional student data sets did not alter the resulting six-category scheme, although we were alert to this possibility. In coding later interviews with UR alumni, over 85 percent of codes from the first code-book were reused, and fewer than 15 percent of codes were new. Thus the number of new ideas emerging is not large; most of the new codes are minor variations of original codes. Ultimately all of the new benefits codes could be placed within the broad parent categories developed in the initial analysis; they are listed as noncomparable observations in Table 3.1 and Appendix D.

Student Gains: Robust in Character and Type

The first key finding is that UR is a substantial learning experience. Among both advisor and student observations about student gains, over 90 percent of all gains-related statements were positive in character, reporting a wide range of intellectual, professional, educational, and personal gains as a result of UR. These predominated over both negative statements, which refer to a gain *not* made (rather than to a poor experience), and mixed statements, which were gains that students described as partial, incomplete, or qualified. Among UR students and their research advisors, we found few clear patterns among the small numbers of negative and mixed gains statements, and thus this chapter emphasizes the positive gains observations. Negative and mixed views from comparison students were both more common and more informative, as discussed in Chapter Four.

In addition to their overall positive nature, the categories of student gains are robust—consistent in content and repeatedly strong in representation. Ultimately we analyzed six data sets using the scheme of six major categories of benefit. This qualitative analysis resulted in over ten thousand positive gains observations altogether (for totals by data set, see Appendix D). Despite starting with finely grained categorization of individual interviewees' gains-related observations, we find very broad, recurring patterns. That these patterns persist across hundreds of individual interviews with people who hold widely varying perspectives helps to further validate the findings.

Because of these robust patterns, we can and do draw illustrative quotations from several distinct data sets. The quotations illustrate the ideas, but they are also essential glimpses of the original evidence that we have analyzed and distilled. In this chapter we highlight the interviews with UR students and alumni and draw in research advisors' reports as these illuminate student gains or differ in interesting ways. Many observations also provide clues to how these gains arose, discussed further in Chapter Seven. In this chapter, quotations from interviews are labeled by gender and discipline to individualize them, but they also illustrate the general absence of distinctive patterns by gender or by field. Therefore we do not continue that labeling practice throughout the rest of the book. We discuss student group differences at the end of this chapter.

Table 3.1 presents frequency counts indicating the relative weight of opinion across the six main gains categories for UR students, UR alumni, and research advisors. The number of distinct observations in each category far exceeds the number of people interviewed because each person made multiple statements about his or her gains. Similar figures for the comparison students are presented and discussed in Chapter Four. Appendix D presents detailed breakouts for each major gains category, by sample group.

TABLE 3.1

Student Gains from Undergraduate Research, as Reported by UR Students, Alumni, and Advisors, in Number and Percentage of Observations

"Parent" Category: Group of Gains-Related Codes	Number of Observations by UR Students (N = 76)	Number of observations by UR Alumni (N = 56)	Number of Observations by UR Advisors (N = 80)
Personal/professional	310	428	335
Noncomparable subcategories	—	59	85
Category total as percentage of all positive gains	25%	21%	19%
Thinking and working like a scientist	248	386	527
Noncomparable subcategories	46	—	—
Category total as percentage of all positive gains	24%	16%	23%
Becoming a scientist	151	327	450
Category total as percentage of all positive gains	12%	14%	20%
Skills	214	404	169
Noncomparable subcategories	—	2	5
Category total as percentage of all positive gains	17%	17%	8%
Career clarification, confirmation, and refinement of career and education paths	131	245	348
Noncomparable subcategories	—	—	4
Category total as percentage of all positive gains	11%	10%	16%
Enhanced preparation for career and graduate school	90	356	169
Noncomparable subcategories	30	160	59
Category total as percentage of all positive gains	10%	22%	10%
Miscellaneous and general gains	11	13	92
Category total as percentage of all positive gains	1%	1%	4%
Subtotal, comparable gains only	1,144	2,146	1,998
Total, all positive gains observations	1,231 (100%)	2,380 (100%)	2,243 (100%)
Negative gains observations	51	257	140
Mixed, partial, or uncertain gains observations	54	88	112

Categories of Student Gains

The six major categories of student gains are:

- Personal/professional gains
- Gains in thinking and working like a scientist
- Gains in becoming a scientist
- Gains of skills
- Enhanced preparation for career and graduate school
- Clarification, confirmation, and refinement of career and educational goals and interests.

As Table 3.1 shows, these six categories account for over 95 percent of the positive statements by students and research advisors about gains made from undergraduate research. Table 3.1 also shows that some 90 percent of positive statements were directly comparable in character across data sets. A small number of comments fall into subcategories that are not directly comparable across all data sets but do align with the six major categories. Comparability of comments becomes especially pertinent for the analysis in Chapter Five, where we look at how students' gains endure over time and transfer to other settings. We now discuss each gains category in turn.

Personal/Professional Gains

At 25 percent of all gains statements, this category was the largest among student-reported gains and remained sizable in interviews with UR alumni (21 percent) and research advisors (19 percent). Although students experienced these gains primarily as personal growth—enhanced confidence and new collegial relationships—they in fact contributed to students' growing sense of themselves as professionals capable of doing "real science." Our label "personal/professional" indicates how internal changes in confidence fostered growth of an external professional identity. "Now I know I'm a decent scientist," one male chemistry student put it.

Gains in Confidence to Do Science

Over three-quarters of students' personal/professional gains observations describe gains in the confidence to do science: to conduct research, learn new skills with increasing independence, solve problems, make decisions—"to get in there and try it and mess up, and if it doesn't work, try it a different way." These gains reflect not just higher self-esteem, but students' awareness of their own new capacities, and the personal significance of these new capacities: "It made me more confident in mathematics, just knowing that I can explain it to other people and I can research and I can write a paper" (female UR student, mathematics).

Faculty recognized this growth of confidence and affirmed its importance. They noted students' movement from tentative to assured decision making and their growing willingness to try a new procedure or pursue an experiment on their own: "You can see it a mile away. When they approach a new piece of equipment, it's more, 'Well, where's the manual?' [laughs] 'Don't waste my time teaching me this, just tell me how to turn it on and I'll figure it out.' Self-confidence, maturity" (research advisor, chemistry).

As they gained confidence in their ability to do research work, students began to recast their identity as members of the scientific enterprise. Their phrase "feeling like a scientist" indicates a strengthening bond with their project as they imagined themselves, plausibly, as scientists—contributing results that other scientists might use or read about in a journal: "In the middle of last summer, when I was finally starting to hit my stride in my work, I realized that there was a threat that I might actually *produce* something" (male UR student, chemistry).

Students gained a sense of achievement when they realized their work was original, even if in small ways—"making the conversation two-way," as one alumna put it. "To be respectable in the scientific community," said a student, "you have to have something new . . . to even be acknowledged. And you know, I had something new right then, and I definitely felt good" (female UR student, biology).

Being taken seriously by their advisor was important. Students described having their ideas listened to, being entrusted with complex equipment and expensive materials, and feeling relied on to accomplish a job: "The professors have a lot of trust in you. They don't think you're going to blow up their laboratories, try to forge your data or anything. And so you don't have someone looking over you saying, 'Okay, you're doing it right,' or saying, 'No, no, don't do that!' It does give you a lot of power. . . . I know that I can go in there and get things done" (female UR student, chemistry).

Giving a presentation—a talk or poster—fostered students' communication skills and helped consolidate their scientific understanding and also prompted them to recognize how far they had come: "I was a little bit proud of myself. . . . I mean, I was presenting material to faculty and discussing things I would not have understood a couple months back. That made me feel pretty good that I had learned so much" (female UR student, chemistry).

Advisors too noted the impact of preparing and presenting work on students' sense of achievement and developing professional identity.

Recognizing this, many departments took pains to create presentation opportunities at the end of the summer. "By the time they've put their poster up on the last day," said one biology advisor, "they really do feel as if they've not only contributed something but they're part of something."

Presenting at outside scientific meetings and interacting there with professional colleagues were more rare but especially powerful experiences for some students. Students remarked on being taken seriously by "grown-up" scientists who treated them as peers, discussing and debating their work as with any other colleague: "At first it was a little overwhelming. . . . I'm just an undergraduate and these people have their doctorates, and I've studied their research. . . . But after a while, I realized that . . . there's some things about my work that they don't really understand yet—I have to explain it to them. So it made me feel really good. . . . The experiences I've had have given me enough confidence not to run and hide" (male UR student, physics).

Opportunities to present at disciplinary meetings did not typically arise until students' research had matured and generated reliable results constituting a genuine scientific contribution. Other scientists took students seriously because they had something worthwhile to share. Thus, conferences were not artificial educational experiences, but authentic scientific events in which students were held to professional standards and encountered professional customs in situ. One advisor said, "Watch them explaining what they've done, . . . it's this big epiphany when they realize that what they're doing really is important, and that somebody somewhere else actually cares about it, and they get into real scientific conversations" (research advisor, chemistry).

Developing Collegial Relationships with Professionals and Peers

The preceding examples foreshadow the second main subcategory of personal/professional gains: new, close working relationships with their research advisor and their peers. Summer research was often students' first chance to work alongside faculty as partners, and they noticed how their relationship in the research lab differed from the more stratified relationship typical of the classroom: "I really feel like I'm just kind of a partner of his. There's not really any kind of hierarchy, like, 'I'm the advisor and you work for me.' We've got this project, and we're kind of using both our minds and our tools to figure it out" (male UR student, chemistry).

Faculty noticed this difference too, and they encouraged the emergence of equality from confronting an unsolved problem together: "It's not this student-teacher relationship, it's a more collegial relationship.

We're basically on fairly equal footing here. . . . I can give them the benefit of my general experience in thinking about mathematical problems, but I don't have any more specific insight into this problem. And it's wonderful when a student comes up with something and I say, 'Well, that's really neat! I never thought of that.' And they just beam" (research advisor, mathematics).

A psychology student observed the same phenomenon: "It makes you feel proud when something you said is important to her . . . like something she hadn't thought of before." Thus, being taken seriously and making authentic contributions appear strongly in students' reports about how this collegial relationship arose: "She gives me a lot of responsibility . . . she finds my results more interesting than I do, sometimes. I really appreciate the fact that she's there to help support me. I don't know—she just makes me feel like I'm a real scientist" (female UR student, biology).

Students also valued personal relationships with their advisors. As a mathematics student put it, "You have more insight that teachers are people too." Advisors knew that their students observed them as human beings and family members, and entrusted them with personal details beyond what they normally shared in the classroom: "They really get to know you as a scientist, they know how science works, but also as a *person*, you know. Because you can't spend all that time without talking about your family or your vacation, and learning about what they like to do, and going out and doing stuff with them" (research advisor, biology; emphasis in original).

Research advisors also noted the longevity of their relationships with research students. They helped students make career decisions and prepare applications, but also recounted long-lasting connections with former research students who visited the lab, gave seminars, acknowledged them in doctoral dissertations, sent wedding and birth announcements, and became personal friends and even house guests.

Students also developed new types of relationships with each other. Joining a community of like-minded researchers working toward common goals, they learned to "bounce ideas off" each other and value the different perspectives this provided: "[When] somebody's just across the bench, and . . . you can solve their problem for them, then you see that it's worthwhile to ask somebody when something comes up. Try it a few times yourself, just so you aren't always pestering people, and so that you'll have a good chance of figuring it out yourself, you know—owning that problem—but then go to other people" (male UR student, physics).

Working with other students was both supportive and fun. "There's happy, chatty talk [in the lab]," noted one biology advisor. But advisors also saw group work as teaching a crucial professional skill: "They learn science is a collaborative process. My students . . . see each other outside the lab, . . . they're here until seven at night and they talk chemistry over breakfast. . . . If they're going to be doing science, they need to be able to talk to other scientists. They need the collaboration, they need the input of other people" (research advisor, chemistry).

• • •

In sum, the category of personal/professional gains emphasizes students' gains in confidence and growth of meaningful, collegial relationships with research advisors and peers. While students primarily discussed these gains in terms of personal growth, they glimpsed within that growth their development as future professionals, a facet that research advisors emphasized even more strongly.

Thinking and Working Like a Scientist

This category was second largest in the first-round student data, at 24 percent of all observations (Table 3.1). It remained significant among observations from alumni (16 percent) and was the largest category among research advisors' observations (23 percent). These observations are of two broad types: gains in knowledge and understanding of science and the research process, and gains in the ability to apply knowledge and skills to a specific research problem. Thus, these gains represent intellectual growth of various types.

Gains in Conceptual and Theoretical Understanding

Students reported gains in their understanding of concepts in science and mathematics: building deeper understanding, connecting ideas within and across fields or topics, and solidifying concepts already learned. "Some of the stuff, [research] actually made it really make sense . . . it really clicked," marveled one engineering student. Research "tied together issues" and placed concepts in context. "One thing I have learned," noted a male UR student in biology, "is that I don't know that much. . . . I've learned to look at the bigger picture and see everything's place inside it. I guess I had kind of a microscopic view of things before—just looking at one specific action of, say, cell development, but never actually thinking about how all these different genes could be interacting."

Some students discovered connections between research and course work. For example, they noted ideas that they had previously encountered in classes, but now understood more deeply or saw as more important after using them in research. Their advisors observed this "search for relevance" too: "'Oh, you mean *this* is what you were talking about?'" laughed one chemistry advisor. Conversely, concepts, techniques, or skills encountered during research resurfaced in the classroom in newly meaningful ways: "When I take classes that use chemistry that I've used in research, it seems more straightforward. . . . It reinforces things, so that it makes it much easier when an underclassman comes and asks me a question on their homework, since I've been forced to not only learn it the first time but learn it the second time when I did it for research" (male UR student, chemistry).

By presenting their work or teaching others, many students discovered, as this biology student did, that "I needed to actually know what I was talking about it in order to communicate it." Fielding questions was another place where knowledge was tested and solidified, showing "what you know, and what you need to know." "Doing the actual presentation and the practice, and getting questions from people," said one chemistry student, "I learned more about the project than I probably learned the first half of the summer. . . . It just really helps to synthesize it all together and figure out for yourself, in your own words, why you're doing this and what you're trying to find."

Gains in the Ability to Apply Knowledge and Skills

Students' gains in the ability to apply their knowledge and skills to a research problem came about through engaging in authentic research. These gains form three tiers of decreasing size—a pyramid with a broad base and narrow pinnacle. Many students discovered they could apply their knowledge and skills in a real investigation; some began to see how to select problems and frame questions so that they can be investigated; and just a few came to understand how the investigative process shapes the knowledge that is discovered. This pyramid of gains, increasing in sophistication but decreasing in frequency, shows how research can move students from application to design and then to abstraction—but it also shows that this is a difficult and slow progression.

Most comments in this subcategory address learning to use critical thinking and problem-solving skills in a research context. "Real-world" research experience provided an opportunity to learn by doing. "You can read about how the whole process works, but until you actually do it, you don't really necessarily always put it together," said a female biology student. Pursuing one problem over several weeks intensified and sustained students' interest. "When you're really interested, like you will be with research, you just learn so much more," said a male chemistry student. In turn, this applied learning enhanced students' problem-solving skills: "The research you're doing is something that hasn't been done, so you have to sort of forge your own path. It's much more problem solving oriented and . . . there's no set track for you" (male UR student, mathematics).

Students exercised their data analysis and interpretation skills and developed an array of problem-solving strategies. "Research really does help you to learn to detect your own dumb mistakes," said a physics student. Students learned to apply classroom learning, but also saw its limitations in solving problems "when there's no right answer yet." "I think there's only so much you can get from classroom learning," commented one chemistry student. "You get into the lab and you say, 'Okay, this should work.' No, it doesn't work! Because there are so many other considerations that you have to make. And that's the kind of thing you can only get from research."

As the summer progressed, a few students began to see not only how to advance their own project, but more generally how to frame a problem for systematic investigation. "You have to figure out the right questions, first of all, and then figure out how to pursue those questions," said a mathematics researcher. Students were excited by the opportunity to "think critically and creatively." "Now what can I change to have this effect, and to have this outcome? That's a whole new experience for me," said a chemistry student.

When research became more self-directed, it also became more rewarding. "Getting directions from above and carrying [them] out . . . is not nearly as exciting as figuring out on your own," said a female chemistry student. "I love that kind of insight you get. . . . All of a sudden you know it, and it wasn't there before," said a male physics researcher.

Finally, a few students' observations reflected a more sophisticated understanding of how knowledge was built. These students began to rethink what it meant to call something a "fact." "As a student you're handed this as fact . . . and you don't question that. But what you find out in research is that a lot of things need to be questioned," said one chemistry student. "We can stand on the backs of people who have figured out . . . but scientists have been wrong in the past. You have to do experimental work and explain why it's going this way."

As a male biology student put it, "You're not so much concerned with what other people have thought about something, because you're having to do it yourself." In this way, students became more skeptical and less accepting of knowledge authorities. They developed their own abilities to analyze and find flaws in arguments—"not just learning what the teachers want me to learn." "Realizing that your professor is not God, and does not know everything, is very important," said a female chemistry student. "[My research advisor] has more wisdom than me, he's more experienced in this field. But . . . I still have a lot to contribute to this because I am still capable of my own thought. I am still capable of thinking critically about a problem."

A few students realized that science was a human process of constructing ideas rather than a way to tap into universal truths. Giving up a simpler view of science could be dismaying, but comments like the following reflect the most mature epistemological understandings that we encountered among students and mark a transition to more complex and adult ways of knowing (Baxter Magolda, 1999; Perry, 1998; see also Nuhfer & Pavelich, 2001):

I was . . . going into it to find truth with a capital T. Whereas, when you get into the actual process, it's very ambiguous. Everything in science is a model to describe reality. We're not really studying reality as such; we're studying this model of reality. (male UR student, physics)

• • •

What I found out is that often what research does is just to explain how something could happen, or probably happens, and not necessarily how it does happen. 'Cause it's very hard to say if something happens for sure. . . . So I think that has helped me a lot in understanding science better. (female UR student, chemistry)

These remarks clearly reflect a richer type of intellectual development than the more general gains in critical thinking and problem-solving skills that were reported by many students and are commonly referenced in the literature. Helping students "learn about science," or understand the intellectual and social processes of how scientific knowledge is constructed, is often a goal of teachers and curriculum developers (Hodson, 1992; National Research Council, 1996, 2000). Learning about science is distinct from "learning to do science," the intellectual and procedural skills needed to carry out an investigation—though such understanding is often assumed to be self-evident within, and a collateral benefit of, laboratory work. In our study, "learning to do science" was a gain realized by most students at some level, and one that students and advisors readily identified. We noticed, however, that both experienced research students and their advisors found gains in "learning about science" much harder to identify. If these gains are difficult to achieve in well-designed, highly mentored, intensive ten-week summer research experiences, then it is no surprise that they are rarely achieved in less intensive learning experiences among less mature students. Chapter Five describes how some insights about the process of science emerged later, long after summer research had ended.

Becoming a Scientist

"Becoming a scientist" describes gains in professional socialization, as students took on the attitudes, behaviors, and understandings of working researchers. As they adopt these attributes, students also begin to identify themselves as researchers. Research advisors' observations on these gains are substantial, at 20 percent of the total. Among students, 12 percent of students' gains observations fit this category, and 14 percent of alumni observations, as seen in Table 3.1.

"Becoming a scientist" is of course related to "thinking and working like a scientist," but this category emphasizes students' growing awareness of the everyday conduct of science—not just as an intellectual activity but as a social and cultural enterprise and as an adult occupation. These categories begin to merge as students' understandings mature (see Chapters Five and Seven), but for novice researchers, these understandings are distinct. Thus it is not surprising that students and advisors offered different but complementary perspectives on "becoming a scientist." Students began to recognize some shared research norms and practices, but did not fully realize the extent to which they were being exposed to, then adopting and becoming adept in, professional practice. However, they did recognize a shift in identity—"feeling like a scientist," in their language. In contrast, as full, credentialed members of the profession, research advisors readily recognized these developing behaviors and attitudes as novice versions of their own professional practice. Through experience, advisors had come to recognize these changes as indicators of students' identity shift. Given both their interest as scientists in developing future members of the profession and their interest as mentors in seeing their students mature into adulthood, advisors were pleased when they saw these transitions commence. Thus, within the "becoming a scientist" category, over half of advisor observations described changes in students' conduct and manner as students began to show curiosity, initiative, and willingness to take risks and pursue their own ideas: "They slowly build up their success and their self-confidence of being able to get to do more complicated things, where you increasingly let them operate on their own . . . and make, ultimately, some individual decisions, right or wrong, about what they want to do next. And that's important, to start to not see themselves as just technicians, which they inevitably are [at first], but to actually begin to make some minor decisions" (research advisor, biology).

As students became increasingly independent, they became more proactive in proposing experiments and explanations, seeking affirmation rather than direction. "[When] they can see where they are going with the project, and think through it and think ahead . . . then I know they've really gotten a grasp of what they're doing," said a biology advisor. Sometimes these transitions were quite striking: "Students really have fun when they approach me and say, 'I know you always say I should at least run it by you before I use expensive reagents, but I did this on my own and look what I got!' And there've been a few that have just done it, around the sides without letting you know. . . . That's a real transition point . . . when they want to surprise you by bringing something of themselves to it. And when you see that happen, you think, 'Okay, we're all set here'" (research advisor, biology).

"Becoming a scientist" began as students gradually assumed ownership of their project. Claiming their "own little puzzle," they invested more deeply in the project. "They're coming in earlier in the morning, they're getting excited about what they're doing," said a physics advisor. A chemistry advisor noted, "They realize that this is a *big thing* that they're getting involved in . . . and doing something significant requires a lot of time." A biology advisor described, "They understand that it's not the way it is in the canned lab, where you do it once, and, right or wrong, it gets written up in your lab report. That's not the goal . . . the goal is to get it so it works, and to get it so it works well. And that requires a certain sort of effort, and willingness to just continue to put in that effort, and the mental energy and physical energy to get it done right."

This student's comment exemplifies how research advisors saw students taking ownership: "There comes a point where you have to say, I checked my experiment, and I know that I did things correctly, and I'm coming back with different numbers, but I will stand by these and support them. This is my data, this is what I got. . . . And I know that this means we need to push our project in this direction" (male UR student, biology).

In addition to changes in behavior, research advisors noticed new understandings of how science is done. Students learned "the feel of research"— the care and time required to prepare and carry out experiments, the need for attention to detail, the tedium of routine laboratory tasks, and the everyday pitfalls of scientific work. "The first time through, things don't always work. That's a strange lesson for students," said a chemistry advisor. "The geniuses like Einstein, you never think that he ran into a dead end, but he did," concurred a physics student. "To get through all that and to know what we know today in the sciences, is just amazing." And a biology advisor said,

> *I think they learn that science is really boring [laughs]. And that's the key—if they can know that science is boring and still do it, and still stick with it, then they have the makings of a really good scientist. Because . . . the first time you learn to do surgery on a rat is really exciting. . . . But when you're doing it for the fortieth time . . . there's nothing new and exciting about it. But you're doing it because it's part of the end goal of learning something. (research advisor, biology; emphasis in original)*

Coping with setbacks and uncertainty in research was new to many students, more accustomed to readily achievable laboratory tasks packaged in three-hour blocks. "I just always kind of expected that you do your experiment and you get a yes or a no," said one student. "But it's not that way—you get a lot of gray areas and a lot of maybes." Learning to deal with these failures—accepting them as normal, emulating their advisors' calm, problem-solving responses, persevering to analyze and reattack the problem—thus became an important temperamental test. Students judged their ability to cope with frustration and failure to indicate whether future work in science was a good fit for them. "That's a part of being a scientist, dealing with that," said a chemistry student. And a physics student pointed out, "You can't get too emotionally distraught. . . . You have to just step back and deal with the facts as they are and say, 'Okay, I've messed up. I need to correct this. It'll take a few hours, but then we'll move on.'"

Research advisors also recognized these temperamental requirements, whether natural or acquired, and tried to help students gain perspective on the ups and downs of scientific work: "I reassure people that tangible progress is not always correlated to how good you are—a lot of it's luck. . . . The best educated are the students who've come up against problems and have had to think around them. . . . It seems like small consolation at the time, but it's not a bad thing, it's a good thing" (research advisor, chemistry).

With time, students came to recognize these gains as useful in science and for life in general: "I think the perseverance that it takes, the patience to be able to just keep working and not giving up on things, that is something that I think will be useful in other areas—learning to not expect things to happen right away, and suddenly, magically, you have all your results" (female UR student, biology).

Research advisors readily identified these behavioral and attitudinal shifts, but also noted that not all students made such shifts in full. "All of the sudden they have an active idea of how to fix it or change it or do something different—that's the transition," said one chemistry advisor, then adding the caveat, "I don't think everyone has that transition."

Thus, what distinguishes this category from "thinking and working like a scientist" is the repeated linkage that research advisors made between specific professional behaviors and understandings, and adoption of a scientific identity. One psychology advisor gave an example: "One thing that I think they have really gained over the summer is . . . experience working with each other, dividing the work, deciding who's gonna do what, how to approach it, working on things together. All the kinds of things that if you do collaborative research you need to be able to do."

Students' identification with a project continued well beyond its actual duration. "Students come back and visit, and they say, 'See that *box* there? That's the box I made.' 'My box'—and they call it that," recounted a chemist whose students built instruments. Yet advisors knew that adopting a researcher's identity did not necessarily mean that students would pursue research as a career choice. Thus the category describes professional socialization not in terms of entry to a career, but as "a sense of being on the inside of science." Once students have made this transition, said a physicist, "You're dealing with mini-colleagues." A chemistry advisor told this story: "These three students are having a conversation. . . . I was eavesdropping on and off as I was working, and I thought, just listening to them, they're scientists. They're sitting there having this conversation about the project: Well, wouldn't you do this? What if you did that? And that's just such a leap from when they started in the lab."

Skills

Observations about gains in skills were common among both students and alumni, at 17 percent for both groups, and ranking third among the six gains categories. Skills represented only 8 percent of advisor observations, smallest of the six groups. By far the most frequently reported skill gain, accounting for over half the observations in this category, was improved communication skills. Other skill gains were laboratory and computer skills, organization of work and time, collaborative work, reading and comprehension, and information retrieval.

Among communication skills, students emphasized gains in their ability to construct and give an oral presentation, respond to questions, and defend their ideas. Formal and informal oral presentation was a significant and planned component of summer research. Students worked through ideas aloud with their advisor, explained experimental procedures to each other, and began to develop formal posters or talks to culminate the summer's work.

Gains in communication skills were wide ranging. Some students reported greater comfort in facing an audience, while others learned how to organize and edit a presentation. "I used to become very nervous doing a public presentation of any sort, and that's much less the case now. I still get a little nervous, but that's actually a positive thing, because you need a little adrenaline going," said one physics student. Even students confident about their general presentation skills found that presenting scientific work stretched them in new ways: "I don't have problems getting up in front of people and talking at all, but talking about scientific things is a completely different matter. . . . You want to get your point across to the people, to understand it, but you don't want to go so in-depth that they get lost" (male UR student, physics).

Practicing in front of peers—sometimes repeatedly—was one way to learn how to make their work clear and comprehensible to others not immersed in the same subject: "We had been in it so long that we would say something and not realize we hadn't explained it, because you get so narrow-sighted sometimes. . . . Sometimes things that make sense to you don't really make sense, you know?" (female UR student, mathematics).

Thinking aloud was sometimes uncomfortable for students, but it improved both the smoothness of the presentation and the conceptual clarity behind it. Peers helped to spot where more explanation, or less, was needed, where logic was faulty, and where an example would assist. Students developed argumentation skills and learned how to think on their feet:

> It's not an easy subject, nuclear physics, but it can be understood if you just spend some time at it. And then you have to present it to some students who don't know what's going on and a bunch of professors who know exactly what's going on. The professors are giving you leading questions to exactly what they want you to understand, and then the students [are] asking you questions about what they don't understand, and basically the whole subject gets covered. It's a great exercise, getting in front of people and speaking. (male UR student, physics)

By the end of the summer, only a few students had done much formal scientific writing beyond a poster. Indeed, at the time of the alumni interviews, ten of fifty-six UR alumni had published or were actively working on coauthored papers; eighteen more expected to be listed as contributors to future publications from their research group. A few were writing formal final papers: some would write a senior thesis later in the year, and just five veteran researchers were coauthoring manuscripts with their advisors. This likely explains why relatively few UR students reported gains in writing skills. Those who did learned to give and receive critique—a new and sometimes humbling experience for students, many of whom thought of themselves as strong writers. As they saw their research advisors mark their work with "a lot of red," students learned disciplinary standards for "the right style and the right word" and grew thicker skins.

As with speaking, students learned how and when to use early collegial feedback to save time and improve their writing—not trying to "write the perfect paper on the first try." A female biology student noted, "I've always been a self-revisionist. . . . Usually I agonize over it for twenty or forty hours before I give it to somebody. . . . But it's a lot easier, I think, to hear someone read it and say, 'I don't understand that. This is what it says to me, what do you want it to say?'"

Students perceived communication and other new skills as highly transferable to graduate school and work. Skills gained through hands-on work—for instance, "discovering how to actually use lab techniques, instead of just reading about them"—were more likely to be remembered, they felt, and built confidence at "doing science." "I used to sort of have this anxiety about lab classes, 'cause I didn't feel that comfortable, and I was afraid of the lab. . . . It's really helped me get over that" (female UR student, biology).

Students gained skill with managing, analyzing, and interpreting data and grew more alert to data that needed closer scrutiny to separate "something wrong" from "interesting physics." Again, they saw such skills as highly transferable. "I feel like I could approach another field—in the sciences, anyway—and be able to make some progress," said one chemistry student.

Working with others fostered gains in critical thinking and communication, but collaboration was itself a valued "real world" skill seen as useful in future work settings. "It's frustrating, but also good that you deal with it," said a male engineering student. Other students mentioned gains in their ability to plan, organize, and document their work. The following comment reflects both a new organizational skill and an attitudinal shift toward "becoming a scientist":

> *Time management, that's a big deal. I was flipping through my lab book today and saw days where I can't believe I only wrote half a page or a page in my lab book. What was I doing all day [laughs] that I only wrote that much? And I know now that you want to get in and get as much as you can, because the lab time is the precious time and the analysis time is—you have lots of time for that. (male UR student, chemistry)*

Gains in their ability to read and digest scientific literature enabled students to extract more and better information from articles "as opposed to just looking at a paper and seeing gobbledygook." Students learned how to find scientific information and how to quickly sort through literature or catalogues to find what they sought.

Research advisors noticed the growth of skills among their research students and the confidence that these gains generated, but they saw gains in skills as nearly a matter of course. They were more interested, as we discuss in Chapter Seven, in students' development as budding scientists, where temperament, habits of mind, and adoption of professional behaviors and understandings outweighed specific skills.

Enhanced Preparation for Career and Graduate School

The final two categories relate directly to students' future career and education plans, together accounting for 20 to 25 percent of gains observations. The first category addresses observations about how undergraduate research prepared students for postbaccalaureate work and study—increasing their readiness and affording concrete advantage in attaining a desired future post. We distinguish these from observations about how UR influenced students' career ideas and choices for postcollege work or study, discussed in the last gains section.

Observations about enhanced preparation for career and graduate school account for 10 percent of student observations, 16 percent of alumni observations, and 10 percent of research advisor observations. In the early interviews, these observations are prospective: students anticipate their future careers and imagine how the benefits of their UR experience will apply in the future, but they do not yet know if this is truly the case. Chapter Five addresses career preparation as viewed two to three years out of college.

The largest group of observations notes the value of UR as a real-world work experience. For students intending to pursue graduate school, UR was "a taste of what science research is like . . . a taste of reality, almost," as one biology student put it.

> *For a long, long time, science seemed to me to just be learning from books—and it hasn't been until recently that I've found out that people actually need to* write *the books based on information they discover. I was kind of scared that I had been going through high school seeing myself as a scientist, or wanting to be a scientist, and wondering whether research science would just be completely different for me, and undesirable. (male UR student, biology; emphasis in original)*

Though conducted within the protective walls of their campus and under the supervision of dedicated mentors, the summer research experience was closer to real scientific research than was course-based laboratory work. Working a forty-hour week, getting paid, and holding responsibility made summer research like a "real job." Working on a meaningful research problem required independence and effort and helped students to envision applying the same capacities as future professionals. "It's nice to have faculty there, but [my research advisor] really taught me this summer how to cope with your own problems, propose your own solutions, . . . set your own goals. And I think that's going to be really important for medical school and in the future" (male UR student, chemistry).

Building career networks was also useful career preparation. Students counted on their research advisors to provide career advice, letters of recommendation, and entrée to their own collegial networks. Through contacting colleagues about research issues or meeting them at conferences, students had met other scientists who might use their findings or help them land a job. In addition to such pragmatic benefits, these experiences also showed students how scientists use professional networks to draw on others' expertise, share resources, and promote their work—another aspect of professional socialization, or "becoming a scientist." "In the scientific world," noted a biology student, "it's kind of like you *need* to see these people, and you get used to knowing what their work is."

Research advisors fostered the careers of former research students years beyond graduation and noted concrete outcomes of UR that benefited their students as well as themselves, such as published articles, student awards, and scholarships. In contrast, for students, most of these career benefits were not yet realized at the time of our first interviews.

However, they did anticipate immediate application of skills and knowledge derived from research in their senior courses and thesis work, and later to a range of work and graduate school settings. "There are skills you can really use in any science field. Just learning how to plan, learning how to be careful, and how to take care of mistakes, and recover from mistakes. I think that's something you can really apply to any field" (focus group student, biology).

Only a small proportion of comments, just 18 percent, reflected instrumental views of the benefits of UR, such as how research experience would enhance their résumés for graduate school, medical school, or jobs. This finding is consistent with a separate analysis of students' motivations to pursue UR, in which only 17 percent of over two hundred motivation-related statements noted the instrumental utility of UR in achieving particular career goals. In contrast, 41 percent of statements about motivations addressed students' intrinsic interest in the field and desire to experience research, and another 16 percent cited goals of clarifying and preparing for future career and education goals. We see no substantial differences in motivation between the liberal arts college students in this sample and separate samples of public university students in campus-based undergraduate research programs (Coates, Liston, Thiry, & Laursen, 2005; Thiry & Laursen, 2009). This is likely due to both the strong intrinsic interests of students who seek research opportunities and the emphasis on interest in research advisors' criteria for selecting students, discussed in Chapter Seven.

Clarification and Confirmation of Career and Educational Goals

The influence of undergraduate research experiences on students' post-baccalaureate plans is of substantial interest to those who advise research students, promote research programs as part of undergraduate science education, and support such programs materially. Institutions commonly link research participation to graduate school attendance, but a causal connection has not been established. Indeed, about 11 percent of benefits-related statements in both student and alumni interviews and 16 percent of advisors' statements described how UR experiences enabled students to clarify, confirm, and refine their future plans. As for career preparation benefits, these were prospective comments about career intentions that were not yet realized. In Chapter Five, we discuss alumni initial career paths following graduation and their retrospective views of how UR influenced their pursuits.

In their statements about career influences, only a few students indicated that UR had prompted a significant change in their plans. In the first student interviews, seven students stated that doing research had clarified for them that a future in research was "not for me." As one woman explained, "I really enjoy doing research, but I can't see myself doing it for my entire life. I don't see myself in a lab, day in and day out."

A substantial motivation for most students was the chance to try out research as a possible future path, whether a career or in graduate work. Thus, discovering that research was not a good fit was a useful clarification that helped to send students in other career directions, as it was for this male biology student who was considering becoming a science teacher: "I came to the conclusion that I don't really want to be a researcher for the rest of my life—and I think I already knew that. And [research] is interesting, but I think I have other areas of interest where I'm doing a lot more."

The value of research experience was notable for two particular groups of students, despite their lack of interest in research careers. Premedical students gained insight into how medical research led to clinical advances and into the uncertainties inherent in interpreting research results. Future teachers valued learning "how science works" so they could teach science as a living process of discovery rather than a staid body of fact. "I decided I wanted to be a high school teacher. . . . Not only can I talk about biology, 'cause I love biology, I'm excited about it, but I also have the research foundation to how these things are built up" (female UR student, biology).

In the first interviews, no student said that a research experience had *introduced* the idea of going to graduate school or pursuing research; many had come to college with these possibilities in mind (see Chapter Five). Among this group of largely middle-class, mostly white students attending liberal arts colleges, students had already encountered, at home or in college, the possibility of graduate work. Thus, research served to test a prior interest rather than introduce a new one. Indeed, many students undertook research for the express purpose of exploring their graduate school interests. The effect of UR experiences on career plans appears to differ for other student groups (Chapter Six).

Thus, instead of broad changes in career direction, most students described more subtle influences on their plans, such as a growing certainty in their plans to pursue graduate school: "I think if I hadn't done research work, I wouldn't have a very good idea of what graduate school would be like, . . . of what science was really all about. It's one thing to study science, but it's another to work on and solve problems" (male UR student, chemistry).

Another large group of observations described refinements in students' choice of field. Many confirmed an area of particular interest, discovered how their interests meshed with particular fields of graduate study, or developed a firmer preference among several choices. Some reported greater focus or increased interest and enthusiasm for a chosen field, and a few were introduced to a new field altogether. Research advisors had observed the same developments, and with their longer perspective, had seen them play out in students' decision making: "It helped me decide what I like about chemistry. . . . Being in class, it's more, 'Oh, I have to turn in this homework assignment and study for this test,' but in research, I really enjoy chemistry a lot more. . . . It helped me decide that I like organic a lot better than p-chem [physical chemistry], which isn't really something I can do just from taking a class" (female UR student, chemistry).

Again, clarity was valuable to students whether it helped to identify a possible field or to rule one out: "I know I'm not as interested in nuclear physics as I had originally thought, and so I don't think I'm going to pursue that. But it has given me the experience to know what research is like and what is required out of it" (male UR student, physics).

In the student interviews, career intentions, like career preparation, were still hypothetical. Students gained confidence in their career ideas through hands-on experience of "what it's like" to do research full time. At this stage, students were thinking hard about "what was next." These concerns were strongly reflected in their motivations to pursue research. Yet they were still a year away from graduation, and many comments reflected students' uncertainty and openness to other ideas that might arise. In contrast, most alumni had taken at least initial steps toward a career or graduate work, and their career commentary was less hypothetical, as discussed in Chapter Five.

Group Differences

Although we examined the student gains data for differences in the nature or intensity of outcomes among different student groups, we found few patterns. We paid particular attention to gender differences. Treating the original UR student samples as populations of all students doing UR in a particular summer, Catherine Riegle-Crumb conducted a statistical analysis of gender differences in gains frequencies. She found that, per capita, women reported higher numbers of personal/professional gains—confidence and collegiality—than did men; there were no other statistically significant gender differences. In her analysis, gender strongly interacted with discipline and college; when combined, these equate to the student's department. She thus concluded that "there does not appear to be a strong gender trend that completely transcends these other factors" (Riegle-Crumb, personal communication, 2002); a larger sample would be needed to detect any such trends. Strong departmental variation in factors such as overall climate and the numbers of women faculty and other women students have been suggested to explain substantial variation in women's STEM degree attainment (Sonnert, Fox, & Adkins, 2007). Differences by ethnicity could not be studied in the four-college sample because of the small number of students of color, but outcomes for students of color are the focus of a separate study described in Chapter Six.

Despite disciplinary variations in how research is conducted, we were struck by the similarity of students' comments across mathematics, engineering, and the sciences. However, having multiple UR experiences, particularly within the same research group, did appear to matter. In our student sample, approximately half the students were new to research, while one-quarter had prior UR experience on the same campus and one-quarter had prior UR or internship experience off campus (see Appendix A for details). Students with longer research experience did report stronger gains, especially the higher-order gains in "thinking and working like a scientist"—the ability to propose research questions and design investigations and the understanding of how knowledge is constructed. As noted, these sophisticated understandings take time to develop. Other studies have also reported stronger gains or greater impacts for students with longer research experiences (Coates et al., 2005; Russell, 2006; Zydney, Bennett, Shahid, & Bauer, 2002b), and we have observed developmental differences in the nature of student gains (Thiry & Laursen, 2009). These results suggest that having early UR experiences may enhance students' gains and develop transferable skills useful earlier in their college careers. But we also have evidence from other studies that students must be developmentally ready to make certain gains from a research experience, and that designing projects for beginning college students can be challenging (Hunter, Thiry, & Crane, 2009; Thiry & Laursen, 2009). Thus offering research to younger students also brings additional challenges of its own, as well as having an impact on research advisors' own scholarly progress (Chapter Nine). The desire to offer the gains provided by UR through alternate means and earlier in students' college careers is a strong impetus behind many efforts to develop other types of classroom-based, research-like experiences.

Finally, it is fair to ask whether students' gains are specific to the liberal arts college setting of this study. As discussed in Chapter Two, the literature generally indicates wide alignment of student gains across study settings. In our own work evaluating structured UR programs at research universities, students have reported the same benefits as described here (Coates et al., 2005; Hunter et al., 2009; Thiry & Laursen, 2009). University students' gains were qualitatively indistinguishable from those reported by the liberal arts college students, but we saw more cases of students whose research experiences did not offer the same level of gains and who had decided not to continue in science or research. Conversely, we have noted the absence of some of these gains in a work-focused internship program at a national laboratory (DeAntoni et al., 2001). Lopatto (2008) notes some variations in the strength of gains reported by undergraduates at colleges versus universities that are related to whether the gains were taught implicitly, through research advisors' teaching and modeling, or explicitly, through formal program elements such as workshops. Chapters Four and Six further address the issue of what determines the nature and strength of outcomes from a UR experience.

Conclusion

It is clear from the evidence that apprentice-model undergraduate research is a powerful learning experience. Our six main categories of benefits to students are robust across multiple data sets in this study and have proven equally robust in understanding student gains from apprentice-model UR in other settings. Such benefits are multifold, encompassing students' personal growth, gains in knowledge and skills, preparation for post-baccalaureate education and careers, and understanding of themselves as future professionals. These are powerful assists for those who further pursue science, mathematics, or engineering; they are also highly desired outcomes of any liberal education.

A theme that rings across the interviews is that undergraduate research yields these gains through authentic experience: students are engaged in real scientific problems to which neither they nor their research advisors know the solutions. Like more experienced scientists, students' work is embedded in a community of practice as they interact with fellow scientists in their research groups, departments, and broader research communities. They see and learn from how their advisors think out loud, solve problems, and cope with everyday setbacks and ambiguous results. By tackling an authentic problem, students also learn authentic skills and adopt authentic practices.

Chapter 4

Are the Gains from Research Unique?

STUDENT PARTICIPATION IN research as undergraduates is widespread, but some students still do not have access to or interest in these opportunities. In fact, the majority of STEM undergraduates nationally do not participate in research (Boyer, 2002). At the four colleges in this study, too, many STEM students did not engage in summer research on campus. Some applied for a research position and were not selected, and others found alternative opportunities that better matched their interests and goals. What may nonparticipants have missed by not participating in summer research on campus? And what may they have gained through alternate experiences, including internships, jobs, or course work? And does the context and duration of the research experience matter? Do students make similar gains through academic year research or off-campus research at universities and government laboratories?

Using the analytical framework of benefits identified for research students in Chapter Three, we discuss whether the benefits derived from participation in summer research at liberal arts colleges may be gained elsewhere, including alternative types of research experiences. This analysis is novel, as the literature on internships and other preprofessional experiences largely focuses on career-related outcomes and does not address more general benefits (Thiry, Laursen, & Hunter, 2010).

Varied Professional Experiences of Comparison Students

We studied these questions through a comparison sample of students who did not participate in summer UR on their campuses. Though identified by their departments as nonparticipants, we discovered that many had in fact found off-campus research experiences or engaged in other forms of on-campus research, such as senior theses or independent study projects, during the academic year. Thus, the research experiences of the comparison sample of students allow us to determine whether the gains made by summer research students at liberal arts colleges are applicable to research in other contexts. Because many comparison students did engage in a research experience, we refer to the main sample of students who engaged in summer research on their home campus as "UR students" and comparison students who had engaged in research in other forms as "alternative research students," "late research students," or, collectively, "comparison students with research experiences." To better understand what comparison students did or did not gain from their alternative experiences, we first describe their diverse undergraduate experiences. Demographic details for the comparison student sample are given in Appendix A, and the study methods are detailed in Appendix B.

About one-fourth of the comparison students applied for a research experience on their home campus and were not selected. Although half of these students were able to find other jobs or internships in their fields, only three went on to participate in research at an alternative location. Thus most students who were not selected for UR did not find research opportunities elsewhere.

More often, however, comparison students chose not to participate in summer research on their home campus because they had different interests and educational goals and sought professional development experiences that would better meet their needs. The range of students' experiences is set out in Table 4.1.

TABLE 4.1

Distribution of STEM Educational Experiences Within the Comparison Student Sample (*N* = 62 Students)

Experience	Number of Students	Percentage of Interview Sample[a]	Notes
Late research on campus	16	26%	42 percent of students conducted
Alternative research off campus	15	24%	some form of research. Five students had multiple research experiences.
Internship off campus	28	45%	
Clinic program on campus with off-campus client	10	16%	
Course work and general college experience	62	100%	42 percent of students participated in research-like classroom activities. 15 percent of students had only these experiences and no preprofessional experiences.

[a]Percentages do not total to 100 because some students engaged in multiple experiences.

Altogether, nearly half of comparison students participated in some type of research experience. Some of these students, labeled alternative research participants, pursued an off-campus summer research experience on their own. These students found opportunities that more closely fit their interests than those offered on their home campuses. Some students had experiences that rivaled those of their peers who stayed on campus, but a few found themselves in labs where they received little or no guidance and engaged in tedious, routine tasks. Still others, labeled "late" research participants, undertook a senior thesis project or conducted independent research on campus during their senior year. Late research experiences differed from summer research experiences because they were situated later in students' undergraduate careers and were generally independent projects that did not involve collaboration with a lab group.

Internships or summer jobs in students' fields of interest were another common professional experience for comparison students. The range of internships reflects the varied interests of comparison students. Students undertook internships in industry (typically in engineering or technology firms), education, health care, environmental organizations, and community agencies. Some of these students worked in real-life settings and engaged in authentic, independent work under the guidance of a mentor, while others received little or no direction and engaged in meaningless tasks irrelevant to their career interests.

A small number of comparison students participated in the clinic program offered at one college. In this long-standing educational program, students work in small, interdisciplinary groups of four or five students to solve a real-world problem for a sponsoring company. The program provides opportunities for juniors and seniors in the computer science, engineering, mathematics, and physics departments to work on practical, applied projects of significance to business and the community. Students work closely in teams under the guidance of a faculty member, student team leader, and company liaison and must work within budget and scheduling constraints that add to the authenticity of the experience.

A few comparison students had no professional, out-of-class experiences at all. However, many STEM courses on the four campuses, particularly upper-division classes, contained a research-like component, in which students engaged in small, open-ended projects, either individually or in small groups, that included elements of authentic scientific inquiry.

Many courses also required substantial written work, extensive literature reviews, and oral presentations where students shared ideas and debated their work with each other. Although students in the UR sample also took such classes, they rarely discussed their course work during interviews. Thus, comparison students' experiences in STEM courses provided the means to analyze whether the gains achieved by summer UR students could be achieved instead through course work.

Overview of Findings from the UR and Comparison Student Interviews

Overall, students' comments about participation in research and other undergraduate experiences were positive from both UR and comparison students, at 91 percent and 82 percent of all comments, respectively. The primary differences, then, between UR and comparison students rest not in their gains or positive comments, but in what they *did not get* from their experiences as demonstrated by their negative and mixed comments. Students' negative observations described what they did not gain during college, and their mixed observations referred to areas in which they may have made limited or weak gains and did not yet feel confident and independent. Mixed observations also included comments in which students asserted that they had made gains but, by their descriptions of those gains, had not achieved those gains at a developmental level appropriate for a college student. Table 4.2 compares UR and comparison students' positive, negative and mixed observations on gains derived from all sources, and Appendix D provides detailed frequency counts.

Because of the variability among students' experiences, identifying the sources of gains reported by comparison students is essential to understanding the nature of gains among various undergraduate experiences. The comparison student interviews were coded using the same analytical framework for UR students discussed in Chapter Three. Although new codes were identified from the comparison data, no new analytical categories were discovered. To differentiate the source of experience for comparison students, codes were created to reference both the specific benefit and the source of the gain. For example, separate codes were developed for "gains in general critical thinking skills from course work," "gains in general critical thinking skills from internships," and so forth. This allowed us to carefully delineate the sources of student gains and identify which sources led to particular outcomes. In addition, student quotations are labeled with the source of gain and whether it is a positive, negative, or mixed observation.

Figure 4.1 shows, for each category of gain, the proportion of positive and negative/mixed observations for comparison students that derive from each experiential source, weighted by the number of students participating in each type of educational experience as listed in Table 4.1 (see Appendix B for details). Because of the weighting, if the sources contributed equally to any given gain, the proportions on the corresponding bar in Figure 4.1 would be equal at one-sixth of the gains from each source. The shading in Figure 4.1 displays the six sources of gains as three pairs: research experiences (alternative and late), work experiences (internships and clinic), and campus experiences (courses and general). As is evident in the figure, research experiences often yielded a disproportionate fraction of positive observations, while course work or general college experiences often yielded a larger proportion of mixed or negative

FIGURE 4.1

Population-Weighted Sources of Gains Reported by Comparison Students with Multiple STEM Education Experiences

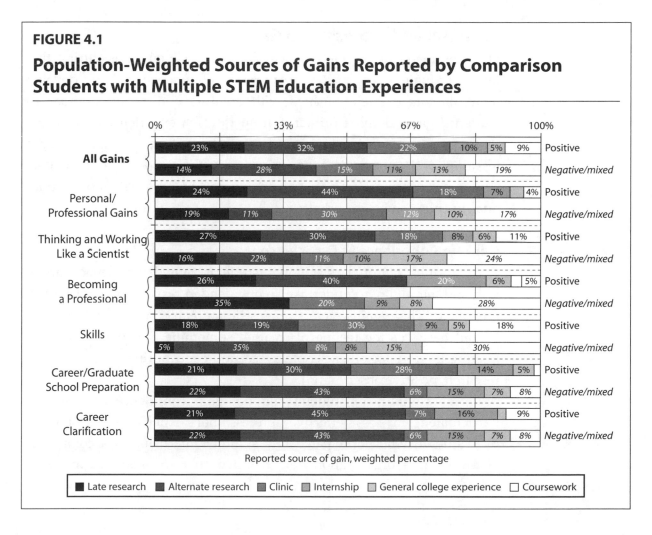

Reported source of gain, weighted percentage

Late research ■ Alternate research ■ Clinic ■ Internship □ General college experience □ Coursework

observations—again, reflecting not a negative response to courses but failure to make a gain.

The analysis for population-weighted sources is described in Appendix B. Contributions of less than 4 percent are shown but not labeled.

Comparison and UR Students' Observations on Gains from UR and Other Professional Experiences

The types of gains identified by UR students applied remarkably well to alternate experiences; however, there were substantial differences in the distribution of those gains between the two groups. For instance, comparison students spoke less about personal/professional gains and gains in scientific thinking, yet they discussed gains in skills and career preparation more often than UR students. Table 4.2 contrasts UR and comparison students' observations in the six major categories of gains.

Personal and Professional Gains

Students made numerous personal and professional gains during their undergraduate years, including increased confidence and the development of collegial relationships with mentors and peers. Comparison students' gains derived primarily from research experiences, suggesting that research experiences in a variety of contexts can yield significant professional and personal growth. In contrast, the majority of comparison students' negative observations came from students with no, or poor-quality, professional experiences.

Gains in Confidence to Do Science

Through their out-of-class activities, students gained confidence, particularly in their ability to undertake an open-ended project and contribute to their field. These gains were strongest for research students: "The thing I liked best was the feeling of creating something and polishing it and making it ready for other people to see, and contributing to science" (late research, positive observation).

Some comparison students did not gain confidence because they participated in less effective professional experiences. Comments by a student who participated in a summer internship at a community environmental organization demonstrated that she had not made the

TABLE 4.2

Student Gains from Other Professional Experiences in Comparison with UR, as Reported by Comparison Students and UR Students

"Parent" Categories: Grouping of Gain-Related Codes and Major Subgroups of Each	Positive Observations (% of All)		Negative and Mixed Observations (% of All)	
	Comparison Students (62)	UR Students (76)	Comparison Students (62)	UR Students (76)
Personal/professional gains	*11%*	*23%*	*3%*	*2%*
Increased confidence	7%	17%	2%	2%
Establishing collegial working relationships	4%	6%	1%	<1%
Thinking and working like a scientist	*23%*	*22%*	*6%*	*1%*
Application of knowledge and skills	18%	13%	5%	<1%
Increased knowledge and understanding of science and research work	5%	9%	1%	1%
Becoming a professional	*8%*	*11%*	*2%*	*1%*
Demonstrated gains in behaviors and attitudes necessary to become a professional	4%	3%	<1%	<1%
Greater understanding of professional practice	1%	2%	<1%	<1%
Identification with and bonding to science and/or professional fields	3%	6%	2%	1%
Skills	*20%*	*16%*	*2%*	*1%*
Communication skills	10%	7%	2%	<1%
Laboratory, organizational, and other skills	9%	9%	1%	<1%
Enhanced career/graduate school preparation	*12%*	*9%*	*2%*	*<1%*
Real-world work experience	7%	3%	1%	<1%
Networking and résumé enhancement	5%	6%	1%	<1%
Clarification and confirmation of career/education paths	*7%*	*10%*	*2%*	*3%*
Clarification of career and graduate school intentions	2%	5%	<1%	1%
Increased interest/enthusiasm for field	5%	5%	2%	2%
Total number and percentage[a]	*1,649 (82%)*	*1,219 (91%)*	*374 (18%)*	*120 (9%)*

[a]Subgroup percentages may not sum due to rounding. Appendix D includes the actual frequency counts and a detailed breakout of categories.

transition to becoming an independent learner during her internship. Thus she still lacked confidence in her mastery of her discipline: "I feel like I could learn how to do a lot of things if someone taught me. I'm a little sketchy in chemistry—if you tested my confidence in that, I might not be so high at times, because it's really hard. I just don't understand it like other people" (internship, negative observation).

Developing Collegial Relationships with Professionals and Peers

Through research and other authentic experiences, students built collaborative relationships with faculty members or other professionals in the field. As with other gains, research seemed to be the most successful experience in helping comparison students establish a mentoring relationship. A student described the distinct benefits of working side by side with a faculty member outside class: "It's nice to work with someone and become interested in the same thing that they're interested in, and work together toward that goal. And they almost become like a peer—you both have the same goal in mind, and they're entrusting you with a lot of responsibility" (alternative research, positive observation).

Some comparison students did not have the opportunity to work closely with a mentor. Though students derived many benefits from participating in the clinic program, they did not work as closely with a faculty mentor as did their peers in summer research on campus: "And with clinic, our professor definitely gets to know all of us really well. But we don't really see him in his element because we're working for the company, we're not doing what he does" (clinic, mixed observation).

Because of the atmosphere of intellectual engagement and faculty accessibility on the four college campuses, many students developed friendly relationships with faculty. Small labs and research-like activities in courses fostered close student-faculty interaction, though not to the same extent as did research experiences: "[I did not receive mentoring] to the extent that some of the people who have done undergraduate research, as far as their relationship with their professor that they did research with. But I feel comfortable with several different professors who will ask me what I'm doing after I'm done here" (no research experience, mixed observation). Indeed, for many nonparticipants, the opportunity to develop a close personal and professional relationship with a professor was the primary aspect of research that they felt they missed: "In retrospect, the mentoring sounds like it would have helped a lot. Just working one-on-one with a faculty advisor, where I can find out more about that person and see how they like doing what they do. . . . My relationship with my [academic] advisor was very, very formal and not very personal at all. I think I would have enjoyed having a personal relationship with him" (internship, negative observation).

Less often UR and comparison students developed working relationships with their peers. Course work, internships, and clinic yielded the greatest gains in peer collegiality. Since students in these contexts typically received less mentoring from faculty and other professionals, they often supported each other in group projects. Although clinic students had less interaction with faculty than did UR students, clinic was particularly successful in fostering collaboration among students: "In the clinic team, we can work on each other's strengths. Some of us have strength in public speaking, some of us have strength in writing or research or experimentation" (clinic, positive observation).

Overall, students developed collegial relationships with mentors and peers through a variety of experiences, not limited to research. However, research experiences were the most consistently successful method of fostering mentoring relationships with faculty or other professionals, while clinic and course work were more successful in fostering peer collaboration.

Thinking and Working Like a Scientist

From the broad array of educational activities in their undergraduate years, comparison students learned to apply their scientific knowledge and skills and enhanced their understanding of the scientific research process, as well as their understanding of the discipline. The nature of intellectual gains differed between comparison and UR students: comparison students reported gains in generalized critical thinking and problem-solving skills, while UR students, and comparison students with research experience, developed more specific research and scientific thinking skills.

Comparison students developed general critical thinking skills from their course work and from the intellectual atmosphere on the liberal arts college campuses, but course work, even with inquiry-based labs, did not usually foster understanding of the research process or research design. Although research fostered gains in scientific thinking for some students, poor research experiences also led to a lack of gains in this category for a few students.

Gains in the Ability to Apply Knowledge and Skills

The quality of the research experience, particularly in mentoring and the student's level of responsibility for the work at hand, was crucial to developing scientific thinking, as seen in this speaker's contrasting research experiences:

> *Before I came here, I worked for one summer in a molecular biology lab. While I learned a technique that most people don't know before their sophomore year, it wasn't authentic. It was as authentic as my mentor could make it while he's writing a whole bunch of grants over the summer. As opposed to here, where every single week, I have to report to my lab group and say, "Well, this is what's going on, and we've found this band," and thinking about what am I going to do next. So I think that that gave it the authenticity. . . . I had a role in this lab. (alternative and late research, negative and positive observations)*

While science courses did contribute to some intellectual gains, they were less successful than research in increasing students' understanding of the process of scientific research. In the following example of an observation in which a student asserted a gain yet had not achieved it, a student recounted how he had "learned" the research process from scientific coursework. However, he simply described "cookie-cutter" labs rather than the open-ended process of scientific discovery: "And in terms of how to go about doing research, I think I've learned that from the labs that I've done. They tell me I need to do this, and then I can do this. You just learn that along the way in your education" (no professional experiences, negative observation).

Students also grew in their ability to apply critical thinking and problem-solving skills to their research project. Through research, students applied these skills in a way that they did not through their regular course work. Most comparison students did not gain this ability through course work alone: "When you're in a class situation, other students will be doing the same thing, and the professor will have done it for the last four years with the same class and they'll know what to expect. But when you're doing summer research, you're asking a question that's never been asked before. And the professor knows just as little about it as you do, potentially, and so it definitely provides an opportunity for critical thinking and problem-solving" (alternative research, positive observation).

Comparison students more often gained general critical thinking and problem-solving skills, as fewer of them had the opportunity to apply problem-solving skills to a research project. Their courses and the stimulating academic environments on their home campuses had honed these abilities. In fact, almost all of comparison students' observations about general intellectual skills referred to course work or the general campus environment, which encouraged critical thinking, reflection, and examination of issues from multiple perspectives: "That's [critical thinking] built into the study here—because a lot of times, especially in the upper-level classes, you're given a very sketchy outline of a problem and told this is what your [computer] program needs to do. And it is up to you to figure out how your program is going to do this" (computer science major discussing course work, positive observation).

Gains in Conceptual and Theoretical Understanding

Through research, students gained conceptual and theoretical understanding, appreciated the relevance of course work, and understood connections within and between disciplines. Students who had participated in summer research on their home campus made twice as many positive comments in this area as did comparison students.

Comparison students occasionally made negative or mixed comments about their understanding of the discipline. For example, one student found the complex conceptual knowledge required in her upper-level classes difficult to understand, and her off-campus research experiences had not helped in this area. She had access to authentic work in both of her research experiences but did not move toward greater responsibility on the project and became stuck in an entry-level capacity: "I love logic and problem solving, and I love doing experiments, but I get lost in all the theory. And sometimes [in] the higher-level classes, I just needed to go slower. It's hard for me to really a get a good understanding of it and keep up at the same time" (alternative research, negative observation).

In sum, comparison students who had intellectually challenging research experiences made greater gains than nonresearch participants in the ability to apply critical thinking and problem-solving skills to research and in understanding the process of scientific research. Many students who did not participate in research made strong gains in general critical thinking from their course work, but research-like experiences in courses did not provide the same depth and intensity as research experiences.

Becoming a Professional

Through out-of-class experiences, students began to adopt the behaviors and attitudes necessary to become a professional. Although this category was originally termed "becoming a scientist," we renamed it for the comparison group because many of their professional experiences occurred in fields outside science, such as business, marketing, government, or philanthropy. As in other categories, research experiences yielded the bulk of comparison students' gains.

Despite their gains in other facets of becoming a professional, some comparison students failed to gain a greater understanding of the real-life practice of scientists or other professionals. Most of these students either did not engage in any professional experiences outside the classroom or had research or internship experiences dominated by busywork.

Learning to Work and Think Independently

Through research and other professional experiences, comparison students described changes in learning to work and think independently, taking responsibility for their own learning, and taking initiative to solve problems on their own. Students, particularly those who had done research, began to pay careful attention to details in their projects and took pride in the results of their work. Many internship students also worked on real-world projects in which they were responsible for an important component of a larger project. They managed budgets and organized and implemented project activities, holding greater responsibility than they had experienced in course work. One internship student described her experience: "When I did the summer work, they'll tell me, 'All right, we have this problem. We don't really know how you want to solve it—go to it, analyze different possibilities.' And so in that way you learn to work independently and to study independently" (internship, positive observation).

While many comparison students became self-reliant and independent learners, some students had no opportunity for independent work outside the classroom. A student described her shortcomings as a learner, which had not been enhanced through any professional experiences: "I see myself as an active learner, but a lot of times I don't have the motivation or the means to become more active in my learning" (no professional experiences, negative observation).

Developing the Temperament of a Scientist

Many comparison students who undertook research came to a new understanding of the nature of research work. Students who had ownership of a research project described learning to cope with failures and setbacks that they experienced in the lab. In contrast, students with no research experience, or with poor-quality research experiences that involved only simple tasks, had no basis for reaching these new understandings. A student whose summer research experience at a government laboratory had emphasized routine data collection techniques reported its lack of impact on her thinking about the process or nature of scientific research: "I've done all of that since I was twelve, really. My undergraduate research hasn't affected that, because I've done it already" (alternative research, negative observation).

Understanding Professional Practice

A few comparison students described gains in understanding how scientists or other professionals practice their profession. Research and other authentic experiences let students observe how scientists and other professionals undertake their day-to-day work. Research students observed faculty or government scientists discuss and write grant proposals and journal manuscripts, undergo peer review and publish, and attend conferences to present scientific papers. Comparison students in other settings observed professionals coordinating and managing project budgets, time lines, resources, and personnel. A student who conducted summer research at a government laboratory described his observations of scientists: "I would attend weekly staff meetings and faculty meetings, where everyone would talk about the progress of their work. And where we would actually spend most of the time [was] talking about getting funding for the next round of work. I'd say—that's a lot closer to what I would be doing if I went on to be a professional in one of these fields" (alternative research, positive observation).

Through the challenges of authentic research work, some students learned how scientists or mathematicians think about problems and saw this as a new perspective that they would need to adopt to succeed in the profession. However, other comparison students, particularly those without research experiences or who were isolated in their off-campus research experience, did not gain a better understanding of the habits of mind or everyday practices of scientists. For example, when asked how scientists think, this student described physical work environments rather than approaches to problems: "People think in different ways. Some physicists, theoreticians, think exclusively in small, cold rooms with math and computers. Other physicists, experimentalists, think in large, cluttered labs full of lasers" (alternative research, negative observation).

Students gained an understanding of professional practice and began to develop an identity of a professional through a variety of undergraduate experiences. Course work alone, however, did not foster the same types of gains as did internships, off-campus or academic year research, or clinic. However, the quality of the experience, particularly in terms of support and guidance from experts who can serve as models of professional practice, was integral in fostering professional gains.

Skills

One of the most common benefits mentioned by comparison students and, to a lesser extent, by UR students was gains in skills. Students gained written and communication skills, mastered new research and laboratory techniques, and developed organizational skills. While courses offered fewer benefits than out-of-class experiences in some categories, they were a significant source of skills gains for comparison students.

Communication Skills

Comparison students reported gains in oral communication skills, learning how to present in a professional environment and to defend an argument. However, the nature of student presentation varied across different contexts. Within research experiences, students made formal end-of-summer presentations and sometimes had the chance to present at professional conferences, while presentations in courses were largely limited to an audience of peers and the instructor.

Presentations to a variety of audiences were a large and deliberate component of the clinic program. Students provided regular feedback on their progress to their industry clients, and each team wrote a summative report and presented its final results to the campus community. As one clinic student described it, "You give presentations similar to what you might give in a working environment. It's usually for a corporate working environment, around a report that really focuses on your progress and whether you're in the budget and how the time line's looking. A little different from scientific presentations, but still really good for organizing your material and being able to present it" (clinic, positive observation).

The general intellectual atmosphere at the four colleges also fostered extensive discussion, debate, and critique both within and outside class: "The liberal arts education itself involves a good degree of postulating theses and coming up with arguments to defend them. It's being able to justify what you think, or why you think something, that seems to be a crucial element to being here" (general college, positive observation).

Some comparison students noticed that their peers who had participated in UR had gained better presentation skills and were better able to justify and defend their ideas: "I think that's something that I might have missed out on by not doing research. Just in the sense that I think people who did it had a lot of room to come up with ideas and work on their problems. And I get the impression that maybe that's helped them in their courses. Some of the people I know who have done summer research have been somewhat more driven in coming up with concepts or trying to defend their ideas" (general college, negative observation).

Comparison students augmented their presentation skills in a variety of contexts, but course work was the primary source of their gains in writing skills. In courses, students often submitted formal lab reports and conducted scholarly literature reviews as part of writing assignments: "We've done a lot of writing where the professor will tell you, you need to write this as if it could be published. It's never been anything that really would be put forward, but it was just the format, and how high the quality was supposed to be" (course work, positive observation).

Other Skills

Students also gained skills in laboratory and computer techniques, organization and planning, and teamwork. As might be expected, research students discussed laboratory techniques more often than nonparticipants did. Repeated use of specific equipment and the real-life consequences of mistakes in research fostered greater gains than in the classroom setting, as the following quotations highlight:

> I got a lot of skills—working with the PCR [polymerase chain reaction (machine)], knowing how to actually clean and sterilize and do all the instruments. To have knowledge of all of this, to be able to say, "I've done it so many times that I'm not making any more mistakes." (alternative research, positive observation)

• • •

> So I have a little bit of everything, but nothing if you're comparing this to research—nothing like knowing every time you pick up a pipette that you know how to work it exactly. I'd probably have to think about it a little longer than other people. (course work, negative observation)

Overall, comparison students with research experience described the development of laboratory skills and oral argumentation skills. But their gains in more general presentation skills derived from a variety of contexts. They also described gains in writing skills more often than did UR students, primarily from formal writing assignments in their courses.

Enhanced Preparation for Career and Graduate School

Students' undergraduate out-of-class experiences helped them to feel prepared for careers or graduate school, strengthened their résumés, and provided opportunities to network with faculty and other professionals. Unlike other categories in which comparison students' gains derived mainly from research, internships and clinic were also significant sources of enhanced career preparation.

Real-World Experience, Résumé Enhancement, and Career Advice

Comparison students described the career benefits from engaging in an authentic, real-world experience more often than UR students. From internships, students directly experienced the nature of work in the careers they explored: 'It took something that was kind of abstract to me—'I'm going to be a clinical psychologist,' or 'I'm going to be in a field of psychology someday'—and it made it real. It showed me what it really is' (internship, positive observation).

Students in the clinic program benefited from their engagement in a real-world project: "It's a year of real-life experience, doing everything from project design to budgeting. A company that I recently applied with does a lot of this sort of stuff, based around the engineering aspects. And I think that I've got some real-life experience doing those exact sorts of things" (clinic, positive observation).

Students saw the real-world benefits of experiential opportunities as something that could not be gained through classes. Courses, even those that stressed real-world applications, did not provide a professional environment that helped students feel ready for similar contexts in the future. "I think [clinic and research] have been some of the highlights of my education here," said one student. "They've been the most realistic applications of the theoretical and background information that I've learned here. They're a lot more relevant to the work I'm about to go out and do, than most of the classes that I've had here" (clinic and alternative research, positive observation).

While internship students often compared themselves negatively to UR students in terms of confidence, research skills, or quality of mentoring, they compared themselves positively to UR students in terms of career preparation and real-world experience: "I think I have a little more experience than students who have done research. They know a lot about research topics and their area, and they're good at technical stuff. But when it comes to [the] real world, as far as working with other people and knowing how things are done in a company, I think I have a little advantage in that area" (internship, positive observation).

Although internships helped students to feel prepared for careers, research was the only experience that directly helped students feel prepared and confident in their readiness for graduate school: "Doing something of this size on my own, was something that I think that if I hadn't done it, I would have felt less prepared to go to grad school" (late research, positive observation).

In contrast, students with weak research experiences did not gain an understanding of what graduate school would be like. These students were often isolated in the lab and did not have the opportunity to learn about "real" research or life as a graduate student. The following comment highlights that students who do not learn about the research process or engage in independent work through UR can develop major misconceptions about graduate school: "I'm not quite sure what to expect. I assume it'll just be college with more physics and less humanities" (alternative research, negative observation).

Some comparison students mentioned career benefits that were not discussed by UR students, such as receiving career and graduate school advice and information, letters of recommendation, and help in securing UR, internship, or career positions. The initial UR interviews were conducted with rising seniors, whereas the comparison interviews were conducted with graduating seniors, so career advice was a more prominent topic for these students, as this comment illustrates: "I was able to talk to him about career options when I was making my decision between companies, as well as personal issues. This professor graduated from here so he could relate to that. . . . It was a great relationship" (clinic, positive observation).

Networking

Networking with scientists and other professionals helped students make professional contacts that could benefit them in their future careers. Research offered many opportunities for networking, but some students built professional networks through internships and other experiences: "The director of marketing and the VP themselves are friends of mine. And I still e-mail them. And a lot of the engineers have friends who are in marketing at Sun Microsystems or Intel, which actually are my top two [career] choices. And I was able to send my résumé directly to these people, so that was really good, connection-wise" (internship, positive observation).

• • •

In conclusion, a variety of experiences, including internships, the clinic program, and research, offered students the opportunity to engage in authentic, real-world work. Through these meaningful, experiential opportunities, students felt they received greater preparation for their future careers than from course work alone. Students who had done research, in particular, felt better prepared for graduate school than did their nonparticipating peers.

Clarification and Confirmation of Career and Educational Goals

Research and other experiences helped students to sustain or increase their interest in the field, learn about graduate school and career options, and clarify or confirm their intentions to go to graduate school or pursue a research career. Comparison students' gains (and lack thereof) in career clarification were disproportionately weighted toward research experiences.

Surprisingly, UR students made more mixed and negative comments in this category. However, the nature of mixed and negative observations between the two groups was quite different. Comparison students were more likely to report that a poor research experience had caused them to change their career and educational plans. Many of these students did not have access to a mentor and engaged in unchallenging, tedious lab work. This small group of students reported that a poor research experience had reduced their interest in a career in research or had not helped to clarify their intentions with respect to graduate school. UR students more often reported no impact because their career plans had not changed.

Refinement of Career and Educational Goals

Out-of-class experiences helped students to clarify whether graduate school or a career in research would be a good choice for them by trying out certain careers they might pursue after graduation. Internships, for example, were highly beneficial in helping students to discern what type of career they desire and what type of work environment might fit their talents, interests, and lifestyle: "It helps a lot as far as what type of engineering I want to do and what type of company I want to work for" (internship, positive observation).

On the other hand, only students who had participated in research were able to clarify whether they would like a career in research: "I have a better understanding of what it takes to be a researcher. I have a better understanding if research will work out for me, if it's something that I want to do" (late research, positive observation).

Other students, particularly those with no professional experiences or experiences that did not match their interests, did not gain clarity in their career or educational goals. I'm sure there is an area of physics that would interest me and drive me wild and make me go screaming into graduate school with my hair on fire. But not at the moment" (alternative research, negative observation).

Research experiences were the most effective mechanism to help comparison students clarify whether graduate school would serve their interests and goals. A student with two research experiences articulated how a poor research experience could have a negative impact on students' educational and career goals: "My first research experience gave me a negative view of graduate school and what it was like. The second one made me feel like, 'Okay, I can be a scientist.' Maybe graduate school is kind of this way, where you just have to publish papers and stuff, but if you can see around that and just do what you're interested in, then it might be good for me" (alternative research, positive and negative observations).

By the same token, good research experiences motivated a few students to pursue graduate school, especially those who had previously become discouraged in their majors. One student described how her research experience contrasted with other experiences: "I had an awful class schedule this last spring, and when you're trying to decide if you want to spend six more years doing this, it was extremely crucial for me to have this research experience. Because the field that I'm gonna go into in grad school was one of the classes that I didn't like—but I worked in that field during the summer and I realized, I like doing the research, I just didn't like the class. So it was important for me to have that positive experience to continue on" (alternative research, positive observation).

Participation in research also helped some students discover that research was not a good fit for their interests, goals, or temperament, particularly for students who were considering multiple career options at the start of their research experience: "After having done research in a medical lab, I kind of decided I don't want to do research in medical lab for my career, even though I enjoyed it for the summer. . . . [It] affirmed that I wanted to go into medicine, and in this direction" (alternative research, positive observation).

Increased Interest in the Discipline

Through course work or real-world experiences, students also expressed increased interest in their discipline or a particular field of study. Course work bolstered comparison students' enthusiasm for their major: "I've had a few classes that have really convinced me that there's a lot of beautiful math that can be done . . . and in the geometry class that I'm taking now, we're looking at a lot of unsolved problems. And it's taking classes like that that have kept my interest up in the discipline" (course work, positive observation).

In contrast, a few students lost interest in their discipline or abandoned their career and educational goals because of poor-quality research experiences. Without adequate intellectual challenge or support from more experienced scientists, these students lost interest in the work. Therefore, the quality of the research experience determined whether it had a positive or negative effect on students' future plans. A student describes how a poor experience deterred him from pursuing research:

> When I came to college, my plan was to do molecular biology research. I thought that was a pretty exciting field. But the more I did it . . . I found pure research to be pretty mechanical. I felt a lot of times that some sort of well-designed robot could be doing my job. There wasn't a lot of creativity in it at all. And there wasn't a lot of human interaction. I found myself just being in a lab, sort of doing monkey work. Maybe it was an interesting experiment, on the whole, but the day-to-day procedures were pretty isolated interactions. (alternative research, negative observation)

• • •

In sum, research and other undergraduate experiences helped students to clarify or refine their educational and career goals. A meaningful experience was critical in helping students to determine whether their future plans were a good fit for their personality and interests. Students' experiences highlight the significance of research in contributing to students' decisions to remain in or leave scientific fields. Poor research experiences served to turn off students from the discipline, while good research experiences increased student interest in and commitment to the field. We discuss students' career choices further in Chapter Five.

Conclusion

Students received the greatest benefits from their undergraduate education if their course work was supplemented with meaningful, experiential work in their field. While the four liberal arts colleges in this study offered a rigorous education in a scholarly environment, courses were constrained in their ability to offer authentic access to a scientific community. Courses provided skills that students would need to succeed as professionals but did not offer a real-world context in which to apply these skills.

Inquiry-based laboratory work within courses gave students a small taste of scientific research, but not to the extent offered by out-of-class, intensive research.

Real-world experiences, including internships, jobs, research, or clinic, provided a range of personal and professional benefits that complemented classroom learning. Both course work and out-of-class experiences helped students gain valuable communication, technical, organizational, and critical thinking skills. Internships helped students clarify their goals and gain insight into the nature of possible future careers and work environments. Through the clinic program, students gained teamwork, communication, and organizational skills, and meaningful real-world experience. More so than their peers, however, students who engaged in an intensive, authentic research experience, whether on their home campus or elsewhere, gained understanding of the process of scientific research and the everyday work and practice of scientists. Other cocurricular experiences offered a host of benefits, but participation in authentic research was the most effective way to socialize novice scientists by helping them to develop the mastery, knowledge, skills, and behaviors necessary to become a scientist.

While undergraduate science education can be augmented by engagement in a variety of high-quality real-world experiences, we find that research experiences fostered the broadest set of intellectual, personal, and professional gains in students. The context in which students engaged in research did not affect these gains, although the quality and authenticity of the research experience were critical to students' growth and development as scientists. Indeed, a poor experience often led students to lose interest in their field or abandon educational and career goals. Students made the greatest gains when they received adequate guidance from a knowledgeable professional, held an appropriate amount of responsibility for a meaningful project, and had the opportunity to work independently, or in effective peer groups, on challenging, real-world tasks.

Chapter 5

What Are the Career and Longer-Term Impacts of Undergraduate Research?

RESEARCH ADVISORS AND institutions have a stake in the longer-term educational impact of their undergraduate research (UR) efforts on students' lives beyond college. Funding agencies and program sponsors wish to know if their investments in UR are affecting the numbers, quality, and diversity of the science, technology, engineering, and mathematics (STEM) workforce. But little evidence exists to document any causal relationship between students' UR participation and their later choices to pursue advanced education or careers in STEM. Our study investigated two questions about the longitudinal impact of UR from students' point of view and with the added perspective of time:

1. How does UR influence students' postbaccalaureate choices about careers and graduate education?

2. What benefits of undergraduate research experience, if any, continue to hold value for students beyond college?

Our evidence on these questions comes from interviews with both UR participants and members of the comparison group as college alumni, two to three years after their baccalaureate graduation. This is not a long time—for many, career paths were still very much works in progress—but these interviews do offer a glimpse into students' initial career moves.

In this chapter we examine current careers and future plans of alumni, discuss their retrospective views on what influenced their decisions about graduate school and career pathways, and examine gains from their college STEM learning experiences that are of lasting significance.

Nature of the Evidence

Postgraduation interviews were conducted with the same people who participated in the earlier interviews as students (see Appendix A). We were able to reconnect with fifty-six UR alumni—74 percent of the original sample—and twenty-five comparison alumni, 40 percent of the original sample. Table 5.1 summarizes career choices for the alumni samples; as section A indicates, the gender balance shifted somewhat in each sample. The distribution of undergraduate experiences represented in the comparison group also differed from that of the original student sample;

TABLE 5.1

Career Choices of UR and Comparison Alumni

	UR Alumni	Comparison Alumni
A. Sample demographics		
Number of individuals interviewed	56	25
Gender distribution in comparison	33 men (of 40)	9 men (of 27)
with original samples	23 women (of 36)	16 women (of 35)
Overall proportion of original student sample	74%	40%
B. Current career status, as reported in alumni interviews		
1. Enrolled in advanced STEM education	61%	32%
a. STEM graduate school	26	6
b. Medical school	5	1
c. Teacher education (master's degree)	3	1 (3 completed already)
2. Enrolled in advanced non-STEM education	1	1
3. Working in STEM-based career in industry, government, nonprofit, or schools	18 (32%)	11 (44%)
a. Subset who are K–12 educators	2	3
4. Working in non-STEM field, transitional or temporary job, or unemployed	3	5
C. Graduate school intentions on entering college, as recalled during alumni interviews		
1. Planned to go to STEM graduate school or medical school	42 (75%)	11 (44%)
1a. Subset who recall this as a long-term ambition	13	4
2. Might go to STEM graduate school or medical school	8	1
3. Did not intend to go to STEM graduate school or medical school	6	13

D. Future career plans, as reported in alumni interviews[a]

1. Pursue advanced STEM education (not enrolled now)	10	4
a. STEM graduate school	7	4
b. Medical school	1	
c. Teacher education (master's degree)	2	
2. Attend non-STEM graduate school (not enrolled now)		1
3. Pursue STEM career, including continuing in current career	**95%**	**80%**
a. Research in higher education (professoriate)	11	2
b. Research in industry or government	13	1
c. Research, unspecified work setting or still deciding	7	1
d. K–12 schools	8	3
e. Medicine	5	1
f. Nonresearch career in industry, government, nonprofit	6	5
g. Uncommitted, but choosing within STEM	3	7
4. Pursue career outside STEM field, including continuing in current career	3	5

[a]Those planning to pursue advanced education are also counted by their career goal following advanced education. Thus, categories 1 and 2 in section D overlap categories 3 and 4, and categories 3 and 4 account for all members of the sample.

in particular, the proportion of research participants increased relative to internship and clinic participants. The low response rate for the comparison alumni means that findings about the career-related outcomes for this group should not be generalized.

We asked both groups about their current studies or work, how they arrived at these positions, their plans for the future, and what had influenced their career thinking and decisions. Alumni discussed the influence of their UR advisor and other professionals, and their use of professional networks in arriving at their current work positions. We also reviewed with alumni our study findings about student gains, asking them to comment and retrospectively evaluate their own gains, including how these may have transferred to their current work. We asked what experiences had led to their gains, so that we could analyze the relative importance of different sources of gains, as in Chapter Four. We coded these gains under the same categories discussed in Chapters Three and Four, and analyzed both for their qualitative content and weight of

FIGURE 5.1

Changes in Emphasis on Student Gains in Alumni Interviews Relative to Initial Student Interviews, from (a) Undergraduate Research Sample and (b) Comparison Sample

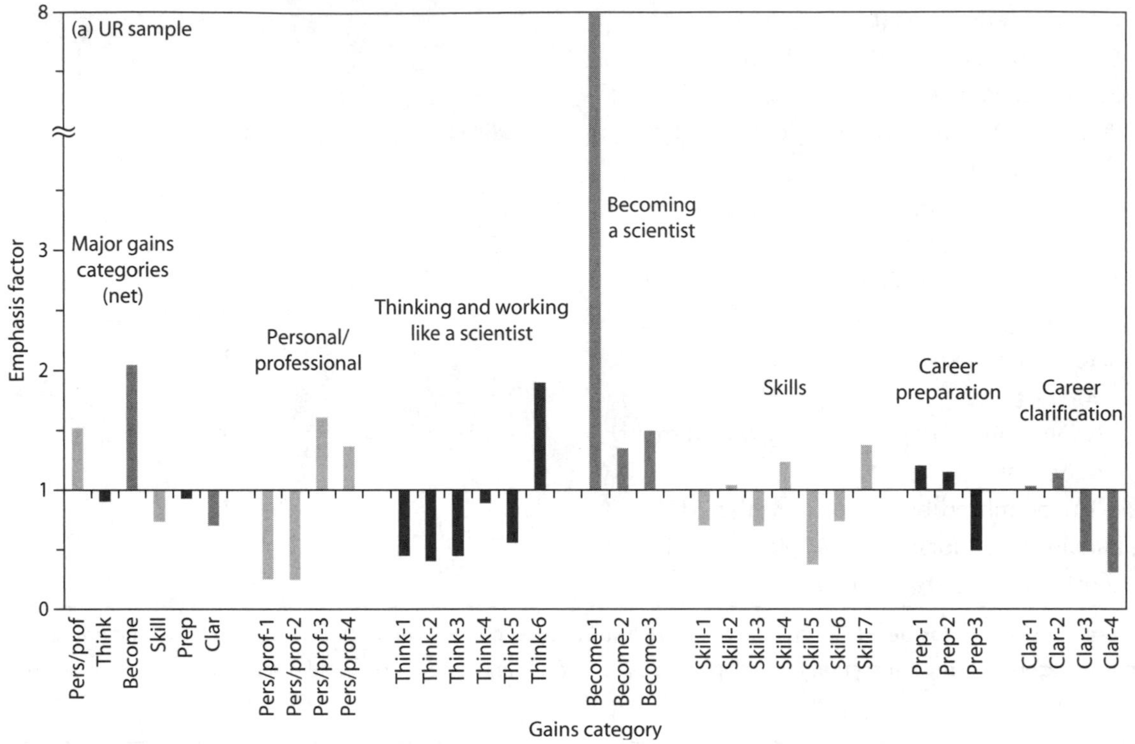

opinion. Again, a few new codes emerged from the analysis, but no major new categories.

Comparing these weights of opinion offers an interesting challenge, because the four data sets reflect both change over time and differences among interview groups. To examine changes in the importance of specific gains over time, we computed the ratio of alumni to students' per capita observations. To better compare these changes in importance between the UR participant and comparison group, we scaled each ratio to the overall size of the gains data set. For convenience, we nicknamed this weighted ratio the "emphasis factor," and we take it as a measure of change in respondents' emphasis over time, scaled to enable comparison across interview samples of different size and complexity (see Appendix B). The relative magnitude, not the precise value of each emphasis factor, is what matters: emphasis factors notably larger than 1 indicate gains that were especially frequent in alumni reports, and thus offer one type of evidence about the longer-term importance of UR. Emphasis factors for selected gains categories for both UR and comparison alumni are displayed in Figure 5.1.

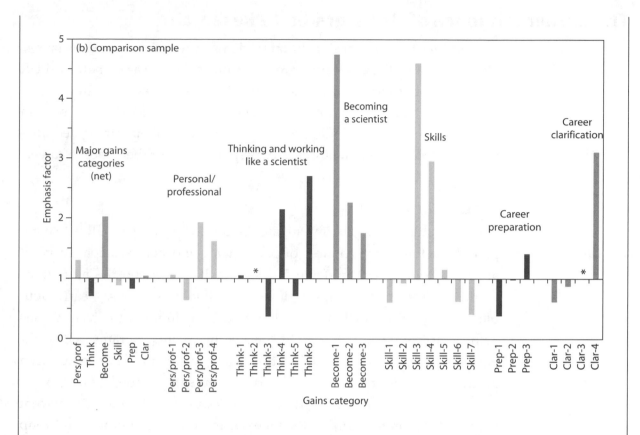

Note: The vertical scale is the same for both plots. Categories are omitted that are not comparable in content for student and alumni data for both UR and comparison groups. An asterisk designates a frequency count too small to produce a reliable ratio.

Legend: Pers/prof: Personal/professional gains; Think: Thinking and working like a scientist; Become: Becoming a scientist; Skill: Skills; Prep: Preparation for career and graduate school; Clar: Clarification and confirmation of career and education goals.

Pers/prof-1: Confidence to do science; Pers/prof-2: Feeling like a scientist; Pers/prof-3: Establishing collegial relationships with advisors; Pers/prof-4: Establishing collegial relationships with peers.

Think-1: Deepened knowledge in field; making conceptual connections; Think-2: Appreciation of relevance of course work; Think-3: Improved critical thinking and problem-solving skills; Think-4: Understanding research through hands-on experience; Think-5: Understanding how to pose and investigate research questions; Think-6: Understanding how knowledge is constructed and its nature.

Become-1: Understanding how scientists practice their profession; Become-2: Demonstrated gains in attitudes and behaviors of a scientist; Become-3: Understanding the nature of research work.

Skill-1: Oral presentation; Skill-2: Writing; Skill-3: Reading comprehension; Skill-4: Computer skills; Skill-5: Laboratory and field skills; Skill-6: Work organization and time management; Skill-7: Collaborative work.
Prep-1: Real-world work experience; Prep-2: Enhanced résumé and job/graduate school applications; Prep-3: Networking with other scientists. Clar-1: Confirmed interest in field; aided choice of field; Clar-2: Increased interest or enthusiasm for field; Clar-3: Introduced to a new field; Clar-4: Clarified and confirmed interest in graduate school.

The Career Influence of Undergraduate Research

We consider the influence of UR on students' careers by several measures. The simplest of these is early career outcomes: What career paths do UR students pursue after graduation, and do these differ from their peers who did not conduct research? Evidence of UR's impact is also seen in graduates' success in finding a career placement, their career decision-making processes, and their sense of preparedness for their chosen career.

Career Outcomes

The most obvious way to investigate the career influence of UR is to compare the actual career choices of participants and nonparticipants: What are they doing now? In Table 5.1, section B focuses on the alumna or alumnus's career status at the time of the final interviews. Nearly double the proportion of UR alumni as comparison alumni (61 percent versus 32 percent) were enrolled in STEM-related graduate programs in disciplinary research, medicine, or education. More members of the comparison group were working in STEM fields and outside. Among both groups, most alumni were still active in STEM work or graduate study (93 percent versus 76 percent, in all), but somewhat more of the comparison group members had moved outside the STEM fields.

A few years beyond graduation is a short time delay to probe career outcomes; indeed the career ideas of many alumni were still very much in flux when we spoke to them. Thus we also asked about their future career plans; their responses are tallied in section D. Several members of both groups planned to enroll in STEM graduate programs. If these alumni are added to those already enrolled, the proportion of UR alumni pursuing graduate work in STEM fields rises to 79 percent and to 48 percent for comparison alumni—still a notable difference.

The high proportion of UR alumni pursuing research degrees in STEM was echoed by their high interest in future research careers. The proportion intending to work in STEM fields changes little from those already in STEM, but the proportion of comparison alumni intending careers in STEM rises to 80 percent. Comparison alumni appeared to be headed toward a wider range of careers, with less concentration in research careers. Thus, from the career outcomes data alone, UR participation appears to associate with:

- Higher likelihood of graduate school attendance
- More probable choice of research as a career path
- Modestly higher retention within STEM-related fields

However, assigning a causal interpretation to these associations would be a mistake, as the evidence in section C suggests. UR alumni reported higher preexisting interest in graduate school as they entered college, with 75 percent already planning to attend and another 15 percent considering it, while fewer than half of comparison alumni had graduate school intentions on entering college. Thus the lower participation rate of comparison alumni in STEM graduate work, both at the time of the alumni interviews and in their future intent, is entirely accounted for by their lower level of intention to do so from the start. That is, these groups already had different interests and ambitions as they began college. In fact, in both groups, the overall proportion of alumni enrolled in graduate school or intending to do so is remarkably consistent with those reporting that intention on entering college—about three-quarters for UR alumni and less than half for comparison alumni. While the proportions are steady overall, they do conceal changes in individuals' decisions, in both directions. For example, three UR alumni reported that UR experience had introduced to them the idea of attending graduate school—not their prior plan—while other alumni had decided not to pursue graduate study after all. We discuss how UR and other experiences shaped career ideas of alumni.

As noted in Chapter Four, the comparison group included a few students who sought and did not obtain UR positions, but most had electively pursued other opportunities that better fit their interests. Many had found internships or jobs in fields that drew on their science backgrounds but emphasized business, policy, teaching, and other applied work rather than research, and their later career activities reflected these initial differences. Comparison alumni more often reported entering college without firm career ideas and more often had made career decisions as undergraduates, not earlier. The comparison students' broad interests, their broader range of careers as alumni, and longer periods of career exploration bear resemblance to groups that have been described in other studies:

- Tobias's (1990) "second tier" of science students, who are talented and well rounded but not so committed to studying science that they are insensitive to poor teaching when they encounter it in introductory STEM courses.
- Talented "switchers" described by Seymour and Hewitt (1997), who switch out of STEM majors because they are bored in introductory science courses that emphasize rote learning and do not capture their incoming interest.
- "At-risk" Ph.D. completers—those who completed the Ph.D. but considered leaving at some point—in Lovitts's (2001) study of graduate

student attrition. Compared with "on-track" completers who never considered leaving, at-risk completers had broader interests and had been more socially and academically involved in their departments as undergraduates.

- A cohort of women who leave science careers because of their discontent with its narrowness, described by Preston (2004) in her study of exit from scientific careers.
- Graduate students who participate in science outreach out of the desire to "give back" to their community, educate nonscientists, and apply their science in the "real world," but who see themselves as out of step with the prevailing ethos in their graduate departments (Laursen, Thiry, & Liston, 2005; Thiry, Laursen, & Liston, 2007).

These studies all identify choice as a significant factor in students' movement out of STEM-related studies or careers. They repeatedly document the existence of a pool of talented science, mathematics, and engineering students whose multiple interests lead them to pursue careers that combine these interests in a more applied way. In statistics used to document the so-called pipeline of educational progress through STEM degrees and into the STEM workforce, however, these students' alternative choices are often counted among the pipeline's "leaks"—as failures to advance in STEM. They thus offer a cautionary reminder to those who track this problem not to elevate some career paths above others when documenting "success," while still attending to losses of capable students—especially women and students of color—that might be prevented.

Career Placement

Given initial differences in students' interests and intentions, career outcomes prove to be a poor indicator of how UR influences participants' career paths. However, several other clues to UR's career influence do appear in our data set. One of these is its impact on students' career placement, or how UR helped students achieve their current position. Chapters Three and Four documented students' belief that their UR and other experiences would help them land a job or gain admission to graduate school; reports from alumni on this topic were much more concrete. While most students did not initially pursue UR for instrumental motivations, two-thirds of UR alumni nonetheless reported that their

UR experience had in fact given them a leg up in a job hunt or graduate school search:

> *They were impressed. I think they saw that . . . I'd be very analytical and that I'd be good with paying attention to details. . . . I don't think I would have gotten my job had I not done research. (UR alumna, chemistry)*

· · ·

> *I'm sure I wouldn't have gotten in some places without [research experience]. I actually got a [graduate] fellowship . . . . That probably wouldn't have happened if I hadn't done summer research, 'cause my grades were average and my GRE scores were average, but the summer research really set me apart. (UR alumnus, physics)*

Similarly, comparison alumni cited job placement benefits from their authentic experiences, particularly from alternative research and internships. More than other sources, these experiences directly contributed to success in securing employment or graduate school admission.

Both groups reported help from their faculty, both research advisors and course professors, in the form of career advice, information, and strong letters of recommendation. In the first interviews with UR students, such assistance was anticipated but not yet realized—thus accounting for its higher prominence in alumni reports. While many alumni reported drawing on professional networks, the nature of those networks depended on the experiences they had pursued. UR and alternative research alumni were more likely to establish and maintain connections in a larger scientific community, while internship alumni were more likely to use connections within the host organization itself.

Career Decision Making

Participation in UR and other educational experiences also influenced postgraduation outcomes through their impact on career decision making for alumni. They described several ways in which these influences were enacted. In some cases, gains initially experienced as personal and emotional changes had led to career decisions. This connection between feelings experienced and action taken is implied by our choice of the term "personal/professional" gains; alumni observations show how that connection plays out. One woman recalled that UR built confidence and fostered a sense of belonging to a scientific community. As her identification with the field grew, she became more assured of her choice to pursue a scientific career:

> *At the time it was very important. . . . It made me much more confident in being in the chemistry department and in just being part of the chemistry family. . . . I felt kind of like an outsider until then. In retrospect, I think that because I felt confident, and more part of a family, I started becoming a chemistry major, you know? Because we had our own little room where we all worked together—and if I hadn't had those types of relationships with my fellow chemistry majors and my professors, I don't think that I would have considered a career in science. (UR alumna, chemistry)*

For another man, feelings of accomplishment from his UR experience had prompted him to attend graduate school in engineering: "Without going through the [UR] program and actually realizing that I could accomplish some of these things in the field, I wouldn't have applied to grad school. It definitely was a huge part of my decision to go, a major factor" (UR alumnus, engineering).

Both comparison and, especially, UR interview groups included many students with long-standing, preexisting interest in attending graduate school. Indeed, "trying on" research to explore this interest was students' most often-cited motivation for undertaking UR. In the initial interviews, students reported that their career ideas were clarified and confirmed, but their stories as alumni show what this really means. Among UR alumni, 82 percent cited their UR experience as influencing their career or graduate school decisions. Many found that they enjoyed research, were good at it, and wanted to do more. They discovered that the lifestyle "suited me" and learned "what research is actually about":

> *First and foremost, it solidified my decision to go straight into industry rather than grad school, because I enjoyed working so much. (UR alumnus, physics)*

· · ·

> *I got from it what I expected to get from it, which was confirmation that I enjoyed doing what I was planning to do. (UR alumnus, mathematics)*

Other students equally valued the opportunity to try research but drew different conclusions. They found a poor fit between this work and their own interests, aptitudes, temperament, or goals. In fact, sixteen alumni reported this type of negative clarification, more than the seven who had stated as students that they had decided not to pursue a research career based on their UR experience:

> *I think it really solidified my ambition to* not *go to grad school in biology. Not to say I didn't enjoy just doing it and learning about it . . . but it really just showed me that I didn't want to do research; that working on one specific thing to learn about and to prove one little fact is not—it doesn't make much sense to me and it doesn't thrill me a whole lot—not what I wanna do. (UR alumnus, biology—emphasis in original)*

• • •

> *It showed me that I was able to do it and that it wouldn't be a problem to do it if I had to in order to get to a certain goal. But I wouldn't want to spend the rest of my life doing that. (UR alumnus, psychology)*

Striking in these accounts of both positive and negative clarification is the repeated emphasis on how UR enabled students to understand the meaning of their choices. By undertaking an authentic research experience, students learned what they would be getting into by pursuing graduate study or a research career. Having now launched down those paths, alumni could better appreciate, in retrospect, the value of that direct knowledge for making a wise choice: "I came into college thinking that I would probably go to graduate school. . . . I didn't really know what that meant, *so I had to find out what it meant*" (UR alumnus, chemistry; emphasis added).

The value of discovering the meaning of one's choice was not limited to UR alumni. In fact, fifteen comparison alumni (60 percent) reported that undergraduate professional experiences—clinic, internships, late or alternative research—had influenced their decision making. While all forms of experiential education had a role in shaping career decisions generally, only research experiences had influenced decisions of comparative alumni to pursue graduate study in particular: "It helped me decide—in a sense, *it acted as an example of what I would be doing in graduate school*—that it's something I love to do. . . . It was the excitement of the research, and the excitement of the findings, and the questions that led me to decide that graduate school and a Ph.D. would be the best solution for me" (late research alumna, psychology; emphasis added)

Most often, comparison alumni had encountered a new field or a new type of career and decided to remain in this field after graduation. Less often, they discovered a business or organizational environment that attracted them, or saw new ways to apply academic or personal interests in a career. For example, one alumna described how a summer job at a marketing firm helped her to clarify that marketing was the right career path for her: "Having the job I enjoyed, having people who appreciated what I did, and knowing that I was good at it [laughs]—all those things. And having the support of friends, family, colleagues—all of that kind of propelled me into this path, and kind of kept me on it as well. All of those things just make you feel like it's a place you belong" (internship alumna, biology).

Another comparison alumnus described how his clinic experience revealed leadership skills that he realized would apply to a teaching career: "There was still a lot that happened in that senior year that helped guide me in that direction. . . . Clinic was part of it—working with people in kind of a leadership role. . . . I was responsible for making sure the work got done. . . . So that hands-on experience was [where I got] the skills that I use today in my classroom" (clinic alumnus, mathematics).

These examples reveal how authentic experiences of any type can help to clarify students' career ideas by showing them the meaning of their career ambitions and pushing them to examine previously unexamined aspirations. Their career choices thus arise not merely out of received knowledge but out of personal, experiential knowledge. This is equally the case whether students choose for or against a given career, and as true of high-quality internships and clinic projects as of research. What matters is the authenticity of the experience. Indeed, authentic field experience is an essential part of the education in other professions, and authenticity may be taken as a defining characteristic of all forms of apprenticeship (Ainley & Rainbird, 1999; Greenwood, 1972; Sullivan, Colby, Wegner, Bond, & Shulman, 2007). As noted in Chapter Four, what is crucial is immersion in the real work of the profession under the individualized guidance of an experienced mentor and within the community formed by the profession (also see Barab & Hay, 2001, for a review of the literature on apprenticeship learning). Alumni observations also make clear the importance of a good fit between the apprenticeship and the apprentice, so that the apprentice is exploring something of genuine interest and testing his or her temperament against the demands of the job. Chapter Seven elaborates on the advisor's role in shaping the apprenticeship experience.

Career Preparation

Finally, undergraduate preprofessional experiences shaped students' post-graduate careers through their role in preparing students to succeed in those careers. Students had anticipated this gain from UR and other experiences; for alumni, this became concrete as they entered work or graduate study and described particular skills that had transferred to new settings.

As Figure 5.1 indicates, the most transferable skills were also the most general: communicating complex ideas to varied audiences, finding and understanding scientific literature, using computers to write programs or analyze scientific data, and working collaboratively. Project-specific laboratory and field skills were least likely to apply in later work or study. As they began work or graduate study, UR alumni discovered that they had relevant skills that some of their colleagues did not and emphasized how they applied skills in new settings. A few comparison alumni also commented on the transfer of generalizable skills, though this was less distinctive in their accounts: as one alumnus pointed out, transferability was not inherent in a skill, but depended on its value in a new context.

More commonly valued than transferable skills, however, was the general sense from alumni that UR or other preprofessional work had prepared them well. As students, they believed that UR was "more real-life"; as alumni, UR experience had facilitated a smooth transition to research in graduate school or industry:

> I came to this lab with a really good sense of how things work. I was very comfortable in a lab setting already, in terms of learning equipment and dealing with people and interacting with everybody. Graduate school wasn't at all a shock to me. The transfer was easy because I'd already done it for two and a half years. (UR alumnus, physics)

• • •

> Research really helped me feel comfortable with being able to be independent in the lab and comfortable developing my own procedures. . . . At the time, I didn't realize how much it was preparing me for a job. . . . At the time it, it was like, "Oh, it's fun to do and it'll help me get a job." But I didn't really realize that it was gonna be like my job (laughs). (UR alumna, chemistry; emphasis in original)

In sum, nearly all UR alumni described enhanced career preparation from their UR experiences: various skill gains and general comfort with self-directed research transferred well to their new work and study activities. In contrast, participation in a real-world work experience that prepared them for graduate school or careers was less significant in the retrospective reflections of comparison alumni. This difference may be largely due to the differing paths of these groups: research experience as an undergraduate maps most directly onto research in graduate school, the most common activity of UR alumni; both undergraduate and post-graduate experiences of the comparison group were more varied.

Overall Career Impact

Data from alumni interviews confirm our original hunch (Seymour, Hunter, Laursen, & DeAntoni, 2004) that within our sample of largely middle-class, largely white students at liberal arts colleges, UR is not a deciding factor in their career pursuits. For most, UR participation helped to confirm and clarify a strong preexisting interest in graduate school and a research career in a STEM field—the interest that led them to try UR in the first place. Comparison alumni appear to have followed different career paths—as they did throughout their college careers, well before the rising senior summer that marks the distinction between our UR and comparison samples.

More significant, the data reveal several ways in which summer UR, like internships, clinic, and late and alternate forms of research, helped graduates to make career decisions, achieve their goals, and succeed in their career pursuits. These career influences are not unique to UR but result from all forms of apprenticeship, which we define as mentored immersion into the real work of a profession. Among the comparison group, such apprenticeship experiences did occur, but were less common than for the UR interviewees. In Chapter Six, we discuss the particular career impact of UR for students from groups underrepresented in the sciences.

Lasting Changes from Authentic Research Experiences

So far we have focused on career outcomes, but how do the other benefits that students originally cited play out in the longer term? We examined how the benefits of UR and other experiences endured over time and which gains became more or less important in the views of alumni. For the most part, alumni confirmed their initial assessments: among both UR and comparison samples, there was little change in the overall distribution of gains observations across the six main categories (see Figure 5.1 and Appendix D). Although the immediacy and intensity of the UR experience faded with time, the same gains they had reported as students remained important to alumni (Chapter Three).

However, specific subcategories of gains stood out in the emphasis analysis (Figure 5.1). Even in the short time since graduation, alumni had come to appreciate and understand aspects of their experience that they had not spotted earlier. As graduate students or working professionals, they could now see more subtle influences on their development that had ongoing personal and professional value. We argue here that these changes were interrelated; they are also those that advisors viewed as especially critical in students' development as young professionals. Comparison alumni placed increased importance on the same set of gains, although the wider range of experiences among this group means that increases with time are less pronounced in Figure 5.1. Specific gains that the emphasis analysis shows to be of long-term importance for UR alumni include:

- Greater sophistication in their intellectual understanding of science
- Clearer understanding of how scientists work day-to-day and why these practices matter
- Adoption of work norms and socialization into the profession
- New appreciation of ways in which collegial relationships with their advisors and other scientists had modeled professional practice and informed their understanding of how science works as a profession

Collectively, we interpret these as showing the growth of alumni as professionals, a parallel deepening in their understanding of both the intellectual and social processes of science. In the first interviews, gains in confidence and "feeling like a scientist" were affective outcomes that fostered students' early formation of a scientific identity. In alumni interviews, these affective benefits had faded (Figure 5.1), as most emotions do, yet intellectual and professional gains had become much stronger in the reports of alumni. Thus, for alumni, "thinking like," "working like," and "becoming" a scientist begin to merge into a self-consistent identification with and socialization into the discipline.

Thinking and Working Like a Scientist

A common goal of undergraduate science education, and a specific goal of faculty advisors working with research students, is to develop students' understanding of the nature of science and scientific knowledge. However, these are sophisticated ideas, grasped by relatively few students even after a summer of intensive research (Chapter Three). When first interviewed, UR students focused on the ability to apply their prior knowledge and problem-solving skills to real research questions. Some 84 percent of students reported gains in this area and discussed it at some length. A rather smaller number of students (25 percent) generalized from practical, hands-on experience working on a specific problem to broader-based insight into how to generate and frame any research problem so it could be investigated scientifically. Finally, only a few students (12 percent) described a still-higher level of abstraction, showing a clearer understanding of how scientific knowledge is constructed. We portrayed these gains as a pyramid, a progression of increasingly abstract ideas achieved by increasingly fewer numbers of students, seen in the dark bars in Figure 5.2. Students' movement toward higher levels of the pyramid is a process that is encouraged by active engagement in research but by no means guaranteed.

As they had as students, UR alumni described acquiring a clearer understanding of how science research is done through the pragmatic experience of working on a particular problem. This specific gain was reported by fifty-four of fifty-six alumni (96 percent), with emphasis on how hands-on project work helped them to understand how investigations are conducted:

FIGURE 5.2

Longitudinal Change in Understanding of the Intellectual Process of Science, from UR Student and UR Alumni Interviews

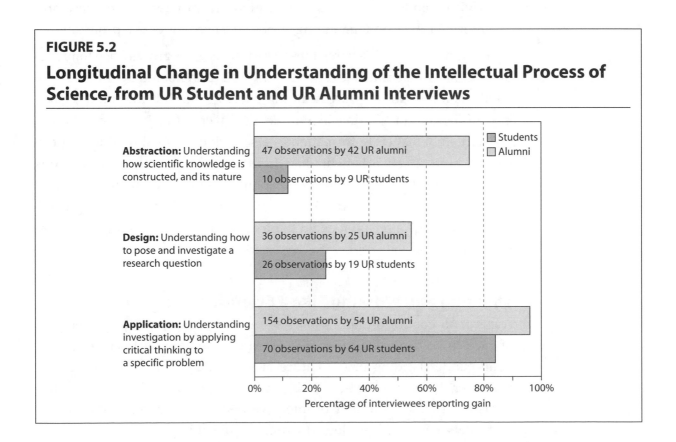

Even though I never got the results that I wanted, I did spend a lot of time thinking, and really, really being a scientist—looking at all that had happened before, and what other people had done in the literature, and trying to come up with a reasonable plan that might actually work. . . . I really did have to learn to consider all aspects of a situation and realize that things really are incredibly complex, and so you can't necessarily fix everything at once. You have to take little bits and play with them, while keeping the big picture in view. (UR alumna, chemistry)

While this lowest level of intellectual gain remained widely cited, the number of UR alumni discussing upper levels of the pyramid increased markedly (Figure 5.2). Nearly double the proportion of alumni (45 percent) reported feeling capable of developing productive research investigations—how to "dive in," "figure out what we want to study," and select appropriate methods: "theoretical or experimental, or both?" Their comments too suggest that many had moved to a higher level of understanding. While that understanding had emerged from hands-on research experience, they could see beyond its particular context to the general investigative process: "What has been of benefit? I'd have to go with the knowledge of the research process itself—you know, the classic scientific model you always hear about. Experience with that firsthand. . . . It's not the specific knowledge I learned about a gene or something, it's the idea that I can apply that method to anything else I try to do if I need to go about something in a systematic way in which I need to convince others of what I found" (UR alumnus, psychology).

At the top of the pyramid, the strength of alumni reports was even more surprising. Fully 75 percent of alumni specifically referenced a clearer understanding of the nature of scientific knowledge. After their summer research, UR students were not consciously aware of changes in their epistemological views—indeed, most had difficulty comprehending the interviewer's questions on this topic—but over time, alumni had come to see knowledge construction as a constantly evolving process. Alumni saw scientific knowledge as evidence-based but open-ended, provisional, and even fallible, and they could articulate how research practice yielded knowledge that had those properties:

Growing up or in high school, you know that there are scientists. You know they do research. But you don't really know the mechanics of how that research comes to exist. . . . You imagine a scientist saying, "Oh, I wanna know more about this—I'll do some research on it." But finding out that research is sort of an ongoing legacy, that one generation tackles part of a problem and then new problems sprout off of that, and it's sort of an ongoing continuum of researchers over the history of science. It's not just isolated individuals with ideas springing fully formed from their heads. I think that the literature review that I had to do, and the bit of experience I had in collaborating with some people that were part of this larger research group, really drove those ideas home. (UR alumnus, physics)

Among comparison students, developing a more sophisticated understanding of the nature of science and construction of knowledge was also rare initially, but it became more important to individuals and more common across the alumni sample. As in the initial interviews, research experiences were the major source of such understanding: half of all comments came from alumni who had participated in alternative research, while one-fourth referred to classroom experiences. Only one comparison alumnus reported that his research experience had led him to a deeper, more complex understanding of the mutable, incomplete nature of scientific knowledge:

I used to think it was more black and white in high school, and with maturity it obviously appears to be gray. . . . If you get down into physics, it has a lot of gray. [laughs] Like quantum mechanics, that's gray. Kinda made me realize, there is no pure science. . . . There are basics, but the more you dig, the more nebulous it becomes, and the more questions you get. And you never answer the questions—you only create more questions. And there never will be a true answer. Because there's just, the more you learn, the more you discover, the more you could ask more questions! (late alternative research alumnus, physics)

The greater rarity of this type of epistemological growth among comparison students may be attributed to their lower rates of participation as students in any form of research and to the uneven quality of those experiences. Too, rather fewer of the comparison alumni were enrolled in STEM graduate programs where they engaged again in research. It is likely that many alumni consolidated an understanding of the nature of science only after they had encountered additional examples of the research process in their senior year or in graduate school, and retrospectively realized that they had met these ideas before. While it is difficult to cleanly separate multiple influences on the new understandings reported by alumni— including UR but also postgraduate experience and general maturity—we have quoted many speakers at some length to include both the content of their insights and their attribution of these insights as originating in UR experience.

Only a few other studies have carefully probed for intellectual gains from UR. Kardash (2000) found only modest gains in what she called "higher-order skills," including developing insight into how to generate and frame research problems for systematic investigation. Rauckhorst, Czaja, and Baxter Magolda (2001) described student transitions in their "ways of knowing" using Baxter Magolda's (1999, 2004) epistemological reflection model. The most common change was from "transitional knowing" to "independent knowing," meaning that students start to believe that most knowledge is less than absolute and move from searching for truth to thinking for themselves. In their study, no students had reached the highest level of Baxter Magolda's model, contextual knowing, in which knowledge is shaped by its context and its veracity is debated according to that context.

These reports, like our findings, may both encourage and discourage practitioners who seek to foster students' understanding of the nature of science. It appears that active participation in UR offers the potential for students to move through a sequence of intellectual gains, from application to design to abstraction. Few undergraduates move through this sequence in a first summer of research; these gains may be realized only after additional research experiences help to highlight general principles, as research advisors also pointed out. While research does help students develop a more sophisticated understanding of the nature of science, it takes a long time for such understanding to become explicit.

Becoming a Scientist

In parallel with their deepened understanding of the intellectual practice of science, alumni gained deeper understanding of how scientists work day-to-day. Indeed, both UR and comparison alumni emphasized this more than any other enduring gain (Figure 5.1). Over time, alumni could see how engaging in research had taught them the practical importance of certain scientific work habits and had afforded the opportunity to see professional standards modeled in context. These enduring benefits thus shaped their later work practices. For example, alumni placed greater emphasis on developing tolerance for tedious procedures, patience to "deal with repetitive things," and recognition that failure was not necessarily their fault; that's "just how research is." As one chemist put it, "There's times you wanna really blow something up, because you know everything's just a mess and nothing ever works smoothly. . . . You have to take the good with the bad and try to learn as much from negative results. And that's a big adjustment. I learned that entirely from undergraduate research" (UR alumna, chemistry).

Not only had alumni learned to cope with frustration, they had begun to relish it. Complexity became an enjoyable challenge, and solving problems fostered creativity: "You sit around and you're like, 'Well, method A didn't work. Let's try method B.' And then, 'Method B didn't work; let's try method C.' And eventually there's a pride in determining the method that will work, and so you just sort of keep at it. . . . You come up with the esoteric, crazy ideas that you hope, someday, one of them will work, and you'll invent the next transistor or something" (UR alumnus, chemistry).

Most interesting were the linkages alumni described between their increased understanding of professional practice and their understanding of how knowledge is constructed. Everyday scientific habits were no longer mere procedures, but shaped the nature of the knowledge that was thus derived. For example, one alumnus linked laboratory record keeping to original work, recognizing the long-term implications of neglecting to take careful notes when conducting a novel experiment: "You know, you were told to do these kinds of things, take proper notes, during your first year of chemistry. But you don't see the significance. . . . But when you are actually doing research which has never been done before, then you want to know how you came to those conclusions. . . . That's something that I think was very much an important part of research that I learned" (UR alumnus, chemistry).

Another described how interacting with and watching his advisor had shown him how scientific knowledge was shaped by professional norms of acknowledging others' intellectual contributions and laying one's own work open to scrutiny. Again, his account reflects the relatedness of his intellectual and professional development:

> [I learned] how you should conduct your work—some of these more subtle gains that I think are very significant. Like seeing your professor at work in that environment—it gives you an idea of how you should conduct yourself. . . . Like giving credit to the proper people, how you have to find the people that did the work before you, and how you have to acknowledge their contribution. . . . And just seeing how honest the whole process of doing science is. . . . Like, even when our calculations . . . don't fit very well, we have to acknowledge that. It's not like we can fudge the numbers and make things fit. . . . It was the first time that I got exposed to it, and . . . I admire how scientists conduct themselves in their work. (UR alumnus, mathematics)

Collegial interactions with their advisor, peers, and other scientists were a powerful source of these new understandings. Alumni had benefited from constructive criticism and collegial input to check out "a crazy idea," and had learned to work collaboratively. However, they now saw as well that colleagues had modeled for them the professional culture and real-world workings of research. Practices that had seemed idiosyncratic were now revealed as common: "We worked with three labs. . . . It was only afterward that I realized, 'Oh, why did we work with so many labs? And what does it mean that they're all next door to each other? And what does it mean that they talk to each other?' That sort of collaboration is something, I think, in terms of what scientists do on a day-to-day basis, that's something that I learned" (UR alumna, biology).

Another UR alumnus realized in retrospect that his UR experience had given him a glimpse into the role of professions in society and what it might mean to pursue a professional career: "It was my first taste of—this sounds funny—but, playing with the big kids, I guess. Of doing something that was really contributing to a larger world that I was growing up into, in a way that having a video store job at home or a dining hall job at college wouldn't necessarily give me. It gave me a sense of how scientists and engineers fit into society. It was the first real experience with that kind of job, quite apart from the learning experience with that kind of employment" (UR alumnus, physics).

Comparison alumni similarly reported lasting value from observing and participating in the day-to-day practicalities of research and other professional work. Like their UR peers, they learned how professionals practice in their fields and absorbed professional ethics, values, and norms. These gains were reported primarily by alumni who had participated in alternative UR and, to a lesser extent, internships.

UR alumni clearly recalled the powerful effects of working with their research advisors as colleagues and having their ideas taken seriously, and began to maintain long-term relationships with their advisors, as their advisors likewise reported. However, with hindsight, alumni saw more clearly how their research mentors had both guided them and modeled the profession for them:

> I am still definitely in touch with my advisor. . . . We built a very strong mentoring relationship. An advisor that encourages you, helps you resolve certain problems that you run into, or helps you understand things, like analyze certain outputs of your work. . . . But also, I guess, my advisor provided extras, like an example of a work ethic and how you should approach your

work and how you should feel about your work. And those are still principles that I use today when I do my work. . . . He was a model for how you should conduct your work. (UR alumnus, mathematics)

As for the UR alumni, collegial relationships with faculty, professionals, and peers became more important over time for comparison alumni. As in their initial interviews, these observations came primarily from alternative research and the general college experience; participation in late research or senior thesis projects did not yield the long-term relationships with faculty that resulted from more intense, alternative research projects in the summer, out of which mentoring relationships grew that had endured beyond graduation.

Conclusion

The outcomes that UR alumni emphasized in longitudinal interviews reflect their growth in understanding science as a human enterprise and their socialization into the profession: "becoming" scientists. Spurred by their UR experience and consolidated by later experience and insight, more sophisticated understanding of the intellectual processes of science was strongly coupled to understanding its cultural and social processes. These insights emerged as alumni realized that their student research had in fact been an authentic experience of their field, and that their advisors had provided not only concrete assistance and moral support but role models for the future.

These lasting changes thus help to explain just how UR and experiences like it influenced the career choices that alumni made. Research experience gave students considering a research career in science, engineering, or mathematics the chance to test their fit with the profession, enabling them to choose or rule it out based on personal, experiential knowledge of what that choice would mean. This outcome was not unique to UR; it also emerged from other experiences of authentic professional work under a mentor's guidance. However, lasting changes in professional socialization, as well as actual career and education choices that emphasized STEM research, were more commonly seen among the UR group. This is due to a set of related factors: preexisting interest in graduate study and research careers that motivated students to pursue UR, high-quality experiences of "real science" through research as undergraduates, and their higher rate of pursuit of STEM graduate study, where intellectual and socialization gains from UR were reinforced and deepened. Seen in retrospect, UR and other authentic experiences marked a leap in learning, a transition to adult approaches to life and work, as this final quotation highlights:

> *You're still growing up. I guess I'm still growing up now, but it's kind of a small milestone to be thinking, "All right, my PI [principal investigator] is not the one making this happen, telling me what to do every five minutes. I need to make this happen and get the results in a certain period of time, and I need to do whatever I need to do to get it done." And I guess it made me adapt to that kind of growing-up attitude. . . . I'd say it was a larger leap on my growing-up scale than just the normal steady incline of maturity. (UR alumnus, psychology)*

Chapter 6

How Do Minority Students Benefit from Research?

SO FAR, WE have discussed undergraduate research (UR) programs for students in general. When looking through the lens of race, an additional layer of complexity emerges. Historically, only white students were permitted, encouraged, or had the financial means to attend college. The legacy of this historical difference persists: 24 percent of whites age twenty-five to twenty-nine hold a bachelor's degree, while only 16 percent of African Americans and 10 percent of Hispanics the same age hold a four-year degree (U.S. Census Bureau, 2007). (Asian American students are not considered underrepresented in STEM fields; their proportions in STEM are higher than in the U.S. population at large, and they complete higher education in greater proportions; U.S. Census Bureau, 2007.) The underrepresentation of some ethnic and racial groups is even more pronounced within the science, technology, engineering, and mathematics (STEM) fields, both throughout higher education and in STEM careers. African American, Latino, and Native American students comprise about one-third of the school-age population but only about 11 percent of people in STEM occupations (Chubin, May, & Babco, 2005). Moreover, white university students experience different educational, social, and economic realities than their African American, Latino/a, and Native American peers.

Many programs seek to remedy these inequities and diversify the STEM talent pool by recruiting minority students into the sciences and supporting them to pursue STEM-related careers or advanced education. (We prefer the term *underrepresented groups*, but it can be unwieldy in repeated use. We use the term *minority* here to indicate minority within STEM, recognizing that demographic trends mean that in many settings, nonwhite racial and ethnic groups are no longer minorities in the overall U.S. population.) As noted in Chapter Two, many of these programs choose undergraduate research as a central vehicle for this work (Alexander, Foertsch, & Daffinrud, 1998; Auerbach, Gordon, May, & Davis, 2007; Barlow & Villarejo, 2004; Clewell, de Cohen, Deterding, & Tsui, 2006;

Fitzsimmons, Carlson, Kerpelman, & Stoner, 1990; Foertsch, Alexander, & Penberthy, 1997; Good, Halpin, & Halpin, 2000; Hotchkiss, Moore, & Pitts, 2006; Jonides and others, 1992; Lopatto, 2007; Maton & Hrabowski, 2004; Maton, Hrabowski, & Schmitt, 2000; Nagda, Gregerman, Jonides, von Hippel, & Lerner, 1998; Walters, 1997).

Although there are many variations, including summer and year-round programs sponsored by universities, national laboratories, and professional societies, the frequent inclusion of UR indicates that it is widely believed to be a mechanism by which these societal goals can be accomplished. That is, UR is seen as a means by which to foster minority science students' interest in STEM, enhance their ability to pursue education and careers in STEM successfully, and help them overcome barriers of education and opportunity. In this chapter, we address the question: What evidence supports the common choice of UR as a central strategy for these programs? What special, additional, or much-needed benefits (if any) does UR offer for minority students, and how does the design of these programs foster these outcomes?

We could not explore these questions readily in our four-college study because the number of minority students at these colleges was small. Moreover, students at these liberal arts colleges, as at many other campuses around the United States, participated in "grassroots" UR activities that were hosted by individual faculty or research groups and often were only loosely organized at the department level. Although many features of these faculty-led UR efforts are shared with structured UR programs, especially those located within the research experience itself, here we focus on structured programs that use UR as a central strategy in their efforts to recruit and retain minority students. As noted in Chapter Two, these structured programs include UR along with other activities, they admit a cohort of students as a group, and they often target students early in their college years. They explicitly seek to recruit students from underrepresented groups to STEM majors, support them to successful degree completion, and encourage them to pursue advanced study or careers in STEM fields.

In this chapter, we examine one such program as a case study to identify how UR may contribute to achieving these goals and what elements of the program accomplish this. Certain aspects of UR take on a greater significance to these students, we argue, than for students at large, and these features are thus deliberately enhanced and reinforced through particular program elements. We begin by reviewing the circumstances for minority students that have prompted the establishment of programs to retain, recruit, and move them forward into STEM education and careers—the problem diagnosis to which UR-based programs are responding.

Challenges for Minority Students in STEM Majors

The existence and design of minority-targeted UR programs must be understood within the context of societal racial barriers and their effect on undergraduate education. Minority children are more likely to live in poverty, to have parents who did not attend college, and to be taught by less-qualified science teachers at lower-performing K–12 schools (Darling-Hammond, 2000; Gándara, 1999; Sirin, 2005; U.S. Census Bureau, 2004). They are less likely to know a scientist or engineer and to participate in science enrichment activities outside school (Catsambis, 1995; Eccles, Barber, Stone, & Hunt, 2003; Tsui, 2007). They are also more likely to attend high schools that do not offer the rigorous curricula and advanced courses that provide momentum toward a STEM bachelor's degree (Adelman, 2006; Wilson, 2000). A large study linking high school science education with college science performance shows that these precollege educational factors correlate with lower college grades in the introductory science courses that serve as gateways to STEM majors (Tai, Sadler, & Mintzes, 2006). Campbell (1996) points out that most minority children, about 85 percent, have been channeled out of advanced mathematics and science by the time they are thirteen years old—so it is thus understandable that specific programs have arisen to recruit and retain the "precious few" (Tapia & Lanius, 2000, p. 22) who remain.

Once they reach college, minority students are as likely to enroll in STEM studies as white students, but more likely to switch to nonscience majors and less likely to complete a STEM degree (Anderson & Kim, 2006; Elliott, Strenta, Adair, Matier, & Scott, 1996; Tsui, 2007; U.S. Department of Education, 2000). The reasons behind these losses are multifold. Both stereotyping itself—including labeling, tokenization, marginalization, and negative attitudes—and stereotype threat, the fear of being stereotyped that results in anxiety, self-consciousness, and underperformance, can throw students off an academic path. Students may face a host of challenges in colleges and universities where students, faculty, and administrators are predominantly white, including these:

- Social and academic isolation (Allen, 1992; Cole, 2007; Crim, 1998; Etzkowitz, 2000; Lewis, Ginsberg, Davies, & Smith, 2004; Morley, 2003; Seymour & Hewitt, 1997; Treisman, 1992)
- Racially motivated social exclusion (Rosenbloom & Way, 2004; Seidman, Allen, Aber, Mitchell, & Feinman, 1994)
- Classroom and peer discrimination, including messages of academic inferiority, or of universal superiority for Asian Americans (Allen, 1992; Arnold, 1993; Feagin & Sikes, 1994; Fisher & Hartmann, 1995; Morley, 2003; Seymour & Hewitt, 1997; Olson & Fagen, 2007)

- Stereotype threat (Osborne, 1995; Osborne & Walker, 2006; Steele, 1997; Taylor & Antony, 2000)
- Inadequate faculty mentoring (see Tsui, 2007, for a review; also Cole, 2007; Crim, 1998; Feagin & Sikes, 1994)
- Feelings of alienation due to lack of representation of one's own culture in academic and social life (Crim, 1998; Feagin & Sikes, 1994; Fisher & Hartmann, 1995)
- Loss of emotional support and connectedness to family and community (Arnold, 1993)
- A dearth of role models (Olson & Fagen, 2007; Wilson, 2000)
- Lack of cultural capital, including knowledge of how the academic system works (Lewis et al., 2004; Nettles & Millet, 1999)
- Psychological stress and self-blame resulting from all of the above (Greene, Way, & Pahl, 2006; Osborne & Walker, 2006; Seymour & Hewitt, 1997)

In addition, minority students are more likely to experience financial and family stresses related to socioeconomic status (Arnold, 1993; Ishitani, 2006; Lohfink & Paulsen, 2005; May & Chubin, 2003; Olson & Fagen, 2007; Paulsen & St. John, 2002).

These experiences can have powerful and lasting outcomes. Racial discrimination, even if unintended, has a negative effect on students' self-confidence (Seymour & Hewitt, 1997) and academic efforts, attitudes, and achievement (Osborne, 1995). Students may respond by disengaging themselves mentally or physically from school (Ford & Harris, 1997; Osborne, 1995; Osborne & Walker, 2006)—thus leading to poor course performance, failure to advance through a structured academic program typical of most STEM majors, major switching to other fields, or withdrawal from college altogether.

At the college level, high attrition is seen, for example, among African American students in STEM fields—even among very capable students with high grades and test scores and a record of high school honors courses (Allen, 1992; Brown, 2000; May & Chubin, 2003). Attrition has been ascribed to a complex mix of factors, including financial barriers, inadequate advising, lack of research experience, changing career interests, lack of career information, and poor science course performance (Brown, 2000; Seymour & Hewitt, 1997). But research is still incomplete, particularly with respect to Latino/a and Native American students, and issues are often assumed to apply equally to all students of color despite their distinct backgrounds and cultures (Seymour & Hewitt, 1997). Weak academic preparation may be an issue for students who come from underserved, especially urban, high schools (Tapia & Lanius, 2000; Wilson, 2000). Lacking the cultural capital to succeed in the academic system, working-class and first-generation college students are also less likely to persist in college and are underrepresented in the sciences as a group, and racial minority students are more likely to be the first in their families to attend college (Wells, 2008). Overall weak social and academic integration with peers and faculty is a significant cause of student withdrawal from college (Morley, 2003; Pascarella & Terenzini, 1991). Early models of programs to recruit and retain minority students in STEM fields thus deliberately sought to build student cohorts, facilitate student interaction centered on their academic work and shared STEM interests, and connect students with faculty (for example, Fullilove & Treisman, 1990).

The Choice of UR: The Case Study of SOARS

In comparing this list of challenges and risks of poor outcomes that minority students face, and the benefits derived from undergraduate research that we and other researchers have reported (Chapters Two and Three), it begins to be evident why UR is so often identified as a central vehicle for recruiting, retaining, and supporting minority students in STEM (Tsui, 2007). Gains in confidence and building collegial relationships with peers and faculty directly address factors that contribute to attrition. Gains of practical skills and in critical thinking and problem solving enhance students' credentials as well as their confidence. And socialization into the identity, understandings, and behaviors of a scientist may be expected to nurture both students' interest in science as a profession and their ability to pursue it successfully. Although these gains have only recently been documented by research and evaluation studies, they have long been postulated by practitioners and theorists. Thus it is not surprising that UR is a commonly chosen vehicle for minority student–targeted programs.

To understand the particular outcomes of UR for minority students, the relationship of these outcomes to the broader goals of recruiting and retaining minority students in STEM, and how both the short-term outcomes and broader goals may be achieved, we focus on one program as a case study. SOARS (Significant Opportunities in Atmospheric Research and Science) is a program for STEM undergraduate and graduate students that is hosted at the National Center for Atmospheric Research (NCAR) in Boulder, Colorado (Pandya, Henderson, Anthes, & Johnson, 2007; Windham, Stevermer, & Anthes, 2004). In its goal "to broaden participation in the atmospheric and related sciences by engaging students from groups historically underrepresented in science and preparing them to succeed in graduate school" (SOARS, 2008), SOARS is typical of structured UR programs targeting minority students (see Chapter Two). As a longstanding program with documented success in supporting students through undergraduate STEM degrees and into graduate programs, SOARS is also exemplary. Thus, like the four-college study of faculty-centered UR efforts, this structured program offers a best-case scenario for examining the outcomes of UR for minority students and the program elements by which these outcomes are achieved.

The evidence discussed in this chapter derives from an evaluation study of SOARS conducted by our group in 2003–2004 (Melton, Pedersen-Gallegos, & Donohue, 2005). Data were gathered from over one hundred hours of observations of thirty-four SOARS events, workshops, and meetings and from in-depth, qualitative interviews and focus groups with:

- Sixty-nine current, alumni, and discontinued student participants in SOARS
- Ninety-eight current and former SOARS mentors, including science advisors, peer mentors, and community and writing mentors
- Forty-three well-placed observers of SOARS activities, including lab managers, steering committee members, and program staff members.

The interviews addressed participants' background, experiences with SOARS, perceived gains and challenges, and advice to the SOARS program. They were recorded, transcribed, coded, and analyzed with a process like that described for the four-college study (Appendix B).

Program Description

The SOARS centerpiece is a ten-week summer immersion into a research experience at NCAR's Boulder laboratories or an affiliated laboratory. Students, then known as protégés, conduct research, write technical papers, and present their research at an end-of-summer colloquium. They attend weekly workshops to develop and refine their scientific communication skills. Each student can participate in SOARS for up to four summers, starting the summer after their sophomore or junior year, and on into graduate school if desired. About ten students from around the United States join the cohort each year. They receive summer salary, free housing, travel funds for professional conferences, and academic-year support in the form of mentoring and monitoring, and financial support for graduate school if needed.

SOARS establishes a strong and formal mentoring structure, providing each protégé with up to four volunteer mentors, each with a different function. All students have a science mentor to guide the student's research project and a writing mentor to coach the student on scientific communication. In addition, first-year protégés have a community mentor to help navigate scientific and local culture, and a peer mentor—a returning protégé who receives leadership training and models effective scientific and professional practices. Protégés work on research projects in a wide variety of atmospheric science topics, prepare and host a professional development seminar, socialize at many informal and formal events, and live together in a housing complex near the lab. The program targets students from groups that are underrepresented in the sciences and those who have worked to overcome educational or economic disadvantage in their personal and family lives. At the time of our study, the protégé group was 36 percent African American, 33 percent Latino, 13 percent Native American, and the rest white, Asian American, or multiracial. About two-thirds of protégés were women. (More details about the program are available at the SOARS Web site. See also Pandya et al., 2007; Windham et al., 2004.)

Student Gains

SOARS students reported gains from their participation that strongly paralleled the gains reported by students in the four-college study (Chapter Three). They identified:

1. Personal/professional gains, including:

   - Increased confidence as a result of engaging in hands-on work
   - Growth in sense of responsibility
   - Sense of belonging to the supportive and collaborative protégé community
   - Establishing a collegial relationship with a research advisor

2. Gains in thinking and working like a scientist, including:

   - Developing and applying critical thinking skills
   - Learning how science research is done
   - Increased sense of the relevance of their course work, and better preparation to undertake subsequent course work

3. Gains related to "becoming a scientist," including:

   - Developing a professional identity
   - Learning how to present themselves professionally

- Growth in understanding how scientists practice their profession
- Understanding science in political and global perspective

4. Gains in skills, including oral presentation, writing, social interaction, leadership, time management, computer programming, and working collaboratively with colleagues

5. Enhanced career preparation, including:

 - Networking with strategically important contacts within professional circles
 - Strengthened applications for graduate school and jobs
 - Presenting and publishing research work

6. Career clarification and refinement, including:

 - Insight into science careers, particularly in atmospheric science
 - Increased interest in and likelihood of going to graduate school

Although these gains are highly comparable to those made by the students in the four-college study (Chapter Three), some take on particular significance for students from underrepresented groups because of the historical exclusion, by policy or practice, of racial minorities from well-paying white-collar jobs and the tenacious presence of institutional, cultural, interpersonal, and internalized racism. These gains center on professional identity building and how this is fostered by students' gains in skills, abilities, and confidence and by their interactions with researchers at NCAR and in the larger professional community. These gains thus help to explain the finding discussed in Chapter Two that UR participation has an impact on minority students' decisions to pursue graduate school that is not seen in studies of majority students.

SOARS protégés reported a tremendous sense of accomplishment at the end of the summer. In rising to the challenges offered by their research project, they felt empowered, which raised their aspirations, motivated them to succeed, and prepared them to feel confident in other situations. One participant said:

> *I'm the first person to go to high school, even, in my family—so to go to college was even a bigger deal. SOARS . . . showed me that I could go further than where I was, and I had never realized that before. And I'd never met anyone who was in a higher position, besides professors at school. And I found that pretty exciting—just seeing that you can do it, doing the presentations, or doing the work, seeing that you could actually achieve that. You could do it on your terms, and you could do it—[that] is a big deal.*

On realizing they could "do science" at SOARS, first-year protégés began to consider graduate school more seriously. Their peers and mentors assured them that they would be prepared and that they would merit acceptance to elite programs: "I saw other protégés who, after SOARS, were willing to go to grad school, and they were getting accepted into these very recognized schools. Of course that motivated me to believe that I could be accepted. . . . Seeing the others going into grad school, I said, 'Well, I have to do it myself!'"

Students' confidence also increased as they began to think like scientists. As they gained the capacity to think critically and pursue their own ideas, they began to view themselves as budding scientists: "The longer you're here, the more starts clicking. You start thinking like a scientist, and everything starts falling into place. That's what I wanted to learn when I got here—'How do people think?' And I'm starting to implement their ideas into my own, and I'm starting to formulate my own ideas, and I'm starting to get a big picture—like a big puzzle is starting to come together."

Learning that science is not a collection of established black-and-white facts was a surprise to many SOARS students, as it was for majority students (Chapter Three). Unexpected problems became more tolerable when students realized that this was a normal part of the scientific process and did not reflect their own inadequacies as a researcher: "[I'm] learning the hard way—obviously, not everything—like, *nothing*—in science goes the way you want it to go. And you design an experiment the best way that you possibly can, and there's still going to be problems, glitches. Things are going to break and the equipment's going to go missing. [laughs] It's just how it goes" (emphasis in original).

Starting with their research advisor and peers, SOARS protégés were embedded in a professional scientific community and built this further through presenting their work at conferences, meeting other scientists, and gaining entrée to their advisors' networks. One student described the impact of these experiences: "Oh my gosh, that was so important! Networking is the key of succeeding professionally. They sent me four times out to conferences, and they sent me also to minority conferences. And it was great. That's something that they should always [do] . . . they should always save lots of money to send students for conferences."

Just as important, they learned how to behave in a professional setting, how to meet new people, and how to develop professional relationships— "not just stand there and look pretty, but put on my professional hat," as one student put it. As they became more comfortable in such settings, students felt a sense of belonging within the scientific community: "They treated me more like a real scientist, and so I really worked up to that. And I rose to the occasion. I ended up being on three different publications; I was just working all the time. But it was wonderful—I mean, it was very, very rewarding. I was just entrenched in the science, and no one treated me like, 'Oh, this little college kid. . . . ' And I'm like, 'Yeah, yeah, I know it—I'm doing the equations, I'm working it out.'"

Finally, protégés valued the many forms of financial support provided by SOARS. With significantly more minority families living below the poverty level than white families, financial support more often took on importance in enabling these students to attend college. For some, their SOARS salary paid for tuition and books for the following school year. Some protégés received scholarship support to attend graduate school if funding was not available from their school, and others received financial aid as undergraduates.

Critical Program Elements

The gains realized by minority students undertaking UR with SOARS are quite parallel to those made by mostly majority students undertaking UR at the four liberal arts college (Chapter Three), but certain gains are even more strongly emphasized by these students. In examining SOARS and other programs like it, we realized that the features of these programs could be grouped into three categories:

- General features of undergraduate research that offer desired benefits and foster desired outcomes for all students, including minority students
- Features of undergraduate research that are especially valuable for minority students and are thus purposefully amplified and reinforced in programs targeted to these students
- Additional features that are not standard in undergraduate research per se but that address other needs of minority students, and are thus added to UR as part of the overall program.

Program elements in each of these categories are shown in Table 6.1 and discussed below.

General Features of Undergraduate Research

The first column of Table 6.1 lists several features of undergraduate research that are common to both faculty-led UR and SOARS as well as other minority student–serving programs. Multiweek engagement

TABLE 6.1

Common Program Elements of SOARS and Other Structured Undergraduate Research Programs Targeting Students from Underrepresented Groups

General Features of UR	Features of UR That Are Amplified	Additional Elements That Are Nonstandard in Faculty-Led UR
Student engages intensively in a summer-long research project.	Early entry is enabled and encouraged.	Academic-year workshops, tutoring, or study groups augment academic and study skills and ameliorate any gaps in K–12 preparation.
Project is authentic; authenticity is employed by research advisor as a teaching tool and tempered to moderate student's experience of difficulties of authentic research (see Chapter Seven).	Multiyear engagement is built in or encouraged to ensure that student gains are achieved and deepened.	Summer bridge programs augment academic skill and build a student cohort around shared academic interests.
Individualized mentoring is provided by an experienced researcher, who is also a professional role model.	Multiple mentors ensure that each student receives high-quality mentoring to meet scientific, career, and affective needs.	Academic advising monitors student progress, catches difficulties early, and directs student to academic and career resources.
Project is carefully selected, with size and scope matched to the student's preparation, interests, and time frame (see Chapter Seven).	Formal professional communication is emphasized, including writing as well as oral presentation.	Financial support ensures that student has the opportunity to complete college.
Student makes gains on multiple personal, educational, and career dimensions (see Chapter Three).	Conference travel is funded to increase student opportunities for professional socialization.	Community or peer mentor helps to navigate local culture and smooth the transition.
Oral presentation of scientific work is an authentic and multifold source of gains; conference travel enhances this for some students.	The peer community is built and reinforced through peer mentoring, seminars, leadership training, and social events.	Program staff offer advising and personal and logistical support through college life.
A research peer community develops and is an important source of support, assistance, and pleasure.	People of color are visible leaders and role models of success in STEM and other professions.	Diversity is valued, and race is an asset.
A summer stipend and housing assistance are provided.	Program infrastructure, leadership, funding, and staff are institutionalized to ensure program continuity and quality.	
Multiyear engagement is possible (but not typical) and offers greater benefits.		

in an authentic scientific project, carefully chosen and scaled to students' preparation, interests, and time frame, is the core. Experienced mentors guide students in their research and offer other kinds of academic, career, and personal support. Students are financially supported so that they do not need other summer work. Scientific communication is an important activity that is scaffolded, supported, and developed throughout the summer and yields growth in confidence, deeper understanding of one's project, collegial connection, and understanding of how scientists practice their profession. When all of this is well done, students emerge with a broad array of educational, personal, and professional gains.

Across these features, the critical importance of authenticity is evident in students' scientific endeavors and further made visible by how students are positioned to interact within a professional community. The linkage between authenticity and student outcomes is evident in SOARS students' reports of the same gains as reported by students in the four-college study (Chapter Three). SOARS research advisors described their forethought in planning and preparing for student research projects that were authentic yet achievable, and identified explicit practices and teaching strategies stemming from authenticity that were very much like those used by advisors from the four liberal arts colleges (described in Chapters Seven and Eight):

- Interacting frequently, even daily, especially early in the summer
- Fostering collegiality through research group meetings, lunch, and conversation
- Encouraging questions and using problem-solving dialogue to probe for gaps in understanding, foster deeper comprehension, and help students weigh alternate approaches to a problem
- Normalizing the everyday setbacks and challenges of research so that students did not become frustrated or discouraged by obstacles
- Assessing students' needs and adjusting their advising approaches to strike a balance between challenge and support while fostering independence
- Offering academic and career advice and professional development, often by sharing stories of their own career experiences and obstacles

It is these common features, we suggest, that have led to the widespread selection of UR as a central strategy in minority student–serving programs, to appropriately take advantage of the educational advantages of UR.

UR Features Amplified in Minority Student–Serving Programs

In addition to the benefits they reported in common with majority students, SOARS protégés reported certain benefits that were especially important to them. We see in the data from students and mentors that these benefits result from a set of design choices and program practices that collectively function first to ensure that every student makes these gains and then to amplify gains that most directly counter the most common barriers to minority students' participation in STEM professions. Table 6.1 lists these features that are deliberately enhanced or amplified in minority-serving programs; we elaborate on each below.

Early Entry and Multiyear Engagement

SOARS recruits students as early as their sophomore year, and some other minority-serving programs are open to first-year college students. The early start in research, because it is coupled with the chance to participate for multiple years, increases students' opportunity to engage deeply for an extended time, and thus to make greater gains (Chapter Three). Early entry into research may draw students into science and motivate higher academic performance for the rest of their college career, while students who entered college with poor academic preparation may benefit from a longer run-up time over several summers to achieve independence and self-direction. Longer engagement also fosters identification with peers as fellow scientists and bonding with them as friends, which may be particularly important for students otherwise at risk to leave the field. As one protégé put it, "It keeps you in the pipeline. Like when you get so fed up with school and everything, and you come back to such a supportive community, it gets you back on track. . . . It's a good way to retain students and it's a good way to push them to keep going to grad school, too, because you form relationships with people here, so you get to see how well they progress."

Emphasis on Communication Skills

While communication skills were important in UR as conducted at the four liberal arts colleges, the design of SOARS formalized this emphasis and committed much more of students' time to developing these skills. SOARS emphasized writing and communication skills through a weekly writing workshop, writing and presentation assignments, and interaction with an individual writing mentor. Students cited the value of writing assignments that were practical and applicable to their research and built skills useful in their course work. Like the four-college UR students, they cited a wide range of gains from making presentations: learning how to tailor a presentation to their audience, developing confidence, overcoming nerves, and learning to critique and review others' work. The end-of-summer colloquium was a formal and festive event that marked a milestone in students' professional development.

SOARS' choice to emphasize formal writing and presentation skills is not surprising. The intensive workshop and revision process can ameliorate individual issues of academic preparation and polish students' performance. Close work with mentors and peers over drafts and practice talks builds collegiality and teaches professional norms of critique. The multifold gains that emerge from presenting may be especially powerful in developing minority students' confidence and scientific identities.

Off-site conference presentation was an even more powerful experience for UR students who had it. For students at the four colleges, this authentic experience was relatively rare: it was legitimately earned only when students' work had progressed to the point at which it could be shared with the broader disciplinary community. The design of SOARS preserved but amplified this feature of UR by providing extensive financial and logistical support for nearly all students to undertake conference travel. Multiyear participation allowed many students to achieve meaningful results that could be presented not only at student-focused research conferences, but as authentic contributions to professional meetings in their discipline.

The SOARS design choice to increase the emphasis on writing relative to what we observed in faculty-led UR may have both pluses and minuses. Writing is a transferable skill that supports students' academic work. Because writing an article is the culmination of a scientific research project, this act may be an important symbol for students of belonging to the profession (Alexander, Lyons, Pasch, & Patterson, 1996), and perhaps especially so for students from groups that have traditionally been excluded from academic circles.

However, signs of resistance to the extensive writing work emerged in the data from both protégés and mentors, which may indicate that the writing requirement was less functional for both groups than was the presentation emphasis. In the four-college study, we found a relatively low emphasis on formal scientific writing in both students' gains reports (Chapter Three) and advisors' discussion of their objectives and methods in working with students (Chapter Seven). But both groups noted the multiple benefits of oral presentation as yielding high "bang for the buck." Thus, it is legitimate to ask whether program goals might be better served by initially emphasizing presentation and then introducing formal scientific writing more gradually. Spending too much time on writing too soon may hinder other kinds of growth—not least, as research mentors also observed, completing enough research to achieve original scientific results that merit formal communication to the field. It is possible to imagine approaches, such as a scaffolded series of relevant and useful writing tasks—beginning, for instance, with an abstract or description of one's research for a graduate school application—that would develop writing skills over time and lead over time to the completion of a formal scientific paper. This is one area where further study and exploration of approaches would be valuable.

Network of Multiple Mentors

The functions of mentors described by SOARS interviewees did not differ from those reported in the four-college study. However, the SOARS multiple-mentor model—which included research, writing, community, and peer mentors—was highly valued by protégés as well as mentors. Protégés could turn to any mentor whom they saw as approachable, skilled, or helpful on particular topics, and mentors could respond to particular issues as a team if needed. Collectively, they formed a safety net to ensure that all students' scientific, educational, and affective needs were satisfied, and made it nigh impossible for any student to fall through the cracks: "You really have to try hard to get lost, to be honest. You have four different mentors that you can talk to. . . . You basically would have to not take advantage of anything to get completely lost, you know what I mean? . . . People are so willing to help."

The team approach was also functional for mentors, as no one mentor was responsible for every aspect of a student's development, and thus helped to reduce burnout, a sustainability issue for any undergraduate research program.

Peer Community

Several SOARS program elements contribute to building a strong and cohesive peer community—"like family," as many students said. In addition to the shared experiences of doing science, rapid development of close and supportive relationships was reinforced by the small cohort size, shared housing arrangements, and group activities such as movies, dancing, camping trips, and "Soul Food Sundays." "I was just in awe of the other students," said one student, "and learned a lot from being in that type of group where we're living together. We're working together, and we're going on excursions together on the weekends, and [sharing] different perspectives on education and family. And finding that I wasn't alone in this struggle to continue through graduate school—it helped me, it motivated me to continue on."

Peer mentors were crucial in shaping this community. They made a point to welcome new protégés, show them the ropes, and ease their transitions. For some protégés, this was their first experience of living away from home. Peer mentors provided encouragement, advice, and friendship; allayed fears that everyone else was "smarter than me"; and took pains to involve new students in social and scientific activities. As successful returning students and experienced researchers, they served as role models and cheerleaders; by sharing their own experiences and stories, they played a strong role in communicating SOARS' norms and culture. Their many functions are exemplified in this quotation:

> [My peer mentor] was like my sister, my mom, my friend, the person I could talk to. . . . The first day I got there, she had cooked for me. And any time she was going somewhere, I had to go! . . . She was going to make sure that I was interactive in everything. . . . And I loved it! She just made the transition so easy. . . . She helped me in a large part to feel at home, and also to feel like I can do something because I'd see that she's done something, and she's accomplished something, and she keeps pushing forward.

The benefit was mutual: peer mentors enjoyed and took pride in helping their mentees build skills and confidence. Being a mentor was an empowering experience, a good way to "practice being leaders." Clearly the design choice to explicitly foster and reinforce a strong peer community addressed students' emotional and social needs, provided practical help in getting up to speed in their work, and helped to persuade them that they legitimately belonged to this scientific community. In their leadership and role modeling functions, peer leaders helped to sustain the program and provided concrete evidence that people of color can be successful in the STEM professions.

• • •

In sum, several features of SOARS are features also evident in faculty-led UR, but are deliberately reinforced and enhanced in programs targeted to students from underrepresented groups. This "belt and braces" approach thus takes the best of what undergraduate research experiences can offer and strengthens it to provide a nearly iron-clad guarantee of positive outcomes.

Additional Features Not Typically Part of Faculty-Centered UR

Programs targeting undergraduate minority students in STEM fields often include additional elements that address needs that are not directly met by UR alone.

Financial Aid

SOARS provided several forms of financial assistance widely recognized by protégés as important to their success. While summer stipends are typically provided, SOARS stipends, like the stipends of other similarly focused UR programs, were deliberately generous; these and other targeted financial aid are critical in enabling low-income students to continue their education. Conference travel provided opportunities for professional networking, résumé building, and "becoming a scientist." While most SOARS students who started graduate school were funded by their departments or by outside fellowships, the promise of financial support for STEM graduate study, though seldom needed in practice, symbolized SOARS support and ensured that motivated students were not barred from graduate work by a lack of funds.

Academic Skills and Advising

Academic year workshops, tutoring, or study groups are common features of minority student–serving programs, as are summer bridge programs that augment what may be variable academic skills (Tsui, 2007). Academic advising may be enhanced and personalized to monitor student progress, spot difficulties in time to remedy them, and steer students to academic and career resources. Because it was not campus based, SOARS did not provide direct academic support, but the SOARS director stayed in close touch with students throughout the year to monitor their grades, provide academic and personal advice, and intervene in cases of difficulty.

Approaches to Diversity

Any program seeking to support students from underrepresented groups in STEM must attend in some way to issues of race, ethnicity, gender, and class. This might pose challenges given that SOARS was hosted at a laboratory with a primarily white male population, located in an affluent and predominantly white community. However, SOARS students commonly reported that race was not an issue: "Coming here was like, it was no color, it was no race, it was no size, it was no nothing. You were just another person."

Two main factors contributed to this atmosphere. First, mentors, leaders, and other lab members endorsed the SOARS goal to increase diversity in the atmospheric sciences and valued their opportunity to help achieve it. Diversity of people provided a valuable diversity of thought, they felt, and righting past wrongs was important. Although some mentors wondered whether they should broach the "iffy topic" of ethnicity in the workplace, most strived to model their values rather than stating them aloud and to approach their mentoring roles in a "color-blind" manner. Although this approach can ignore key differences in culture and lived experience, mentors' respectful treatment of protégés, genuine caring about their success, and modeling of their shared field and chosen profession ultimately was what mattered most in the mentoring relationship, as others have found (Campbell & Campbell, 1997; Lee, 1999). As a result, very few difficulties around race, ethnicity, and gender were reported to occur at the lab.

Second, the closely knit, multiracial protégé group provided a supportive and collegial community that achieved the critical mass needed to provide a safe haven, foster social integration and academic support, and reduce perceptions of racism (Allen, 1992; Gándara, 1999; Murguia, Padilla, & Pavel, 1991; Tinto, 1993). Race in the protégé community instead became an asset as students gained understanding of other cultures, developed respect for differences, and developed interpersonal skills. As a result, they became more comfortable in their own identity as women or as persons of color and saw how they could combine this with their identity as scientists and engineers.

With race a less salient issue among protégés, stereotype threat and the resulting loss of confidence were diminished. Senior students showed junior students that members of their race do thrive and succeed in the STEM professions, increasing confidence and raising aspirations. In general, the protégé community enhanced students' positive racial identities, which researchers have found to protect against the negative effects of classroom and peer discrimination (Sellers, Caldwell, Schmeelk-Cone, & Zimmerman, 2003; Wong, Eccles, & Sameroff, 2003). The Meyerhoff program, Louis Stokes Alliances for Minority Participation, and others have also reported the importance of the learning community to minority

STEM students (Alexander et al., 1998; Clewell et al., 2006; Maton et al., 2000; Summers & Hrabowski, 2006; Nagda, Gregerman, Jonides, von Hippel, & Lerner, 1998; Walters, 1997).

Institutional Commitment

In faculty-led research, the personal motivation and interest of individual faculty largely sustain their efforts to involve undergraduates in research, even where these are coordinated at a departmental level. For a structured program, however, extra resources are needed to build and uphold the amplifications and additions that we have enumerated. At NCAR, upper administrators made their support visible and actively recruited mentors, garnering high participation rates of scientists, engineers, and others as SOARS mentors. The lab funded the director's salary and put significant effort into fundraising to sustain the program. The SOARS director played several critical functions, including:

- Recruiting students and guiding them through the application process
- Recruiting mentors and matching them with protégés
- Setting high expectations of protégés and upholding these expectations with flexibility when needed
- Establishing communication norms through a respectful attitude and skilled listening
- Providing individualized advice to protégés on personal and career issues
- Resolving problems raised by mentors or protégés in their mentoring and other interpersonal relationships
- Promoting a collaborative culture that encouraged protégés to give and receive help when needed
- Monitoring protégé progress through one-on-one meetings and academic-year contact
- Using professional networks to foster opportunities for protégés in college and in the profession
- Communicating SOARS norms and culture to protégés and mentors through one-on-one meetings, training sessions, visibility at program events, and "management by walking around"
- Securing funding and reporting to funding agencies and other stakeholders
- Gathering information and feedback to document SOARS' work, assess its effectiveness, and improve the program

Support staff members were critical assets in student recruitment and application processes, program planning and logistics, and support for students' field work and conference travel, both during the summer when students were on-site and during the academic year. The steering committee aided in student selection and mentor matching, provided program direction, and engaged additional stakeholders. In addition, the strong protégé community played a role in sustaining its own future. As the program director put it, "Protégés are not just participants in the programs, but contributors to its very structure and shape."

Longer-Term Career and Educational Outcomes of SOARS

The results of this study identify positive student outcomes from SOARS and key program elements that help to achieve these. Because SOARS has an explicit goal to retain students through their STEM majors and into graduate programs, it is legitimate as well to examine students' postbaccalaureate educational and career progress as important, longer-term outcomes. Compared to the four-college study—where, as we have argued, students' career outcomes were predicted by their incoming interests and were not a direct result of UR (Chapter Five), and where UR is just one component of an overall educational experience (Tobochnik, 2001)—career outcomes may be more directly claimed as resulting from programs like SOARS that augment students' education.

Among the students interviewed in 2003–2004, 86 percent of protégés planned or had commenced a career in a STEM field, and 55 percent were aiming for careers in research—nearly half in atmospheric and earth science, and most of the rest in mathematics, engineering, or computer science. As of 2008, 65 percent of former protégés who had earned a STEM undergraduate degree had completed a master's degree or were enrolled in a graduate program in a STEM field (SOARS, 2008). This compares favorably with national averages of about 30 percent of STEM students who obtain a bachelor's degree and are enrolled in STEM graduate school two years later (National Science Foundation, 2002).

While on the surface these proportions resemble the high fractions of UR students in the four-college study who pursued STEM graduate work (61 percent) and planned STEM careers (95 percent), including research careers (55 percent) (Table 5.1), there is a crucial difference: only a small fraction of the SOARS students had considered graduate school at all prior to entering SOARS. For example, three-quarters of first-year SOARS students in our study stated that graduate school was a new idea for them, introduced by their SOARS experience. Only three students reported graduate study as a prior ambition—versus the large majority of the students in the four-college UR sample who held graduate school ambitions as they started college (Table 5.1). This echoes prior findings that UR introduces graduate school as a new possibility not previously considered, primarily among students from underrepresented groups (Chapter Two).

SOARS students also described stronger influences on their career plans than the clarification and refinement that dominated the accounts of students at the four colleges. Their SOARS experience had inspired them to higher career aspirations, instilled confidence that they could succeed, and made graduate school seem like a realistic possibility. The time after graduation was no longer "a big, black beyond." Their deepened understanding of what a career in atmospheric science would entail was reflected in one career goal shift peculiar to this field. Initially some 30 percent of new protégés indicated high interest in broadcast meteorology as a career, but by the end of their SOARS experience, fewer than 5 percent held this goal. This shift is just one indicator of how an authentic, mentored experience provided career information that enabled students to see a wider range of choices before them, consider a research career among these options, and make more informed and realistic choices from among a wide array of careers within the earth and atmospheric sciences. Despite the lack of a clear comparison group, it appears that the intensive model of UR, combined with other structured support, achieves its desired goals to advance students from underrepresented groups into the profession.

These findings about the career influence of SOARS are consistent with the literature. In their study of minority students' career paths, Asera and Treisman (1995) note students' needs for information about the culture of their chosen discipline, the structure of the profession, the organization of graduate school, and the breadth of careers related to the discipline. Students' career choices were influenced by interaction with mentors, access to "insider knowledge," and affirmation that they could think and perform like a mathematician (p. 147). Tsui (2007) points out that even among high-achieving minority students, the literature indicates a "critical lack of tacit knowledge about higher education and careers" (Arnold, 1993, p. 277; Seymour & Hewitt, 1997). Significant impacts on career outcomes, including changes of career direction, have been reported for minority students much more often than for white students (Table 2.1). The amplified benefits of socialization into the profession that we have described earlier in this chapter go far toward explaining this outcome.

Conclusion

SOARS and other programs aimed at advancing STEM students from underrepresented groups incorporate undergraduate research as a core program activity, with deliberate modifications to address the special challenges that these students face. Such programs take advantage of the common benefits that students derive from UR, but beyond this they deliberately enhance, amplify, and reinforce some features in order to guarantee that all students have the time and opportunity to make these gains in deep, meaningful, and empowering ways. They augment UR with other program elements to address additional challenges that UR alone does not address. Our analysis of these critical program elements, drawn from the case study of SOARS, aligns well with cross-program analyses by Gándara (1999) and Tsui (2007). Likewise, in selecting elements that foster academic and social integration into a disciplinary community, the design of these programs is consistent with theoretical arguments relating integration to undergraduate retention and advancement (Astin, 1992; Tinto, 1993; Pascarella & Terenzini, 2005). Collectively, the evidence shows the power of undergraduate research as a tool for engaging minority students in authentic science in order to overcome past societal disadvantages and develop individual talent in communities that have not had these opportunities. Whether such efforts can scale up to the point that they cumulatively foster a more diverse scientific workforce is a bigger question, whose answer remains to be seen.

Chapter 7

How Do Research Advisors Work with Students?

SO FAR, WE have focused on the nature, extent, and singularity of students' gains from participating in research experiences, both immediate gains and those realized over time. The next three chapters shift the focus to the processes by which such gains are achieved and by which UR work is both maintained and constrained, based on evidence from our four-campus study.

This chapter presents the methods that research advisors use and how these contribute to the desirable outcomes that research studies have documented. Advisors used opportunities inherent in authentic research projects as everyday teaching tools to meet both their own research needs and the educational and professional development needs of their students. In identifying the variety of teaching strategies, we embed a how-to manual: no advisor used all of these strategies, but collectively they offer good advice for new research advisors about the problems to expect in working with students, many ideas for how to resolve these, and reassurance that certain challenges are normal and inherent in working with novice researchers.

Chapter Eight continues to highlight research advisors' work with students but takes a more global view in detailing how advisors mentor students individually, provide career advice, and monitor and assess student progress toward their learning objectives. Chapter Nine examines the costs and benefits to faculty of doing this work, pinpointing some factors that shape, support, and constrain UR as both an intensive, individualized form of education for students and a scholarly activity for the faculty themselves. In all three chapters, synergies and tensions between advisors' roles as educators and scholars become apparent.

Some of the findings discussed in these three chapters may seem particular to the liberal arts colleges in which this study was carried out. Some details are specific to the setting, but in studies of UR in multiple contexts, we observe significant commonality across well-implemented programs in the functions that are described and in how they are carried out by thoughtful advisors. These functions may be filled elsewhere by people with different job titles or shared among multiple persons, either informally or deliberately, as in the design of the Significant Opportunities in Atmospheric Research and Science (SOARS) program (Chapter Six). In a university research group, the lab director may design the project, the coordinator of a structured UR program may recruit and select students for laboratory placements, and a postdoctoral researcher or graduate student may supervise a student's everyday work. At a national laboratory, these roles may be filled by research scientists and technical and administrative staff. But each can deploy the strategies described here to work effectively with their student researchers.

As seen in Chapters Two, Three, Four, and Six, the nature of positive outcomes for students depends little on their UR setting; they can be achieved in a variety of settings. We argue here that successful advisor practices likewise depend little on the context in which UR is conducted. Thus, the material in these three chapters offers examples of functions that support UR rather than a prescription for how these functions should be filled. Again, this is the reason for our deliberate choice of the term *research advisor*, which emphasizes these functions rather than the job title of the person who may carry them out.

Nature of the Evidence

The findings discussed in this chapter, and in Chapters Eight and Nine, were based on information provided by the eighty faculty in our sample: fifty-five active research advisors, twelve administrators also active as research advisors, seven faculty who normally did summer research but were "taking time out," and six faculty who had limited participation or no longer participated in UR work. Interviewees answered questions about student outcomes, their working methods as advisors, and the benefits and costs of their UR participation, and many raised related matters. While most advisors had not previously been invited to discuss their research work with students, the topic was important to them: interviews were intensive and often continued for two or more hours. Appendix A contains details about the faculty interview samples, Appendix B reviews the study methods, and Appendix C provides the interview protocol for faculty.

The coded data set from these eighty interviews encompassed 5,509 distinct coded topics and nearly 14,000 discrete observations. Nearly half of these addressed three major issues directly connected to advisors' practice of UR, in roughly equal numbers: student outcomes (Chapter Three), the benefits and costs to advisors of their UR participation (Chapter Nine), and how valued outcomes were achieved (this chapter). From advisors' observations on how they undertook their UR work, we distilled the description of approaches used in effective UR work that is presented in this chapter, and we highlight advisors' own words in describing those approaches.

Student Recruitment, Selection, and Matching

For faculty in undergraduate institutions, summer research with students is a critical component of their scholarship. Without graduate students or postdocs, making progress with their own research depends on the effectiveness of their selection and education processes. Research advisors in these institutions constantly managed a tension between meeting their own research needs and fulfilling a strong, shared commitment to both educating students and securing the next generation of research scientists. This tension, apparent in many aspects of advisors' work, surfaced as well in the process in how student researchers were selected.

The processes whereby students were recruited, selected, and matched to particular advisors and projects were clearly socially negotiated. All but three of the nineteen departments in our sample used some type of formal process whose primary goals were to open up research opportunities for a wide range of students and ensure fairness in distributing among advisors students perceived as stronger and weaker. Thus, departments advertised and widely promoted available research opportunities, sought to moderate faculty competition for talented students and fairly share the risks of accepting marginal students, and helped match students to appropriate projects. At these colleges, the selection processes took place at a departmental level, but similar issues and approaches arise for individual advisors and on selection committees for structured UR programs.

Selection committees met to sort and select applicants and match them with appropriate advisors and projects. This process was widely described as negotiating a good balance: they took into account academic performance, preparation, relevant experience, letters of recommendation, and students' preferences for particular advisors and projects, and balanced these with advisors' preferences, direct experience of students, available funding, workloads, and a widespread desire to accommodate a diverse array of students. Selection was also limited by the number of students a department could accommodate. These were lively, often competitive discussions—"rather like an NFL draft," one chair wryly observed.

The formal process was often accompanied by a set of informal processes of recruitment, selection, and matching that operated in parallel with, and often in support of, the official system. Methods included direct personal recruitment, whereby research advisors "kept an eye out" for promising students in their classes, mentioned research opportunities to them, and encouraged them to apply. They were aware that other advisors were doing the same thing, but were careful not to be seen as "poaching" talented students. More acceptable than direct poaching was the widespread use of informal brokering, or "trading" to distribute capable students. "Good students" known to a particular advisor were referred to a colleague whose project was a better fit for the student's interests and abilities, with the mutual understanding that the colleague would make similar referrals.

Another informal practice was gradual incorporation of students into a research group of students over time. Students might begin by volunteering during the academic year, attending research team meetings, and talking to faculty about the research. Research advisors could observe students' interest and capability, while students gained an early experience of hands-on work. Students who thus edged into working relationships with particular advisors established some priority. Although these arrangements skirted the formal process, they clearly served useful functions for both students and advisors.

Advisors expressed some ambivalence about this unofficial system of recruiting and trading, the traditional default system that formal application, selection, and matching processes had been instituted to replace or govern. However, whenever an informal system develops or persists alongside a formal system intended to serve similar purposes, it is fair to assume that the informal system is performing some functions that the formal system meets insufficiently. Paradoxically, as Blau (1974) observes, unofficial practices that are discouraged or disallowed by official rules may yet further the achievement of organizational goals. Informal selection processes had three functions:

- Identify promising students and draw them into the research talent pool. Talented students who do not apply cannot be selected, and shy students who are not noticed or encouraged may be lost.

- Gather direct information about students seeking positions. Advisors need opportunities to observe and assess students, and sharing this information benefits all advisors.
- Allow both advisors and students to make well-informed choices.

The coexistence of formal and informal systems also reveals a tension inherent in advisors' UR work: a shared desire to provide as many research opportunities as possible while still securing sufficient, competent help to push forward their own scholarly agendas. Some advisors were uncomfortable with unofficial practices that they defined as "self-serving," "cheating," or "good old boy" behavior. They worried that under-the-table trading could miss or exclude students who might be both less aware of research opportunities and less confident to apply. However, many advisors acknowledged and accepted the parallel formal and informal systems; some departments that officially frowned on private arrangements turned a blind eye to them. Taken together, these dual systems met valued goals: the formal system emphasized diversity and fairness, and the informal system focused on talent spotting and protecting faculty scholarship. Indeed, it appeared to be hard to invent a formal system that met all these goals well: one department had abandoned its new formal system and had gone back to its informal methods.

Students were expected to be active in pursuit of UR positions and to show initiative by attending seminars, reading about possible projects, and seeking out advisors to discuss research possibilities. Failure to do this was a commonly applied bar to a research placement. As one advisor observed, "They have to work for it." Despite advisors' extensive commentary on matching and selection processes, we received little commentary on them from students. What did communicate were advisors' efforts to be open with students and give them a fair chance.

What Criteria Guided Faculty Selection of Students?

Advisors clearly viewed some students as more or less appealing as potential researchers. Table 7.1 shows the criteria that individual advisors used to select or reject students. On average, advisors raised four positive criteria and one negative criterion each, which fell broadly into three categories: student attributes that were viewed positively or negatively, student group preferences, and departmental and individual constraints.

TABLE 7.1

Criteria for Selecting and Denying Students for UR Positions, as Reported by Research Advisors

Criteria	Criterion Used in Selection		Criterion Used in Denial		Overall Use of Criterion	
	Number of Observations	Percentage of Positive Criteria[a]	Number of Observations	Percentage of Negative Criteria[a]	Number of Observation	Percentage of All Criteria[a]
Student attributes						
Character and temperament	149	53%	49	58%	198	54%
Particular attributes of character	74		27		101	
Motivation, interest, commitment	55		19		74	
Collaborative skills and attitudes; faculty comfort with student	20		3		23	
Academic work	62	22%	5	6%	67	18%
Academic achievements	35		0		35	
Academic preparation or qualification	27		5		32	
Contributions to a project	39	14%	8	10%	47	13%
Skills (communication, lab, project needs)	31		8		39	
Research or related experience	8		0		8	
Risk	0	0%	6	7%	6	2%
Attributes seen as risks to productivity	0		6		6	
Student groups that benefit most	30	11%	0	0%	30	8%
Preference, especially by gender, race, or ethnicity	27		0		27	
Need for preparation for graduate school	3		0		3	
Constraints of resources and time	0	0%	16	19%	16	4%
Limits on numbers or on younger students	0		16		16	
Total criterion mentions	280	100%	84	100%	364	100%

Note: Frequency counts are taken from interviews with seventy-four active or recently active research advisors.

[a]Percentages do not sum to 100 percent because of rounding.

Student Attributes

As Table 7.1 shows, student attributes were by far the most often mentioned factors in selecting students for research positions. Advisors' preferences were shaped on the one hand by attributes of character, behavior, and attitude, and on the other, by some combination of academic achievement and preparation, skills, and research-related experience. While they agreed overall about what characteristics made a student more or less likely to succeed as a researcher, advisors were broadly divided in how they prioritized these: forty-four advisors saw attributes of character, temperament, and motivation as paramount, and twenty-six looked first for well-prepared, academically strong students with good grades.

However, every informant mentioned attributes of character, behavior, and temperament. Notable among these was tenacity, defined as a willingness to persevere and keep trying new approaches to problems. In classes and laboratory work, advisors looked for students who could handle frustrations and "wanted to dig in their heels." Although students reported confidence to do science as a major benefit, advisors looked for early signs of this quality. They liked students who were curious, seemed ready to tackle new things and saw challenges as "fun," and were willing to take risks, work with unknowns, and cope with uncertainty. They also favored students who were ready to express their ideas and speak up for themselves.

Given the need to be productive, advisors also looked for students who were dependable and independent—hard workers who would take responsibility to get tasks done. In face-to-face discussions, they looked for signs that students were eager to learn, interested in their research, and enthusiastic about a project. Finally, they wanted students with collaborative attitudes and good communication skills who could work well with others.

Experience had led many advisors to value these attitudes more than grades, preparation, or skills. One advisor explained, "I will teach them what they need to know, but I need to see that spark of real interest." More pragmatically, some advisors felt that high interest increased the likelihood that a student would actually contribute something useful. Some favored attributes were also those that advisors hoped to see strengthened as a result of UR experiences, and that students reported as positive outcomes (Chapter Three).

As reflected in Table 7.1, advisors were disposed to discourage or reject students who lacked favored attributes or showed others they saw as unsuitable. Students who did not demonstrate interest or enthusiasm were eliminated first, along with passive learners who seemed to avoid thinking about problems. Advisors avoided students who seemed motivated primarily by a desire to build their résumé or obtain a summer job. The second, smaller group of advisors who looked first for "talent" also valued attributes of character and motivation, but inferred linkages between academic achievement and character: intelligence diligently applied was seen as the source of high-quality work; high grades indicated hard work and motivation to learn; lower grades were indicators of questionable interest and research potential.

In contrast, advisors who valued character and motivation over academic record asserted that "grades do not tell the whole story." For them, tenacity and curiosity trumped academic performance alone. They also valued "good lab citizens" who were organized, neat, cooperative, and polite to others. These advisors were proud of their ability to spot a student with research potential. Their success stories often featured "B students" who had flourished in summer research and gone on to be good professional researchers. The prevalence of such views explains advisors' emphasis on students' taking the initiative to approach them about research opportunities. Advisors also paid attention to the match between students' preparation, skills, and research-related experience and their own needs for productive, collaborative coworkers. Computer programming and mathematics proficiency were valued for certain projects, as were students with "good lab hands" who could set up equipment with minimal direction. Advisors avoided students who lacked basic lab competence, found it difficult to master techniques, or were prone to breaking equipment. They valued good professional practice, such as meticulous attention to detail, keeping good lab notebooks, and the ability to communicate well.

Thus, advisors were broadly agreed about what made potential students more or less attractive and what kinds of help they needed for productive research. These patterns were consistently expressed across the sample. It is worth noting that some student gains are presaged by characteristics that advisors select for, but then work to enhance through UR because they see these as characteristics needed in the profession and thus as essential to students' future success.

Student Group Preferences

Finally, advisors were swayed by considerations of which students might benefit the most from research experiences. They favored male students of color, women of all races and ethnicities, and students who were the first in their families to attend college—all of whom have been historically underrepresented in science, technology, engineering, and mathematics (STEM) disciplines—and applicants from schools offering limited research opportunities. Because the four colleges in our study had few students of color, even with these efforts the proportion of students of color in the four-college UR sample was only 11 percent. Gender preference was openly practiced and well supported in eleven of the fourteen departments at the three coeducational colleges (represented by thirty-eight male and twenty-four female advisors), where other selection criteria were equally met. This reflected both a high representation of women faculty in many of these departments and a strong, collective bias toward "giving young women a boost."

It was not clear that gender preference was a response to either contemporary or local concerns. At these campuses, female students were well represented in the life sciences, chemistry, and mathematics and, as at other institutions nationwide, less represented in physics, computer science, and engineering. However, women's underrepresentation was not the main motivation. Advisors were more concerned that without research experience, some capable women would not think of entering graduate programs or science-based careers or might not appreciate the importance of undergraduate research in pursuing these paths. Wishing to improve the self-confidence of their women STEM majors, advisors saw research experiences as effective in achieving this end. They cited successes among their female researchers who realized that they could "do good research" and gained confidence to "stand up for themselves" by "not hiding or denying their abilities," and by "asking for what they needed."

However, several advisors observed that the need for gender preference may be declining in some fields. They noted more confident behavior among recent cohorts of female students; some male advisors observed that current women students were academically stronger than their male peers. Women advisors commented on a shift in rationale from encouraging women to enter STEM graduate programs to preparing them well for the mental and emotional challenges of graduate school.

• • •

In summary, the criteria by which advisors collectively and individually selected students fell broadly into two well-defined patterns of individual criteria and a set of additional group-level considerations.

These patterns reflect differences in advisors' reasons for participating in undergraduate research, their objectives, and definitions of success, and they throw further light on why coexisting formal and informal methods of recruitment, selection, and matching were common. Advisors treated any combination of methods as functional if they effectively provided the information needed to identify and recruit promising students. Thus, talking to students and swapping information with colleagues allows judgment about personal attributes, scrutiny and discussion of written records reveals academic merit, and open departmental discussion of the whole slate of possible students favors considerations of diversity and fair distribution of talent.

Second, individual advisors' selection criteria reflected tensions between their need for research productivity and their desire to meet students' education and career needs. This tension surfaces during student selection, before the summer's UR work begins. Selection criteria also reflect concerns to prepare the next generation of scientists in ways that reflect the national talent pool. Finally, advisors often trusted their hunches about a student's research potential more than information about academic performance, consistent with their widely expressed view that authentic, mentored research can turn promise into professional competence.

Authenticity as the Central Organizing Principle

The principle that guided all aspects of the advisors' summer teaching work was to offer students an authentic experience of research. Paramount in making a student project authentic was the choice of a scientific, technical, or mathematical problem. "It's gotta be answering a question that the scientific community—my little subset of that community—really wants to know the answer [to], and wants to know it now," said one advisor. "The questions we're attempting to answer, if we don't get 'em answered, someone else is gonna do it." At the same time, advisors noted, "You have to have some wisdom about what kinds of things you can do." Many detailed how they chose problems that were "tractable" within the research environment of an undergraduate college; young faculty described the forethought they had given this issue while job hunting. Some had identified a particular niche in their research field; some staked out a portion of a larger collaborative effort; others chose hot topics but used methods that could yield results quickly enough to stay competitive. Said one faculty member, "The research I'm doing is still at the forefront of its field, but it is not developing a whole new subdiscipline. [I'm] able to continue in . . . main-line areas of research rather than truly developing a new subdiscipline, which is what would be expected at MIT or at Berkeley."

Some had found success by finding collaborators who could "fill holes" left by lack of access to instrumentation or time for large-scale experiments. Others focused their research program on one major problem rather than trying to work on multiple fronts.

Despite these caveats, research advisors insisted on the scientific integrity of their student projects: "The science has to go where the science wants to go." Faculty conducted all the normal, everyday work of researchers, taking on certain intellectual aspects of the project themselves, maintaining contacts and collaborations with researchers at other institutions, attending and presenting at conferences, and writing journal articles and grant proposals. Involving undergraduates as fellow researchers changed the tempo and scale of their research but did not alter its fundamental scholarly nature. That is, advisors chose research questions whose investigation could be slowed down but need not be dumbed down.

Once a suitable scientific project was identified, ensuring that students learned from it was not difficult because an authentic project also carried with it the means for learning. Advisors widely agreed that working hands-on, step-by-step, from beginning to end of the research process, was "the very best way to know how science works." They defined authentic (or "real") research as inherently diagnostic, complex, and open-ended and regarded authenticity as the central organizing principle of their teaching methods. An authentic research experience immersed students in creative thought and hands-on work; it pushed them to apply what they already knew in new and synthetic ways to questions that are significant to the scientific community and for which there are no existing answers. Student projects must also entail the problems, risks, and reversals common to all research. Thus, authenticity functioned for advisors as a scholarly objective of their own, as a philosophy of undergraduate research, and as a teaching medium:

> I think probably the most important thing is the process, because you
> can't guarantee success. You can't guarantee a product at the end. And
> so the whole summer's experience centers around that process of seeing

how science is really done. They experience it to a certain extent in the course work . . . but here is where it really comes together. For ten weeks, eight hours a day, and nights and weekends, they are really focusing on this one thing. Here they get to finally use all of those things that we've been trying to teach them; now they see why you need to know that. And they really can solidify a lot of the knowledge that they have a tenuous grasp on from their course work. That really is the heart of it: working through it, seeing how science is done.

Advisors saw authentic research as enabling students to deepen their understanding; apply their knowledge, reasoning, and skills; discover connections among pieces of knowledge; and explore the possibilities of and limitations to research questions. Grappling to make sense of the imperfections and puzzles in real data forced students to think about how their data connected to the questions posed and thus to decide what was appropriate or flawed in their methods. Through intensive hands-on work, they argued, students "come to understand the nuances of research," "the myriad details to be attended to," and "the temperament that research requires," and thereby can "discover whether it is for them."

Developing collegial modes of thought and work was another valued outcome of authentic research. By working alongside their advisors, students learned to appreciate the importance of collegial contributions, including their own. Advisors placed their students in the same boat as themselves, as cothinkers and coexperimenters, powered along by "a shared investment in the project questions and outcomes."

Authentic research also showed students what it meant to adopt science as a profession. Indeed, experiences that enable apprentices to understand the nature of their future working life are near universal in the formal and informal socialization of professionals in medicine, law enforcement, teaching, the military, and the clergy, as well as in traditional trades where apprenticeships were originally developed (Ainley & Rainbird, 1999; Greenwood, 1972; Glazer & Hannafin, 2006; Sullivan, Colby, Wegner, Bond, & Shulman, 2007). An authentic learning experience forces a shift from knowing about something to understanding one's own nascent relationship to a particular body of knowledge and practice. It is simultaneously an intellectual, affective, social, and physical experience with consequences for future lifestyles, attitudes, and identity (Hunter, Laursen, & Seymour, 2007). As masters do for apprentices in other occupations, research advisors carefully monitored their apprentices' experiences, staged their introduction to independent work, decided whether or when to intervene and assist with problems, and supported students through setbacks. Thus, although research experiences were authentic, advisors tempered the degree to which students dealt alone with the full consequences of moving a research project forward on their own.

Advisors' insistence on authenticity was strongly expressed; they criticized research experiences they saw as insufficiently real at both ends of an education-research continuum. Colleagues were open to criticism if they employed students mainly to further their own research productivity or "pushed them to one side" and thus neglected to give students a mentored, collegial, educational experience of real science. Such students— referred to as "technicians," "lab rats," and even "slave labor"—were seen as "extra hands" who did repetitive work and learned specific skills but did not contribute intellectually. This was a sensitive issue; many advisors mentioned a conscious daily choice between their teaching objectives and their own research progress: "I don't look at them as if they were just helpers. If they were helpers, I would do it very differently, and what it costs me would be much lower." A second advisor noted, "A lot of times it involves letting them do things that I could do a lot more quickly. So it's a trade-off. Sometimes I just want to be done quickly."

At the other end of the continuum lay primarily educational experiences in which students learned about the research process by doing projects whose outcomes were already known. These experiences were sometimes referenced as "teaching-research," as opposed to "research-research" or, more skeptically, as "make-work" projects. The topic was controversial: while college administrators looked for ways to give more students some kind of research experience, research advisors were generally opposed to shorter UR experiences, largely because students needed time to understand, grapple with, and make progress on solving problems. They resisted initiatives they saw as simulated research and thus as less able to stimulate the student growth conferred by authentic research.

Advisors constantly negotiated a balance between progress in their own research and a strongly felt professional and disciplinary imperative to educate students. Giving their students an authentic experience was the principle that bridged these two objectives. Throughout this chapter, we highlight the role of authenticity in advisors' approaches to their UR work and their use of real research experiences as everyday teaching tools.

Achieving Authenticity: How Student Research Projects Are Chosen

Authenticity was initially secured by the choice of a meaningful scientific question. That question was then framed to make it amenable for novice researchers under the time and resource constraints of summer UR. Project selection for undergraduates took two main forms:

1. Advisors drew on their own research or scholarly interests as a source of projects, often offering a choice of contributory projects, with each student working on his or her own piece of the puzzle. When projects were longitudinal, with new students picking up where others left off, advisors often had a good sense of project direction. Protocols had been worked out, and the roles for new students were clear. At the other extreme, student work helped to shape the direction of exploratory projects.

2. Advisors who could not easily offer aspects of their own research looked in their area of specialty for problems. They described a perpetual search for unsolved, open-ended, well-defined problems at an appropriate level of difficulty to add to their running lists of possible projects.

Whatever their source, advisors were agreed that good projects should be conceptually and technically accessible to young researchers. A good UR project:

- Must start at a theoretical level that undergraduates are capable of understanding, given their year in school and course background
- Must draw on skills that students already possess, or can learn quickly enough, to give them a chance to progress in the time available
- Should have a modest scope that can be either simplified or extended
- Should have a good chance of producing results within the time frame available.

Advisors avoided projects they defined as "risky": vaguely defined or too capacious; requiring untested, difficult, or complex techniques; expensive, dangerous, or inherently slow; or likely to damage equipment or waste valuable time chasing uncertain results. But risk was an inevitable part of authenticity: advisors told stories of projects that after weeks of effort did not work out, had to be scaled back or subdivided, or turned out to have been done before. Redesign was the norm, and projects commonly changed direction.

The issue of whether, and in what circumstances, students could propose their own projects was widely discussed. Some degree of project choice engaged and motivated students, advisors agreed, and they hoped to see students develop independent lines of inquiry out of their initial work. However, they were near unanimous in rejecting the idea that students should initially propose projects. The capacity to generate a research question and fruitful ways to approach it was acquired only through sustained research engagement, they argued—an outcome rather than a starting point. Their skepticism of student-generated projects was grounded in experience and reinforced by collegial folklore about ill-defined, overdemanding, or even disastrous projects. Advisors also pointed out that students need not generate the project idea in order to develop a sense of ownership and responsibility for it. Indeed, we found no linkage between project origins and positive outcomes for students, including their sense of project ownership.

The Research Advisor's Role as Teacher

A tension between scholarly and educational goals for UR shaped the ways in which advisors identified student-sized projects to tackle a research problem of disciplinary interest and then selected students whom they thought could both contribute to and benefit from research. Once the summer's work began, however, research advisors were unanimous in describing their everyday interactions with students as "very much a teaching thing—I'm always thinking of what I want them to come away with and how I can get them there." They articulated what kinds of learning and growth they wanted to see in students and the methods that they used to enable these:

> It involves a lot of little things, like whether I hand them an article versus make them get it themselves, and how much I work them through the process of making a decision so they can find things out for themselves. . . . I try to think of what things you have to know in order to be able to figure something out on your own—and different ways to frame a question. So I try to work them through that and have them . . . figure out for themselves what they need.

Some teaching methods were overtly planned; others were inherited from advisors' own research experiences or created and reinforced by shared collegial practice. When asked to describe and reflect on their

UR teaching objectives and methods, advisors did so in detail with illustrations. Advisors experimented with their pedagogy and consciously repeated methods that worked well. They were sensitive to variations in students' capacities and needs, and they adjusted their expectations and methods accordingly.

Advisors' understanding of the teaching dimensions of their summer work helps to explain their frustration where colleges failed to recognize the skill and effort entailed in conducting research with students. Some explained that administrators from disciplines without a UR tradition might have no direct experience of the teaching work involved and thus be likely to view summer students solely as paid assistants to faculty scholarship. What is missed by this latter view is the research advisors' conscious concern to prepare students for work as scientists, scholars, and professionals and for aspects of "life in general." In the sections that follow, we describe the chief strategies that advisors developed for teaching through authentic problems.

Role of the Research Peer Group

Research advisors used peer groups as both an important teaching resource and a place to extend students' growth as scholars and professionals. Advisors expected students to learn how to work collaboratively and collegially, and they encouraged students to draw on each other as their primary sources of intellectual stimulation, practical help, and emotional support. Almost paradoxically, by using the group as a first resort, students became more independent in their own thinking and decision making. Some assigned a project to a pair of students as a way to make each more critically aware: the process of mutual questioning "intellectualizes usual routines." In team projects, advisors encouraged members to discuss how to tackle each piece of the project and divide up routine tasks.

Research pairs or teams commonly met with their advisors each week. These meetings served specific functions, teaching that:

- Problem solving begins in the group
- Groups are a sounding board for the development of ideas and a safe and supportive context to practice and critique presentations
- Groups are fertile contexts for project ideas to develop and evolve and for the interpretation of emergent data
- Scientists require good skills in explaining their ideas and in collegial critique, review, and editing.

Learning to contribute to a thinking and working community may be particularly important for women, students of color, and first-generation college students. Indeed, advisors who were active in recruitment and retention programs targeting students of color stressed the contribution of peer learning communities.

Advisors worked to build camaraderie among group members by hosting opportunities for social interaction and fun outside of work. Pizza parties, backyard barbeques, Frisbee and volleyball tourneys, and outings were occasions when advisors opened themselves, and their homes and families, to personal and sociable relationships with students.

Developing mutual reliance within the peer group also helped to optimize research progress. Advisors relied on continuing students to supervise, train, and mentor newer members. Senior students brought newcomers up to speed, facilitated the transition of projects before graduation, and acted as mentors and as intellectual and technical resources. As novice students received practical guidance, seniors learned how to work with assistants and gained in self-esteem by seeing their expertise at work and their significance as role models. Explaining the project to novices also solidified and consolidated their understanding of its intellectual basis. Some advisors connected students to former group members who provided live examples of career pathways, helped younger students "see how they can get there," and built alumni networks.

Advisors' Pedagogical Strategies

Advisors described a variety of teaching strategies that they used with their research students. These addressed common needs, such as starting a new student in research or intervening when a student hit a trouble spot, and made consistent use of the shared research problem as a reliable way to draw students into the project and teach skills and attitudes crucial for research.

Getting Started

Advisors prepared for summer research throughout the academic year, but UR began in earnest in the spring when advisors met with students to discuss and refine the scope of their projects. To students who joined continuing projects, advisors explained what they would be doing, how their work related to the whole project, and what might be accomplished by summer's end. They clarified their expectations for working hours, professional behavior, and safe laboratory practices and might offer preparatory reading, such as past students' papers, posters, and lab notebooks, to help students understand the project's direction and methods.

Advisors described a transition period, typically two weeks, in which students built skills with instruments, computers, and protocols. To get students going quickly, they taught techniques, discussed pertinent literature, and developed team familiarity with the project and the lab. Advisors warned students that the first weeks would be intense: the learning curve was steep, and they might feel at first that they were accomplishing little. As one advisor observed, "The first couple of weeks just kinda kills you." However, immediate immersion of students into many facets of the project at once was seen as highly effective in getting students familiar with the project and sufficiently competent to undertake some work on their own. In the following sections, we look at the teaching methods advisors used to enable their students' intellectual and related behavioral and temperamental gains.

Engaging with the Project's Intellectual Content

Research advisors' discussion of students' intellectual growth was embedded in three types of rich descriptions: what advisors observed in practice, what they expected, and what they consciously built into their ways of working with research students. Advisors were clear and overt about their learning objectives and about how and why they worked in particular ways to achieve them. Their observations were built into the markers of progress that we discuss in Chapter Eight. From the outset, advisors were consciously teaching to achieve intellectual growth. They gave students direct help in unpacking their problem and explained the theories and prior research behind the project. In guided reading and in discussions, advisors pushed students to:

- Use and extend their incoming level of knowledge in order to understand the research questions
- Think about how different pieces of knowledge could be brought together to address a research question
- Look for conceptual connections within their discipline and to related ideas in other disciplines
- Think (and argue with others) about the initial research questions
- Explore connections among ideas that suggested viable scientific approaches.

Deep engagement with their topic led students to learn particular project-relevant knowledge, but also showed them how deep study of any topic enables researchers to make broader connections between particular topics and general principles. One student researcher described how she was drawn into the intellectual heart of her project: "I think that the process of building this project and doing all the background research gives you a specialized understanding. It helped me make connections from what I initially thought of as my little research question back to that broader world. . . . That was a big part of it, seeing how it fit into that bigger picture."

Advisors also drew on their own prior experience of research in order to make the scientific process real, explaining their approach to research questions and why they had taken particular decisions. They involved students in the research design by discussing possible hypotheses, protocols, or techniques. Talking about past and present work was one way to share their enthusiasm, "engage students in the fun of doing real science," and allay some of their students' initial anxieties "about whether they could do any of this."

Problem Solving as Pedagogy

A set of related pedagogical principles, attitudes, and practices was evident in the ways that advisors used conceptual, technical, and other problems as opportunities to stimulate intellectual growth and foster the temperamental attributes required in good researchers. They consciously used naturally occurring problems to leverage intellectual growth. "Throwing students straight into the research" forced them "to apply what they already knew to figure things out" and to "make connections that can make the pieces fit." Undertaking authentic research obliged students to learn that getting good results takes time, practice, and patience, and that "almost no one gets it right first time"—and to cope with the inevitable frustration that this posed. Students also varied in their capacity to suspend prior understandings of knowledge as given or "factual." These early challenges of real science prompted some students to decide that research was not for them.

Fostering Independence

One objective of teaching through problem solving is to enable students to become independent in their thinking, approach to learning, and choices of direction. Independence was valued for its immediate, longer-term, and transferable benefits and was also used to judge student progress.

Research advisors sought to wean students from learned expectations of teacher direction. These strategies came into play when advisors judged that students had enough understanding, skills, and practice to tackle pieces of the work by themselves. At that stage, advisors began to step back and "let the students do the doing." Explaining to students that they were now "independent investigators" who "must do the work themselves," they gradually withdrew from daily oversight, described as "staying out of the way," "being hands-off," or "letting students sink or swim." Making their encounters more formal and deliberate conveyed that they expected students not to present them with matters that they could resolve for themselves. In making themselves less available, advisors accepted the risk that students would make errors, but their disengagement was neither abrupt nor uniform. They watched to see when individual students were ready to take on responsibility while continuing to help other students longer. They also distinguished the kinds of problems that they wanted students to raise with them—anything damaging or dangerous—from those they expected students to handle, and encouraged students to draw on the assistance of peers, lab technicians, and other faculty.

Advisors articulated their reasons for wanting students to develop independence. First, "doing UR is very hard work"—"far more work than just teaching." "It takes up hours and hours and hours of time" and "represents a huge commitment." Advisors needed students to work without constant direction while they traveled to meetings and counted on some quiet office time to write and plan. Students who wanted more direction than advisors had time to give undermined the advisor's research productivity. This issue was of particular concern to advisors approaching tenure, but we have noted the same concerns among graduate students and postdoctoral researchers who supervise UR students.

Normalizing Risk and Uncertainty

Advisors used the inevitable upsets of real science to teach students about dealing with risk. They warned that "doing science is very messy," "research is always risky," and "you cannot guarantee success." A research design may be flawed, methods may not work as expected, equipment may break, and data may be inconclusive. Advisors conveyed the role of trial and error, persistence, and (sometimes) sheer luck in making progress: "sometimes things go wrong all the time"; "you have to serially repeat the experiment"; and "you might not get good results or finish the project." Because they wanted students to understand these vicissitudes as normal, they consciously modeled how they coped with frustration and exercised patience in the face of slow progress. One advisor wryly observed, "I tell them that they will be ready for grad school when they are comfortable in dealing with all the usual frustrations of research."

Judging When to Intervene

Advisors distinguished between the levels and types of problems that students could solve by their own thought and effort and those likely to require help. If a problem was judged to lie within students' intellectual reach, they would "never hand the student the answer" or "solve it for them." They wanted to see students take ownership of problems that research threw at them and succeed by drawing on their own resources—for "their prof to give them the answer is to miss the point."

Making an Effective Intervention

Advisors did not, however, let students flounder amid their difficulties. When advisors intervened, they discussed the possible resources and options open to the student, helping the student to "take a step back," "review the situation," "gain perspective," then think through his or her assumptions, decisions, and methods and the results these had produced. Advisors encouraged students to think diagnostically—to break the project down into component pieces and rethink how they might be reassembled—and to refer to reading that might help them identify what was going wrong.

Talking It Through

Once a student had identified the likely sources of a problem, the advisor offered herself as a sounding board while the student thought aloud about options. Advisors provided hints about possible directions, often by posing questions, but students had to make their own choices about what to do next. Advisors encouraged students to "wrestle with the problem," "use what they knew in creative ways," "stretch themselves," and "take intellectual risks." Sometimes "just sitting down and talking" was enough to get students to think their way through a difficulty. Out of this process, students learned that although their advisor made them struggle, he would also guide them with pertinent questions and suggestions, making it easier for students to take on challenges and persevere.

More Radical Interventions

Research advisors intervened in more active ways when they judged a problem to be beyond the student's capacity to resolve it. Where a student had tried hard without making progress and time was running out, advisors provided more explicit direction: "I sit down with them and hammer out a plan of action." Diagnosing an unfixable design flaw, advisors might "decide that it was time to punt" and significantly modify the approach. They also used "stuck situations" to model the professional practice of asking for advice from colleagues in their networks. This is an example of advisors' judgment in tempering the consequences of authentic research for their novice colleagues.

How Students Responded

Teaching through problems was risky in part because students varied in their capacity to handle, intellectually and affectively, the frustrations of hands-on research. Novices expected research questions and methods to be straightforward and to assume that "if they did everything right, they would get good results." As the summer progressed, they were obliged to deal with increasing complexity and uncertainty. Some students willingly met these challenges: they were responsive to their advisor's suggestions and clues, argued out the options with other students, and "tried a whole bunch of things" to wrestle with problems. When these processes worked well, students gained insight into what they had missed and could move forward. In the process, they improved their mental and technical abilities, learned to persevere, and grew more confident.

However, not all students collaborated in this troubleshooting process. Some hid their problems to struggle on their own; some resisted stubbornly, ignoring or challenging suggestions. Others found it hard to acknowledge that things were not going well and "pursued failing methods in a ritual way." Some could not tolerate the frustrations of research, especially students who, accustomed to doing well, were fearful of tackling open-ended problems. Advisors recalled students who became upset, threw temper tantrums, broke equipment, "failed to come to the lab for a week," and "were emotionally devastated." Some "had a tremendous need to confess failure": they "would unburden themselves mercilessly" to their advisor and, even in their final presentation, would "recount everything that they had tried that did not work." Although advisors observed a general student tendency "to see the walls that they were hitting as higher than they actually are," a few students were frozen by this experience, unable to make a move on their own. This was another reason that advisors recruited students who thrived on open-ended challenges and those who, used to hard work for modest grades, "knew how to dig in." A few students could diagnose a problem and "put it all together without help," but this was both rare and undesirable; even if ultimately successful, those who struggled in isolation missed out on discussion, suggestion, argument, and encouragement from their advisor and peers.

Teaching by exposure to authentic research problems is also inherently risky because some problems are harder than others. Students commonly spent the first half of their summer "pulling their hair out," "just trying to figure out how to approach the problem," and "not getting anywhere." Experiments failed and equipment broke down; some problems could not be fixed despite everyone's best efforts. From these situations, students learned that it is sometimes necessary to rethink or abandon a project that will never produce usable data. Students also encountered the role of both good and bad luck in research. The most dramatic example we encountered was a biology experiment in which all the cell cultures, instrumentation, time, and money invested in the project were lost to summer power outages. Setbacks of these types were not inherently educational, but how advisors responded to them was. Students learned how researchers cope with major reversals and that their advisors did not have all the answers. Advisors widely pointed out that benefits accrued when students learned and grew by being part of the discussion about a change in project direction.

In sum, engagement with authentic, unforeseeable problems offered both an educational tool to enable valued outcomes and an object lesson about the nature of research. The intense, creative conversations prompted by research problems pushed students to take on intellectual and personal challenges and to act independently based on their own thinking. This direct, intensive, individualized focus on problem solving was a central feature of research advisors' pedagogy.

Building Students' Skills

Growth in students' skills was less important to advisors than to students (Chapter Three), yet advisors consciously taught and emphasized particular skills, both to move their projects forward and prepare students for higher-level work.

Reading for Comprehension

Advisors' motives for teaching students to understand and use scholarly literature were both pragmatic and remedial. Students needed to understand their project's conceptual underpinnings and its linkages to bodies of research and to read scientific literature well enough to extract project-related information. That said, few advisors asked students to undertake literature reviews; instead, they scaffolded students' reading in the following ways:

- Compiling packets of preparatory readings that the group met to discuss
- Assigning each student a piece of reading to explain at a subsequent meeting
- Starting with easier literature and gradually progressing to more difficult pieces
- Helping students dissect complex pieces of writing to focus on how experiments were done, data produced, and results interpreted
- Working through articles in a guided sequence to clarify how a project built on prior work
- Using textbook extracts to bring students up to speed on relevant theory.

Students were often overwhelmed by their first efforts to read original papers. They struggled with the formal language and condensed style, got confused, and sometimes gave up. Advisors did not expect students to reach a high level of reading comprehension in the short time available.

Technical Skills

For projects based on lab or field work, an early teaching task was getting students to an adequate level of competence, confidence, and safety in their use of equipment and techniques. Strategies for teaching laboratory skills included:

- Explaining the use of each piece of equipment students would be handling and demonstrating the techniques to use
- Supervising trial runs to ensure that students could follow procedures
- Assigning reading from lab manuals
- Requiring students to conduct a lab inventory to become familiar with its resources
- Teaching the use of particular software for data analysis or programming.

Advisors usually had a short time in which to bring students to the desired level of technical competence. As with much else in authentic research, this did not always happen. One advisor observed that if a student was not competent in a technique within two weeks, she knew from experience that he was unlikely to master it.

Record Keeping

Advisors required students to make a detailed record of their work and taught them how to organize accurate laboratory notebooks. This was a matter of mutual benefit, as advisors needed to stay informed and keep track of complex, longer-term projects with multiple participants, and students intending to continue as researchers needed to learn good habits of data management and recording. Advisors taught record keeping by providing handouts with guidelines on keeping a lab notebook; offering a workshop for new researchers; or requiring students to write weekly activity summaries, a running log of findings, notes on how they interpreted data, proposed next steps, or periodic progress reports.

Advisors impressed on new researchers that thorough records would "keep students on top of their work" and "provide the backbone" for reports and presentations as well as later publication. "In authentic research," one advisor observed, "students learn that they are the ones who are writing the lab manual." Advisors widely observed that learning what and how to record was the most important writing skill that students learned in summer research.

Communication Skills and Formal Presentation of Student Research

As discussed in Chapter Three, learning professional communication includes, but far exceeds, the acquisition of skills. Advisors used oral and poster presentation of research as a vehicle to achieve multiple objectives, including intellectual engagement, organization of conceptual thought, and professional socialization. Formal presentations also served as a motivating, organizing, and culminating focus throughout the summer. As both research advisors and their students made clear, the processes by which professional presentation habits were learned and practiced, and by which intellectual growth and self-confidence were gained, were as important as the presentation itself. By contrast, these advisors saw learning formal writing skills as of less importance at this stage in student development.

Advisors consciously set out to teach students how to explain their work such that others could understand and discuss it. From early in the summer, advisors introduced students to the idea of constructing a coherent story line and accustomed them to talking about their thinking with a friendly audience. Research advisors:

- Guided students through the process of using their records to construct explanations of their research questions, methods, data analysis, and interpretation

- Required students to write and present short reports
- Encouraged students to use the research group as a sounding board for their ideas
- Fostered a safe environment in which to try out ideas and to give and receive critique.

Advisors also modeled for group members how to ask questions that helped the presenter to conceptualize or explain his or her work. They understood that most students did not yet know how to offer a critique in a respectful, supportive way and that "students are at a delicate stage of evolution," fearful of exposure and easily crushed. Learning to give and take critique went well beyond acquiring skills: students needed to understand these practices as essential to the process of building scientific knowledge. At this early stage, however, students often described learning to distinguish between personal and professional criticism as a journey in emotional growth.

Whether they worked alone or on a team, students learned how to organize and present their ideas in intensive, regular dialogues with their advisor. Advisors worked methodically to build students' communication skills by asking questions of increasing complexity and suggesting alternate ways to conceptualize and explain ideas. As they repeated the cycle of summary, presentation, and discussion to teach students that explaining was important "whether or not you had good results," advisors laid down the beginnings of oral argument by anticipating likely questions and discussing how to address them.

As the end of summer approached, advisors urged students to "pull their research together" and used group meetings to structure, rehearse, and refine presentations and swap advice. Although advisors agreed that they would never allow a student to give a presentation without prior practice, critique, and revision, students often resisted this expectation. Understanding that resistance arose from discomfort with vulnerability, especially with teachers, advisors built in regular, informal opportunities to help resolve students' fear of exposure.

At all four colleges, formal presentation of research was a distinctive formal characteristic of UR work: 73 percent of advisors in our sample described oral presentations or posters as a requirement, and others mentioned it as customary. End-of-summer events sometimes drew in the whole campus; some were organized by science divisions or departments. All participating students and faculty, and many staff and administrators, made a point of attending; parents, local employers, community members, and corporate sponsors might also be invited. Presentations were an important way to alert younger students to research opportunities and engage their interest. In the most common format, students' posters showcasing their work were set up in a prominent venue; guests circulated to view and discuss the work with the authors. Alternatively, departments held research symposia where students discussed their work. Similar symposia or poster sessions are also common in structured UR programs (Chapter Six), and preparing for these may add value for UR students in circumstances where most research focuses less on communication skills (Thiry & Laursen, 2009).

All our data sources confirmed that students drew from their advisors, and from the organizational prominence and formality of these events, a strong sense of significance to their professional development. Both students and advisors took pride in describing their group's work and showing student posters. These were festive occasions—a time to recognize good faculty work as well as celebrate and encourage students.

In addition to on-campus events, some departments provided funding to enable students to present posters or talks at off-campus meetings, most often at student conferences such as the National Conference on Undergraduate Research. More rarely, students were supported to present at a regular disciplinary meeting. In our UR alumni sample, 41 percent of alumni had presented their UR work off campus—eight at a professional meeting and fifteen at an undergraduate research conference. Advisors and students consistently observed how these experiences enhanced the beneficial effects of presenting. Achieving results meaningful to others outside their campus and having their work taken seriously drew students into the community of their discipline and affirmed their career aspirations.

Writing and Editing

Learning to write and edit for scholarly publication is sometimes cited as an outcome of undergraduate research. However, we found that student gains in scientific writing were less universal and more mixed than were gains in oral communication—a pattern that reflected advisors' teaching practices around formal writing. In general, student opportunities for real scientific writing were rare. Six research advisors reported that they never coauthored papers with their student researchers because articles were written after students had moved on. Others noted that publishable results were the fruit of several summers' work by multiple students on a larger project, so results could rarely be attributed to individual students. Most advisors did not see it as likely to bring summer researchers to the level of making a professional contribution.

Although the chances of publication were low for most students, nine advisors had involved student coauthors in papers for publication or conference presentation, and five cited journal articles by sole student authors based on their original, independent work. However, at most, 43 percent of the sample had contributed, as students or alumni, to a published paper based on their summer research; 25 percent had not; and the remaining third did not mention this outcome.

The degree to which advisors worked with students on formal writing skills was determined by the ultimate audience for the writing. All advisors worked intensively with students to prepare local posters and presentations and teach the basics of professional writing. Beyond this, some required a formal research report, and in these cases, advisors taught the fundamentals of scholarly writing and editing, using students' papers as teaching opportunities. They introduced the elements of a scholarly paper, showed students how to structure a coherent narrative, explained disciplinary standards, insisted on correct terminology and conventions, and gave feedback on multiple drafts. As students got used to editing and revising, advisors might ask students to critique and edit each other's papers and discuss what they learned from doing this.

Far more rarely, advisors worked with students on a coauthored paper, which sharply increased their efforts. They often began by inviting students "to take a stab at a first draft of a section" or an abstract; met to discuss content, format, and style; and began the emotionally tricky process of teaching professional response to editorial suggestions. They shared some of their own writing in progress or stories about learning to write and worked intensively with students' drafts, "using a lot of red ink" and perhaps "talking them through a paper—if necessary, line by line." In these cases, advisors spent a lot of time reworking, "heavily editing," and "polishing" these pieces to meet professional standards; their hand in the resulting products was evident. Here, advisors not only tempered the consequences of authentic research but intervened to protect their own professional reputations.

Conclusion

Advisors chose projects for their UR students that centered on a scholarly problem of significance to their field. But many attributes of research advisors' everyday work with their student researchers may quite properly be called teaching. Advisors made deliberate and widespread use of particular teaching strategies to serve distinctive, commonly articulated learning objectives. Authenticity in research projects was critical in securing desired outcomes because advisors employed predictable features of real research as teaching tools. However, advisors exercised professional judgment in selecting projects and modifying the degree to which students had to cope, alone with the full consequences of doing real science.

Advisors did not learn their teaching methods in any formal process of professional development. Rather, they drew on customary practice, shared understandings, and their own experiences as student researchers, in turn passing on these approaches to their apprentices. Advisors widely practiced transparency with students about the task at hand, making the reasons for their teaching strategies patent. Students were often uncomfortable but were enabled to understand what was being asked of them, why it mattered, and why their advisor was pushing them to learn in particular ways.

Experienced research advisors may not be surprised by our account of how they do their UR work. Their response may well be, "Well, yes, of course that's what I do." However, we hope that it is useful to new research advisors, those developing new UR programs, and those who support their work, to mirror back the goals that UR advisors set for their students, the methods they use to reach them, the ways their teaching methods work in practice, and the philosophical rationale that binds them together.

Chapter 8

How Do Research Advisors Mentor, Advise, and Evaluate Students?

This chapter continues the discussion of the work of research advisors and how their working methods contribute to positive outcomes for students. Chapter Seven focused on how advisors use opportunities inherent in authentic research as teaching tools to meet both their own research needs and the educational and professional development needs of their students. In this chapter, we see how that work results in an expanded professional and personal relationship between student and advisor. Even after summer research is over, students' professional development is ongoing through advisors' mentoring and career advising work. Research advisors also monitor and assess student progress toward the learning objectives they espouse, both overtly and tacitly, and this chapter lays out how they define and use markers of student progress.

Advisors as Mentors

We have consistently used the title *research advisor* to designate the formal role that faculty and others play with their research students. However, advisors commonly used the term *mentor* to characterize particular aspects of that role as their everyday work with students evolved into an ongoing relationship of individualized support and counsel. How advisors defined and structured their relationships with research students is similar to other practices identified as mentoring (with respect to college science education, see Boyle & Boice, 1998; Cohen & Galbraith, 1995; National Academy of Sciences, 1997; Wunsch, 1994). Mentors relate to students individually and intensively and take into account many aspects of their thinking, behavior, and aspirations.

Research advisors consciously practiced mentoring; they could describe what they did and why, and they used methods that were remarkably consistent across our sample. These methods were not arrived at by formal or collegial decisions but were part of a received tradition from which many advisors had themselves benefited as student researchers. Mentoring was not an open-ended commitment, but was bounded by an overarching concern to give students an authentic, yet guided and supported, experience of real science. In UR programs designed to attract and support students of color, mentoring may be formally structured and its boundaries extended to more aspects of students' lives (Chapter Six).

The dominant characteristic of UR mentoring was intensive engagement throughout the summer (and often beyond) with multiple aspects of each student's research-related thinking and professional growth. As mentors, advisors:

- Modeled professional behavior, notably collegiality, by working alongside students and soliciting their input in research design and data interpretation
- Consciously set a "relaxed," informal, and "approachable" tone that encouraged students to "check in with them," raise questions, discuss problems, and seek feedback
- Used one-on-one conversation to give students personal guidance about both their work and their emergent career ideas
- Fostered social integration that released work tensions and encouraged bonds among research group members
- Allowed students to encounter them as people and gain insights into the intersections between their work and personal lives.

Thus, advisors consciously gave students many ways to answer the question for themselves: "Is this the kind of work that I want to do and the kind of life that I want to live?"

Two mentoring strategies were specifically aimed at getting students to understand that what they were doing was real science. First, advisors offered themselves and their work setting as a model of what real scientists do. They constantly made their thinking and actions transparent and did their own work among their students to show the level of precision and persistence required. Advisors worked largely in real time, letting students see how they worked through scientific problems and interacted with emergent data, and leading students through their analyses. Advisors also shared personal responses to their work, and students experienced at close quarters their advisors' curiosity and excitement, frustration and struggle. A second strategy was to solicit students' input into the work as it evolved. From an early stage, advisors asked students to explain back to them what they were doing and why, as part of an open-ended, running conversation in which they generated ideas together. As students gained in skills, reliability, and independence, these conversations became increasingly collegial. "I don't know the answers, they don't know the answers," pointed out one advisor. "We're a bunch of smart people sitting in a room trying to figure some things out."

Mentoring sometimes included dealing with student problems and bad behavior. Advisors simultaneously made clear to students both their personal support and their expectations. They emphasized that a student's work and behavior could have professional significance for their advisor and set clear standards. When a student behaved irresponsibly or inappropriately, advisors laid aside friendly informality for formal discussion, even admonition. But when students were seen as "doing their best," advisors supported them through discouragement and avoided criticism or "productivity pressures."

Some advisors used the term *cheerleading* to reference their response to students' uncertainty, loss of confidence, or flagging courage; many used the strategy without giving it a name. Cheerleading involved keeping students aware of their own progress and encouraging them to take pride in their accomplishments. Discussing setbacks, especially in groups, invoked a number of mentoring taboos: never criticizing a student for errors, never putting down student ideas, never "being critical with students even when they have gotten nowhere," and never telling a student that he or she "will never make it in research." Instead, mentors encouraged a discouraged student to "see this as not about results but understanding a process" and to "be patient with yourself and think about what you are doing and why."

These mentoring ethics apparently were not universal. Advisors told stories of faculty who criticized students for errors and failed experiments, lost their temper, or called students "stupid." However, the positive mentoring norms we describe appeared to be part of the research culture at the four institutions. One chair noted that a faculty member was denied tenure, despite his research productivity, because his students consistently reported him as a poor mentor.

We have already discussed how advisors used the inevitability of problems and risks in authentic research as teaching opportunities. Here we stress their role in the student-specific mentoring relationship. Pushed to rise to real-life challenges, students did so in the certainty of their advisor's personal and professional support. A student's enthusiasm and response to challenge determined how hard an advisor would push her and established his own level of commitment in terms of time and effort.

Career Advising

Career advising was another activity whereby the student-advisor relationship was extended beyond daily work in the lab. Advisors used individual and research group meetings to help students clarify and develop their career ideas, and they continued these conversations into the academic year. Most advisors did not wait for students to approach them but engaged them in conversations intended to help them make informed career decisions. To students interested in graduate school, advisors explained that research is the heart of graduate work in the sciences and they should be sure that they enjoyed life as a researcher before committing to it. Advisors also explained to students the role of research experiences in a competitive graduate school application. Because first-generation college students were often unaware of the connection between undergraduate research and graduate school, advisors encouraged students who showed aptitude but lacked confidence to think about graduate school.

Some advisors promoted graduate school overtly, including a few who took on only research apprentices who were committed to a scientific career. However, most advisors sought to ensure that students could assemble a competitive application, understood what graduate school entailed, and made "good choices for themselves." They also legitimated decisions against graduate school by students who discovered that they did not like research. Either way, their primary objective was to use authentic research to help students clarify and refine their career aspirations.

Advisors' career-related strategies included both "show" and "tell." By taking a tough line in pushing students to struggle through problems, advisors actively helped students prepare for the rigors of graduate school. Advisors also "tried to put students in the picture" about career options by drawing on their own and former students' experiences in deciding what to do in life. Their advice included a surprisingly high proportion of warnings about graduate school as "a very hard, long road," the impersonal nature of graduate-level teaching, and the hard life of a scientist through and beyond the Ph.D. One advisor advised students that "if they can think of anything else they want to do, they should do that instead." They gave gentle but candid appraisals of students' chances of success in certain fields or at high-reputation schools. One physics advisor was careful about encouraging women to apply to graduate school: "It depends how mentally tough she is to withstand a male-dominated, unfriendly, and competitive field."

But advisors also spoke of the intrinsic pleasures of academic life and sought to interest students in specific fields. Some took their students to visit research labs to experience a graduate research environment, meet a wider network, or participate in cross-institution experiments. Students reported that working in close and extended association with their advisors, and observing how they responded to the ups and downs of research as well as the pleasure they took in their work, settled many of their questions about science as a career.

Despite advisors' efforts to help students clarify their career goals, many students still struggled with uncertainty. Advisors empathized and tried to set students' career thinking in a wider context. They told students that "career paths are apt to be non-linear"; indeed, "people often stumble around before they find the right path," and "some successful scientists have traveled a varied, crooked road."

Career advising was especially important, in advisors' views, for women students. Twenty-two female advisors (of thirty-two) discussed their role in modeling for both male and female students the professional and personal lives of professors in science, technology, engineering, and mathematics (STEM) disciplines. Close observation and interaction with their advisors offered most students their first opportunity to see how faculty related to colleagues, managed their professional commitments, and balanced these with their personal lives. Female faculty saw it as important for young women who were thinking about career options and life priorities to observe some of their advisors' professional and personal constraints and responses and were aware that students would draw their own conclusions. How colleagues' working lives and relationships were modeled could either further the movement toward a more diverse professoriate or reinforce traditional stereotypes. So as they worked closely with female students, female advisors found themselves in a dilemma: they wanted to encourage and support female students who might pursue careers in the sciences, but were unsure how open to be about the problems that they and female colleagues experienced and that their students might directly notice.

Although mentoring and career advising may appear a seamless part of the whole research advising job, they are specific tasks with their own working methods that serve different purposes and require different skills. Some faculty may be more adept than others as mentors and career advisors—roles for which there is usually no professional training and which faculty tend to learn by prior experience, example, and trial and error. The distinctions in practices between "career advising" and "mentoring" (and their consequences for students) have been demonstrated in research (De Welde & Laursen, 2008) although not yet with respect to the work of UR advisors.

Advisors' Markers of Student Progress

As research advisors reflected on the processes and outcomes of their work with undergraduate researchers, it became clear to us that they assess the progress of their students and their own work as advisors in terms of their learning goals. Advisors had developed a distinctive and widely shared set of practical assessment indicators by which they judged a student's progress in attaining particular learning objectives or the set of objectives overall. Advisors were articulate in describing the signs that they looked for in students, and the significance that they accorded to them, but they had no collective term for these student progress indicators, which we have labeled assessment "markers" and gathered in Table 8.1. Markers were the practical means by which advisors judged how far students had progressed in achieving gains that advisors desired, planned for, or observed. Some markers of growth were looked for as outcomes of particular teaching strategies, such as learning through problem solving or presenting their work. Other markers were taken as evidence that a certain consistently applied approach was working—for example, advisors' insistence that students work independently and collaboratively without detailed direction. Finally, some related sets of markers were taken as evidence of cumulative progress.

All growth, and thus its indicators, was seen as ultimately deriving from the authentic nature of the research experience. As described in Chapter Seven, advisors used naturally occurring conceptual and technical problems to stimulate both intellectual growth and the temperamental and behavioral attributes that good researchers need. Indeed, both faculty and students understood that how students responded to problems was one test of their aptitude for research-based careers, including their responses to situations of stress, risk, and uncertainty. Achieving these markers was seen as a necessary prelude to readiness for a career involving research, which was further judged by another set of markers.

TABLE 8.1

Intellectual, Affective, and Behavioral Markers of Student Progress, as Reported by Research Advisors

Markers of intellectual growth

"Critical thinking"

  Showing openness to different ways of approaching research objectives and tasks

  Starting to ask critical questions

  Thinking for themselves

  Developing skepticism; not taking ideas as given

  Showing understanding of why they are doing any task

  Showing creativity in response to problems

  Making connections; understanding relationships among ideas

  Applying prior learning to their research

  Making sense of their data, understanding what their results mean

Understanding the conceptual framework for their work

  Gaining insight into their discipline

  Showing a grasp of the research process

  Developing a more sophisticated understanding of the nature of science and the construction of knowledge

Intellectual and affective engagement

  Showing intellectual engagement in their research work

  Showing commitment to the work, excitement about what they are doing, interest and enthusiasm for research and the discipline

Markers of change in approach to science

Learning through problem solving

  Persevering in the face of difficulties by applying methodical problem solving and trying new directions

  Taking initiative to discuss problems, using collegial networks to make progress

  Showing willingness to work hard, putting in effort to finish a task

Dealing with risk and uncertainty

  Showing willingness to wrestle with problems and take risks

  Treating setbacks as normal; becoming comfortable in dealing with them

  Tolerating uncertainty and frustration

Developing independence

  Beginning to work independently; consulting, seeking critique or confirmation after making a decision

  "Getting on with their work" in a careful and responsible manner

  Using ingenuity to resolve problems; marshaling resources and taking initiative to seek assistance or advice

  Showing confidence in decision making; enjoying thinking and acting for themselves

  Becoming self-directed

(*Continued*)

TABLE 8.1 (Continued)

Markers of gains in skills

Showing confidence in using and applying new technical skills

Planning, organizing, and documenting their own work

Markers of gains related to professional communication

In discussing and presenting their own work

Discussing difficulties openly and revising ideas with others

Explaining, making arguments, fielding questions about their work

Giving, taking, and responding to collegial critique comfortably

From attending professional meetings

Recognizing their contributions as valuable

Starting to take themselves seriously as scientists

Making connections between their own work and the field

Starting to build professional networks

Markers for collegiality and collaboration

Working actively with peers as colleagues

Behaving respectfully with peers regardless of differences of view

Starting to develop and use scholarly collaborations

Markers of career readiness

Realizing that research is or is not what they want to do

Gaining a sense of what career directions and working lifestyles are right for them

Expressing self-knowledge and confidence

Demonstrating intellect, temperament, and skills that ready them for graduate work

Markers of overall UR effectiveness

Developing confidence in their ability to do science

Taking on an intellectual or technical challenge, trying to figure it out

Taking risks

Thinking and acting independently

Persisting, seeing a task through

Working comfortably and appropriately with other researchers

Taking ownership of their work

Showing motivation to meet the demands of the work

Talking about their work with enthusiasm and interest

Being serious and creative about their own ideas and vested in their outcomes

Taking the initiative, offering ideas and proposals, making plans

Seeking input and finding intellectual stimulation in collegial work

Assuming responsibility, making decisions, seeking validation later

Expressing pride or sense of accomplishment in their own work

Adopting the status of belonging within science

Realizing the value of their work and extent of their knowledge

Claiming the status and having this claim validated by their advisor and other scientists

Recognizing that they have "become a scientist"

Claiming the identity of "scientist" and having this identity validated by their advisor

Of all student gains, advisors saw intellectual growth as most dependent on authentic research experiences. They used the term *critical thinking* to gloss an array of distinct but related signs of intellectual development. Advisors looked for these markers in discussing research issues with students, and observed them in action as students worked to resolve problems. In individual and group discussions, advisors used additional markers to discern students' understanding of the conceptual framework behind their project. They also placed great emphasis on signs that students were intellectually engaged in their research work. This marker was distinguishable from, but in practice closely associated with, a set of affective markers of engagement by which advisors judged students' commitment to the work and interest and enthusiasm for research and the discipline. Taken together, advisors used this set of intellectual and affective markers of engagement as indicators of a student's motivation and capacity to go further in research. They also strongly influenced an advisor's willingness to spend time and energy working with any student.

Assessing Overall Effectiveness

Advisors used four particular markers to gauge the overall effectiveness of their teaching and mentoring work. All of these were taken as signs that a student was "becoming a scientist": confidence in her ability to do science, ownership of a project, expressing a sense of belonging within science, and identifying herself as a scientist. Each marker was described as multicausal and cumulative over time, and advisors needed to see all four to be certain that a student aspiring to a research career had chosen it appropriately. Table 8.1 lists individual components of each of these four overall markers.

Demonstrating Confidence to Do Science

Gains in students' confidence in their ability to do research and contribute to science were perceived by students and advisors alike as having both personal and professional dimensions. For advisors, the primary markers of increased student confidence became evident when a student encountered a new situation, roadblock, or puzzle. The student took on the challenge, pursued his or her own ideas, persisted in seeing them through to completion, and worked comfortably with others.

Thus, "being confident" meant that the student could function intellectually and affectively in new situations and work collegially as a professional. Although these increases in confidence were defined as specific to doing science, advisors and students alike viewed such confidence as transferable to other aspects of life. Thus, advisors hoped to see some measure of confidence to do science develop in all student researchers, not only those moving into scientific careers.

Taking Ownership of Their Work

Advisors defined *ownership* as a high level of intellectual and personal engagement in and commitment to the work, and they looked for these as key indicators that students were beginning to think and behave like scientists. Advisors saw students "latching onto" some aspect of the project and making it their own—as "wanting to bring something of themselves to the work." Signs of ownership (Table 8.1) were seen in students' motivation and high presence in the lab, the pride and enthusiasm they exhibited in discussing their work, and their vested interest in the outcomes of their project. Students who were viewed as taking ownership showed creativity, took initiative in generating and pursuing ideas and seeking collegial input, assumed responsibility for their work, and "made it happen." Investment in their project did not happen for all students, and complete ownership—where a student directs, guides, and makes choices about a project—was reported to be rare. However, advisors saw making a piece of work "their own" as a good indicator that a student was becoming a scientist. As one advisor explained, "When you see that happen, you think, 'Okay, we're all set here.'"

From the students' point of view, the opportunity to take control of some aspect of the research—and, in the process, finding that they enjoyed the work and had the confidence to do it—helped them make informed decisions about their future. Like confidence, a sense of ownership in the work, gained through personal and intellectual commitment, was seen as transferable to other work and life situations.

Claiming the Status of Belonging in Science and the Identity of Scientist

These two different but related indicators occurred in tandem. Advisors looked for signs that students interpreted their own activities as scholarly work and were beginning to see themselves as working scientists. The most obvious marker was that at some point, they overtly claimed both the status and the identity.

Advisors watched carefully for signs that students had developed a sense of themselves as belonging to the scientific community. Advisors often observed this outcome among students who accompanied them to a conference or made a presentation. Students' discovery that their results were unique and that professional scientists took their work seriously often prompted their realization that they were doing real science and could make useful contributions to the field. Some moments of recognition were retrospective—for example, when students, in writing up their work, "suddenly . . . realize how much they know," or while talking about their research at an interview, suddenly appreciate that they have accomplished something of value. Some revelations were prompted by external validation, such as coauthorship of a paper.

Although students' awareness that they have become scientists may be sudden or retrospective, advisors described it as an outcome of multiple, interacting processes that built over time. "Feeling like a scientist" was seen primarily as a product of sustained engagement in authentic research. Students needed time to work on a project in a focused, in-depth manner and to refine their thinking and become more efficient and organized. As advisors sought their help, they conveyed the message that they respected and trusted their students and were relying on them. This process required careful observation of a student's readiness: students could feel overwhelmed by the expectation that they make a contribution if it was solicited too early. This caveat underscores the widespread view that for students to become scientists in their thinking and practice, and to identify themselves as scientists, are processes that take time. Thus, many advisors liked students to commit to at least one year of work on a project and generally opposed shorter, "research-taster" programs. Several advisors observed "students becoming really serious about their research" in the summer between their junior and senior years; others described the middle of senior year as a time when extended research engagement culminated in "professional buy-in."

Observing their students over time, advisors assessed students' progress toward these shifts in self-perception, which they typically noted before their students did. However, to stabilize and consolidate these realizations, students had to openly make these claims and have their advisors confirm them. Such claims were treated as inherently valid: advisors offered no examples of disagreeing with a student's self-assessment or of failing to legitimate their claim to a place in science.

How Advisors and Their Colleges Evaluated Their UR Work

How to evaluate the outcomes of UR work has become an issue of concern only recently. Historically research results and faculty's ability to publish or secure grant funding served as assessment enough. For students, summer research was paid employment, and no grades, assessments, or course credit were given. However, with the rise of UR as a preferred educational practice, grant makers, accrediting agencies, and institutions are looking for success indicators. Thus, we asked faculty and administrators what methods of program evaluation and student assessment they used. Institutional representatives commonly cited the rates at which UR alumni entered graduate or medical school. As noted in Chapter Five, this is problematic unless there is also clear evidence that students chose these career paths as a result of their UR experiences.

Deans, chairs, and many advisors were keenly aware of the need for formal indicators of the educational value added by UR experiences. They needed outcomes data to report to college executives, accreditation bodies, and funding agencies and to bolster their grant proposals. Advisors also sought to document the results of their UR teaching for reward and recognition purposes, as well as feedback for themselves. A limited number of institutional strategies for evaluating UR were carried out by faculty, institutional research offices, or learning assessment specialists: student portfolios of their research work; peer review of faculty performance as advisors; end-of-summer interviews exploring students' perceived accomplishments; student questionnaires about their summer research experiences. One group had developed a protocol asking students to "demonstrate their understanding of the processes of science" by framing a research question, developing a hypothesis, designing an experiment to test it, analyzing real data, writing a research report, and presenting their own work. These examples were sparse, and institutional evaluation efforts were often described as poorly developed or even perfunctory.

By contrast, the informal processes by which advisors judged student development and marked particular stages of gain were pervasive, subtle, and profound. As illustrated, advisors employed a set of markers for particular areas of student growth and for broader, more complex, cumulative gains. Advisors widely agreed among themselves and with their students about what kinds of gains occurred. They were equally clear about how these gains were generated, what their markers were, and when such transition had been made. Advisors routinely drew on these observations in drafting letters of recommendation but did not use these indicators as the basis for formal assessment strategies.

As one means to address the need of institutions and UR programs for evaluation methods, our group has developed an online survey instrument, the Undergraduate Research Student Self-Assessment (URSSA). Based on our literature analysis (Chapter Two) and findings on student outcomes (Chapter Three), the core URSSA items address students' self-reported gains and critical elements of their research and mentoring experiences. Other items can be customized to query elements of a specific UR program (Hunter, Weston, Laursen, & Thiry, 2009). Lopatto's (2004, 2007) Survey of Undergraduate Research Experiences (SURE) is another such instrument. The SURE survey takes a similar approach to students' self-reported gains. Future research might explore ways to formalize advisors' system of well-understood markers of student progress and thereby translate faculty's tacit knowledge into an additional, empirically grounded method for learning assessment and UR program evaluation.

Conclusion

Beyond the everyday teaching strategies that they use to help their research students learn from authentic problems, advisors take on other roles that grow out of their close knowledge of students as individuals and build on the trust and collegiality developed in their joint scientific work. As mentors, advisors guided students' thinking, set expectations and held students to them, modeled professional behavior, and shared themselves as people. As career advisors, they supported students' decision making, offered advice and appraisals, and shared their own career-related stories. Faculty were conscious that they served as role models for their students and aware of the messages that students might take from observing their work and lives. Finally, advisors described a consistent set of markers that they used to assess students' progress as researchers, both to note gains in particular areas and describe broader, more complex and cumulative growth. Their markers were sophisticated and subtle, and used in evaluating individual students for graduate school and job applications, but not as yet incorporated into program assessment. Practitioners may find it an interesting challenge to develop creative approaches to using these markers—which depend on close observations of individual students by their research advisor—in a way that is consistently calibrated across faculty and departments.

Chapter 9

What Are the Costs and Benefits to Research Advisors?

BY APPLYING A set of well-understood principles and teaching practices, undergraduate research (UR) advisors can consistently provide an authentic experience of science that is of lasting value to students. In Chapter Six, we discussed the support from institutions that is required to sustain a structured UR program. In faculty-led UR, research advisors themselves are the primary drivers of this intensive, individualized form of education, perhaps abetted by some organizational, financial, and collegial support from their departments and institutions.

In this chapter, we draw on our interview data to understand what motivates faculty to undertake UR each summer, what costs and strains mitigate their involvement, and what benefits sustain it. Understanding this balance for advisors is crucial to determining how and where undergraduate research can be offered in a sustainable and stable form at any particular institution and whether it can be expanded to offer more opportunities for students.

Nature of the Evidence

Observations on the benefits and costs to faculty of their work with student researchers were offered by our sample of eighty UR advisors and administrators (Appendix A). Advisors described why they participated in UR work or had temporarily withdrawn from it, what they gained from working with student researchers, and what it cost them, in any sense, to do it.

Table 9.1 lists the costs and benefits to advisors of undergraduate research and their relative weight. Over half of advisors' observations (section A) identified types of difficulty that they saw as inherent in authentic UR work. These encompass the everyday, ongoing challenges

TABLE 9.1

Costs and Benefits to Faculty of Conducting Research with Undergraduates, as Reported by Advisors and Administrators

Topic	Number of Observations	Percentage of Subcategory	Percentage of All Costs and Benefits
A. Inherent and ongoing difficulties of authentic UR work with students	1,346	(100%)	53%
Everyday challenges of conducting UR work to balance advisors' research productivity needs and their educational and professional objectives for students; how these are managed	464	34%	
Lowered productivity of research in a primarily undergraduate institution and its consequences for advisors	310	23%	
Lack of experience and know-how in managing UR projects and students; negative consequences	49	4%	
Limited and unreliable resources	30	2%	
Issues of time and effort	161	12%	
Balancing UR work with other professional, personal, and family priorities; UR-relevant gender issues	332	25%	
B. Additional strains raised by the changing institutional situation in which UR is undertaken	537	(100%)	21%
Conflict between organically evolved, faculty-led UR and institutional efforts to meet a growing demand for research experiences	128	24%	
Difficulties arising from requiring students to do UR	187	35%	
Unresolved issues of institutional status, value, and recognition of UR work	222	41%	
C. Benefits of doing research with students	661	(100%)	26%
Career-related benefits that arise from research productivity	287	43%	
Satisfactions from contributing to positive outcomes for students	120	18%	
Intrinsic benefits	254	39%	
Total	2,544		100%

that individual advisors faced in balancing their educational objectives for students with their own needs for scholarly productivity and the ways they responded to or coped with these challenges. Section B of the table accounts for another 20 percent of observations about stresses that were provoked by external changes to the situation in which advisors' UR work was done, notably pressures to accommodate more students. These strains were normally latent but were made manifest in circumstances that raised questions about the place of UR within their institutions. Finally, section C categorizes just over one-quarter of advisors' observations on the benefits of doing UR work. Embedded throughout these observations are advisors' statements about their motivations for conducting research with students. These findings are based on data from the four-college study, but we have encountered comparable issues at other types of institutions and among nonfaculty advisors. The form in which these issues present themselves, and how an advisor copes with or resolves them, depends in part on each individual's career stage and institutional context, but the underlying tensions appear to be common across UR settings.

Is UR Teaching or Research? A Fundamental Tension

All of the eighty advisors in our study sample were highly committed to undergraduate research. For thirty-five who specifically discussed this, it had begun with their own experiences of research as undergraduates. (Only six advisors reported that they had not done UR; participation of the remaining 39 as students was undetermined.) Many had deliberately pursued faculty positions in colleges that combined an emphasis on education with expectations of research productivity in their field. These faculty saw undergraduate teaching and research as equally important dimensions of their work and as hallmarks of their institutions: "a real plus to my job," "a passion," "our mission," "one of the things you go to a small school for."

> We feel that it is the best way for students to learn about science. . . . If they really do science, they are also going to learn science. It's more interesting, it's more exciting, it creates a bond between students and faculty . . . . So it's a combination of value to the faculty who want to be in this environment. They want to present papers and publish papers, but they know they're doing it with a different kind of student support structure than at a graduate school—but it's still of value to them. We think it keeps us alive as an institution. [emphasis in original]

Their institutions also communicated this dual emphasis on teaching and scholarship, as these remarks by administrators exemplify:

We look for faculty who are equally committed to student learning and their own intellectual growth.

• • •

We can never compete with U.C. Berkeley, but we want to have some ability to hold our heads up that our faculty are scientists and not just teachers.

Because they valued UR for their students, in their role as teachers, and for themselves as scholars, advisors were highly committed to providing authentic research experiences. That commitment sustained them through periods of difficulty and was validated by both tangible and intrinsic rewards. However, it also kept them juggling educational and scholarly objectives that were sometimes at odds. At an individual level, advisors faced built-in difficulties of doing research with undergraduates and made everyday choices about how to resolve or reconcile these. For example, preserving the high quality of UR experiences while making them available to students with a wide range of aptitude, preparation, and skills—a policy they widely endorsed—inevitably increased the risks to their research productivity. Thus, underlying our discussion is a fundamental question: Is UR an activity primarily concerned with the education of students or the scholarship of faculty? In describing their commitment to UR, faculty uniformly answered "both." They described rewards on both sides and the costs that ensued when these two purposes conflicted.

Advisors' balancing act was dynamic. All advisors described how costs and benefits fluctuated over time, assessing their experiences in terms of better and worse summers, students, or periods of research productivity rather than as fixed costs or benefits. Advisors noted inherent difficulties twice as often as benefits (Table 9.1). This disparity reflects the complex issues that advisors negotiate and the difficulties they must manage or resolve. That most advisors tolerated these stresses most of the time highlights their commitment to providing students with a real science experience. Nonetheless, the balancing effort could be costly. At the time of our interviews, some faculty had opted to "take time out" from normal summer research, and others were considering it. Changes in individual circumstances—becoming department chair, preparing for tenure, meeting family commitments—exposed pressures that faculty accepted in more stable situations, while changes in the institutional setting of UR brought to a head unresolved issues about its institutional role. The nature and predominance of these individual balancing acts at colleges where undergraduate research was a common and important activity for STEM faculty serves to highlight the still greater challenges for faculty that may arise in institutions where UR is less common or less valued, a topic to which we return in Chapter Ten. In the following sections, we highlight the dual importance of research and teaching in discussing the main categories of cost and benefit.

Difficulties of Authentic Research with Students

Many benefits and costs of UR to advisors can be understood as a continuum of payoff and risk to research productivity. At one end of the spectrum, pursuing authentic projects with students paid off handsomely; when experiments and equipment worked, it was possible to "crank things out." On the other end, the inherent risks of framing research problems to involve students added to the normal uncertainties of research, and faculty found themselves "stumbling through a maze with blindfolds on." Where any given summer's work fell on this continuum depended on the student, the project, and luck. Over time, these experiences led advisors to develop detailed theories of how to choose students and projects (Chapter Seven). An advisor new to UR commented: "These three students this summer really dazzled me. I see now that they can go a lot faster than I thought they could. And my first summer was just the opposite—'Oh, how am I ever going to get anywhere working just with undergraduates?' But a larger part of that was that I hadn't picked appropriate projects."

Several advisors credited their research productivity to careful student selection and their practice of keeping "star students" in their group as long as possible: "I am tripling my output because I'm relying on them to be part and parcel of the science. . . . I have to babysit a lot of projects, but . . . these are students who are capable of working with a good degree of independence. And that increases with time, as some of them have worked with me for more than a year. However, I should predicate all this—I just don't take *any* students in my group" (emphasis in original).

But the role of luck was apparent in other success stories:

The last summer, I thought I'd really picked well. But one of them was just luck of the draw. I wasn't very excited about him based on his application . . . but he was amazing. He was really good at trouble-shooting. Usually I'd give students a list of different things to try, and when they didn't work, they might all give up. But I'd talk to him, and about two days later, he'd say, "Well, this worked on the third try and it got great results." And he got beautiful data. . . . It wasn't all mechanical to him—he really wanted to understand the project. And none of this showed up on his application. So that's my indication that I haven't quite learned how to spot them yet.

We begin by discussing the inherent difficulties of conducting research with undergraduates, which even veteran advisors continued to face throughout their UR career. Later we discuss research productivity and other types of benefits to advisors.

Everyday Challenges of Research with Undergraduates

Section A of Table 9.1 lists the difficulties seen as inherent to authentic UR work. In these colleges, faculty were expected to be both effective educators and productive researchers—a job balance that is different from that required in other institutions, but where advisors nonetheless note similar difficulties. The largest group of observations focuses on conflicts between educational and research objectives and how advisors managed them:

I don't really gain an awful lot for having the students—it slows me down a bit because I have to teach them certain things, like the theory behind the work. So by the time they get up to speed, the summer is almost over.

• • •

I refuse to elbow students out of the way so that we can get it done in a timely fashion and get a publication. So the downside for me has been, literally, dozens of lost publications—which counts against me despite the rhetoric. This college counts beans just like the rest.

Students could develop many of the skills and capacities that faculty researchers needed, but they were nonetheless "short-term helpers in a long-term enterprise": "It would take all summer, but I would get a student to the point where they could make the material, and then they were gone. And the next student would start all over again, and I would make no progress. So I've dropped the project completely."

Because training students was a major time investment that was easily lost, advisors tried to hang onto students for more than one summer: "I have a first-year student who went to work at a national lab in her second summer, and I can't possibly say, 'Oh, don't go. Come and work with me again.' You can't be too selfish and deny them that opportunity. But it makes a problem for me."

In some departments, this difficulty was addressed by recruiting promising younger students into a research team where they could remain engaged until they graduated. Other departments opted against this, feeling that it undermined their agreed aim of making research available to more students. Again, the need for productivity explains why so much effort went into student selection. Adherence to formal, more open methods of student selection created greater uncertainty about student readiness; offering research opportunities to students visiting from other institutions inevitably increased the number of short-term assistants.

Advisors also took great care in selecting research projects. In Chapter Seven, we noted the pedagogical demands on project selection: advisors sought projects that were authentic but to which students with varied levels of knowledge and skills could contribute meaningfully. At the same time as they crafted student projects to fit within these pedagogical constraints, they also had to keep their work moving along to yield meaningful progress. One advisor had received the following advice as a young faculty member: "If your problem is dependent on instrumentation not available at this school or on techniques that took you years to learn as a graduate student, you're gonna fail. It's not going to work in an undergraduate environment. So picking your problem and the method to use are critical to you finding success."

The balance was more consistently tipped toward productivity in cases where data gathering would benefit from many hands, techniques were more easily learned, the requisite knowledge or skills were less demanding, and materials and equipment were neither highly sensitive nor expensive. Field researchers and advisors in physics, mathematics, and computer science cited more difficulties in finding student-appropriate projects: "Unlike the experimental sciences where a project might require a lot of detailed work that you can bring undergraduates in to help with, because of the nature of mathematics, students have to have reached a particular level before they can be of any use at all."

Finally, advisors expressed concerns that with authentic projects, they could not guarantee good results. Research was inherently risky; unforeseen difficulties arose, and techniques might be too new, untested, or complex for undergraduates. These outcomes were demoralizing for students but could also have negative professional consequences for faculty.

Lowered Research Productivity

Involving undergraduates in research in any context brings inherent risks of reduced productivity. This was discussed in a second large group of observations reflected in section A of Table 9.1. Whether advisors monitored students' individual projects or engaged them in ongoing work in their laboratory, they risked being less productive than if they had worked alone or employed professional help. First, productivity was highly dependent on student quality. Advisors described experiences with students who never developed interest, enthusiasm, or capacity for independent work; who made insufficient effort, procrastinated, or failed to do the work:

> *Do I get frustrated with the students sometimes? You better believe it. Do they mess up experiments? You better believe that too. . . . Sometimes you're just darn mad that your experiment was ruined by their just not paying attention, not being focused enough, not willing to devote the time to do it. . . . I try not to come down too hard on someone who has made a mistake, because everyone makes mistakes. But if it's repeated mistakes, if it is a general lack of interest . . . I've asked people to leave the laboratory.*

Some students never learned good work skills, were unwilling to think about real research problems, or were unable to handle frustration. Again, these descriptions illustrate why advisors gave so much time and energy to choosing projects and then to selecting and training students. Despite this, some high-achieving students proved to be "a disaster in the lab." This was common enough to explain why many advisors chose students based on direct experience of their workplace temperament more than for their academic record.

Second, working with students took more time and effort than working alone or with experienced assistants and could seriously slow the rate of progress: "There's a real cost to me doing my work with students. If I was to work by myself, I could probably get five times as much done than I do with supervising students in the lab."

The slow pace and variable output of research reliant on undergraduate assistance was evident in advisors' accounts of their presentation and publication patterns. Progress was slower, they felt, than in universities where research groups included graduate students and postdocs. The high demands of supervising undergraduates made it hard to finish a research project and find time for writing. One speaker described a pattern of drought and flood in UR-related publications: "Having students in the lab over the last six years has had a detrimental effect on my number of publications. I don't have the time to sit and write papers, so I shifted my focus to presentations. On my last sabbatical, I wrote up data from the last five years, so then I published a whole slug of papers—and then the record ran dry until the next sabbatical. I think that's true for many people here."

Concerns about negative impacts on their publication rates have also been reported by university faculty working with UR students (Hunter, Thiry, & Crane, 2009). This cost can be significant in environments with typically stronger pressures to "publish or perish" and where lower institutional value is placed on undergraduate teaching than at these four colleges.

Advisors at these colleges also perceived cumulative, longer-term consequences of slowed productivity, notably lack or loss of prestige among their disciplinary colleagues. Collectively these issues—changes in research plans to accommodate student researchers, bad experiences with particular students, low productivity, slow progress, and delayed publication—were especially problematic for faculty preparing for tenure or seeking promotion. Aware of these risks, some chairs allowed faculty approaching a tenure review to opt out of UR for a time.

Costs of Time and Effort

In 12 percent of observations, advisors reported the time and effort involved in undergraduate research. They described the intensity of the setup period, long hours in the laboratory, and the demands of keeping research moving forward while simultaneously teaching, mentoring, and troubleshooting with students. At times, the teaching functions of UR overwhelmed the research effort, and advisors commonly described summer research as "exhausting." "Yeah, it takes a toll," agreed an advisor. "It's also fun, but there's a sense of relief when the school year starts again. Other colleagues see summer as the time of letting go or relaxing. For me, the whole year is building up to summer."

A number of advisors used *burnout* to describe a stage they reached after multiple summers of working with students. "Hitting the wall" was often the impetus for taking a summer off. Chairs and administrators were well aware of this. As one of them noted, "Commencement ends, and you've got a week to get all of your grading done and get your summer research program started. And when that ends, there's about two weeks before things get geared up for classes. So there's not this long gap of summer that is mythologized about academe."

In departments where almost everyone did summer research, faculty depended on each other to "pull their weight" by taking on enough students to provide positions for all those selected. Taking time out placed pressure on colleagues to take on more students. Where tenured faculty dropped out for a summer, untenured faculty felt compelled to pick up the burden, both to work productively toward tenure and to demonstrate their UR commitment. These strains were more keenly felt in smaller departments.

Research advisors described how UR work competed with other professional commitments, such as writing grants and articles, keeping current with the literature, and talking with other researchers. Faculty who were also involved in pedagogical or curriculum development had another layer of duties to balance, as did department chairs and UR program directors. These too are UR costs found in other institutional contexts.

A great deal of time and effort was expended in finding sufficient funds to sustain UR activity. Advisors and administrators cobbled together funds from many sources, writing individual research grants and site grants to support students and materials, raising endowments for instruments and conference travel, and drawing on departmental funds for supplies, equipment maintenance, travel, and new faculty start-up costs. Institutions could ease these stresses and signal their support by assisting in proposal preparation, but where financial or practical support was inadequate or missing, UR operated as a grassroots activity. The number of UR spots for students might contract when individual or site grant funding ended, and institutional funds could be important sources of bridge funding. However, funding current UR efforts, let alone expanding research opportunities to larger and more diverse groups of students, was a widespread concern. While the strains of insufficient organizational or financial support bore heavily on faculty workloads and morale, we did not find that lower levels of such support translated into poorer student experiences. Rather, most student gains directly related to how individual advisors worked with students.

Mentoring student researchers was also inherently time and effort intensive. While advisors developed some reusable strategies with practice, some issues remained constant even for advisors of many years' experience—for example, the persistent question of how much structure and direction to give students. In deciding when to intervene and when to stand back, advisors were constantly aware of time passing. Time issues were also problematic when students continued research during the academic year, when everyone was busy with classes and other activities.

Challenges in Balancing Work and Personal Life

In addition to general observations about time issues, another quarter of advisors' observations concerned the difficulties of balancing UR demands with other professional commitments and their personal, social, and family lives. Prolonged participation in research with students raised larger issues of how to achieve balance among multiple expectations. These same concerns are reported in many studies of academic life (for example, Colbeck & Drago, 2005; Committee on Maximizing the Potential, 2006, 2007; Monroe, Ozyurt, Wrigley, & Alexander, 2008; Rosser, 2001; Ward & Wolf-Wendel, 2004). Here we consider how they influenced faculty decisions about the extent and frequency of their UR participation. This influence was not merely hypothetical: at the time of our interviews, seven faculty (four men, three women) were taking a summer off, nineteen advisors (twelve men, seven women) reported that they had recently taken time out, and in one department, a group of women advisors decided that they would all take the following summer off. Their motivations were mixed: more personal or family time; time to read, write, prepare a new course, or sort through backlogs of research results; and the pleasures of working at their own pace and "just having time to think."

Growing proportions of female faculty and of two-career couples with children had brought both work/life balance and gender issues into departmental awareness in recent years. These changes had reduced faculty willingness to allow professional demands, including UR, to override other life interests. Faculty also questioned whether holding an academic job should prevent them from leading normal personal, social, and family lives. As one administrator put it, "This is just a basic human right." Nineteen female and fourteen male advisors who had children at home described how summer research exacerbated the usual challenges of balancing work and home life. Long and unpredictable hours in the laboratory were especially hard on scientists with younger children: one father noted the irony of spending less time with his children in order to spend more time with other people's children. It could be challenging to arrange summer child care, elder care, or family vacations.

Parents coped in a variety of ways. Some managed their time precisely, setting specific work hours, sharply focusing their research time on particular goals, or coordinating strict family schedules. In two-career couples, some spouses stayed at home or worked part time for a period; where both were scientists, they helped each other with laboratory work or student supervision and traded responsibilities for work and children on a daily basis. Some women advisors made a point to offer each other mutual moral support and practical help, such as covering during family emergencies. But not all managed these balancing acts, with consequences including career shifts and marital discord. Women advisors also worried about how students observed and interpreted faculty work/life balance and how this might affect students' views of their career options (Chapter Eight; see also Grant, Kennelly, & Ward, 2000).

Female advisors also worried that parenting might compromise their academic status. Although most colleagues had ceased to question women's ability as scientists, the issue of how to simultaneously be effective scientists and active family members was less well resolved. They saw having children as disrupting disciplinary colleagues' perceptions of them as "serious scientists" (Colbeck & Drago, 2005; Cole & Zuckerman, 1987). Despite their achievements, they had broken with the normatively approved STEM career trajectory and experienced a reduction in professional status (Long, 1987).

Parents' efforts to meet the competing demands of summer research and family life by good time management and scheduled productivity were discounted by some colleagues because their work patterns deviated from cultural traditions such as late-night presence in the lab (Grant et al., 2000; Hochschild, 1971). Again, women advisors saw these issues as especially relevant to their role as career advisors and role models to their women students. As one observed, "This probably does not make science careers look very attractive to them."

UR administrators understood the sources of these strains in residual gendered attitudes and practices. They took the lead in promoting policies and practices to facilitate work/life balance, modeling and supporting boundary setting, and mentoring colleagues in career management. Advisors described the value of opportunities to take time out, rotation of departmental duties, released time, institutional recognition, increased options for part-time positions, job sharing, and other strategies. While this set of strains was by no means uniquely generated by UR, effectively addressing it was seen by both male and female advisors as consequential for UR's survival at their institutions and for its role in recruiting women into science careers.

Situational Strains Arising from Efforts to Expand UR Opportunities

Balancing the dual educational and scholarly goals of UR was inherently challenging, but most faculty accepted this juggling act. However, advisors described an additional layer of stresses arising from efforts to accommodate a growing demand for student research opportunities. Ironically, these efforts were stimulated by the very success of faculty's UR efforts that prompted institutions to offer more students such a good experience. Where faculty viewed such efforts as undermining control over their UR work, conflict arose between faculty and their institutions over its status and value.

Advisors perceived an increase in the demand for UR opportunities, which they ascribed to three main sources:

- Public and private foundations have come to see research experiences as critical in the production of future scientists. Funders support UR to promote science careers, particularly for students from historically underrepresented groups, or to make research experiences a regular part of science education.
- More students seek UR experiences, partly out of awareness that this enhances their graduate school applications.
- Higher education institutions have become aware of UR's educational value and its role in promoting graduate school enrollment, and thus seek ways to offer UR experiences to more students.

Section B of Table 9.1 summarizes the resulting strains. Unlike the challenges of meeting dual educational and scholarly goals, these strains were not constant: they were situational, provoked by external changes that our interviews captured at particular places and times. These strains were also latent (Parsons & Smelser, 1956): normally hidden, they became apparent only when external forces threatened to destabilize advisors' dynamic balance of objectives. Sociologists recognize such strains as arising from an inherent conflict between the circumstances in which an activity is normally done and the patterned ways in which it is normally practiced. People accept them as a normal cost of doing the activity, but experience them emotionally as low-grade stress. Most of the time, the strains are invisible, but they become manifest when a changing context raises them into awareness, destabilizes coping mechanisms, and forces a more direct response (see Berger, 1963; Ferrante, 2005; Helm, 1971; Merton, 1968).

For advisors, these issues centered on the value, status, organization, and control of what is defined as "undergraduate research." Strains surfaced in situations that advisors viewed as institutional encroachment on their traditional modes of UR work. They could not be reconciled within individual advisors' UR practices, but arose from broad differences between institutional and faculty perspectives. While institutions sought to expand educational opportunities for students, faculty sought to protect their freedom to pursue research as they chose. One-fifth of advisors' observations on the additional strains of UR converge around three main issues (section B of Table 9.1):

- Conflict between organically evolved, faculty-led undergraduate research and efforts to institutionalize UR experiences
- Difficulties arising from requiring students to do UR
- Issues of professional recognition and rewards for summer research advising work.

At these schools, pressures from funders were largely manifested at the departmental level, prompted by UR site grants that obliged the department to take on more students, including visiting students that advisors often described as "weaker." Advisors had some control over how they responded to this expectation; they made good use of increased funding and negotiated student assignments with colleagues. However, taking on more or "weaker" students increased their time stresses, sometimes to the breaking point. One administrator and former chair explained:

> So we put pressure on our own faculty to accept students for the summer program. . . . I twist arms; I say, "We have to take this many students. Who's going to take them?" Sometimes, they're overextended—no question—and they feel pressured to take the less good students because they feel some obligation to do this. . . . And it's a big problem. . . . A lot of people have results they've never written up, or experiments they could have finished if they would just take a summer to do the work and write it up. They feel that they can't take that time. It's a real problem for everybody, but it's a really big problem for junior faculty who have to publish.

This quotation touches on several pressures already discussed. It also points to the sense of moral obligation, widely described and strongly expressed, to give all of their student researchers an authentic science education experience. Advisors were willing to engage in this work even when it conflicted with other imperatives, but commitment to these multiple goals made it hard for advisors, whether they elected to increase these strains by taking on more students or to resolve them by taking time off. Given departments' tacit and explicit expectations that each advisor would take a fair share of summer students, when advisors managed a summer off, they expressed some guilt about colleagues' "taking up the slack." This sense of duty to the collegial UR effort made it possible for the chair (who understood this) to "twist arms." Increased external funding did not necessarily relieve these pressures, because it came with a price tag. Most advisors responded like George Orwell's (1945) carthorse, absorbing additional student demand by increasing their own effort.

A different set of issues came into play when institutions seeking to provide more research experiences attempted to reshape how their faculty practiced UR. Advisors had developed their approaches to student research as voluntary, professional activities, interpreted individually and guided by informal agreements, collective decisions, and disciplinary norms. They were accustomed to autonomy in defining and organizing their UR activities. Institutionally instigated changes intended to accommodate more students thus raised fundamental questions about:

- Risks to the authenticity of projects and student experiences
- The balance between educational and research objectives
- Who determines the content and methods of UR educational experiences
- The quality of apprenticeships for future scientists.

These issues were under strong debate at one college that was beginning to implement a graduation requirement that students complete a faculty-mentored senior capstone project. To accomplish this, science faculty would be asked to mentor more summer students in a shorter, structured program. Advisors viewed such proposals as "diluting" the authenticity of UR experiences, forcing a shift from voluntary professional practice to formal institutional expectation, encroaching on a tradition of professional autonomy, and raising their workload while risking traditionally valued student outcomes. They also expressed resentment at being required to do what they normally offered freely. In the face of these proposed changes, some science faculty withdrew from UR participation; others considered withdrawing but felt torn by their moral commitment to UR and guilty at increasing their colleagues' workload.

In another instance where a department required all its majors to do UR, the problem was not one of diluting authenticity but of obliging faculty to work with students who disliked and resisted research. Advisors recounted "truly miserable summers" with students who lacked motivation, were unproductive, and wasted resources. As one administrator pointed out, the widespread view that research can benefit all students is valid only for students who want to try it.

These experiments also raised the issue of how summer advising should be credited. Indeed, the institutional status and recognition of UR work was discussed not only in these special cases but widely across the sample. None of these colleges had a formal merit system that recognized or compensated advisors' summer work. A few drew salary from external research grants, but many earned no additional salary for summer research. Some administrators described the prevailing college view that UR is a normal part of scholarly work from which science faculty benefit from grants and student research assistance, but concurred that recognition of research advising as teaching had not been institutionally addressed.

Advisors' views about institutional recognition and support for their UR work were both symbolic and substantive. They looked to their institutions for more practical help in preparing grants to pay their summer students. Some sought formal recognition of summer UR as teaching, whether through salary, course release time, credit toward their teaching load, or sabbatical eligibility, but others worried that this would bureaucratize UR and limit faculty autonomy. They argued as an equity issue that a record of directing student research was expected to attain tenure in the sciences, while humanities faculty could pursue their scholarship without any obligation to students. One chair had represented his colleagues' concerns to the college merit pay committee, without success. Another college had offered a modest stipend based on the number of students each advisor supervised, but this gesture backfired. The strength of faculty reactions to honest efforts to make a good thing more widely available surprised and even exasperated some UR administrators.

In these unresolved situations, faculty struggled with a growing sense of dissonance between pressures to take on more research students and what they perceived as insufficient recognition, support, or compensation for the UR work they already did. Well-intentioned efforts to increase student UR opportunities had thus raised from latent to manifest status a set of strains that added to what UR advisors were barely managing to handle at a personal and collegial level. The issues were also symbolic for faculty, partly because the costs of meeting their requests for salary or time were likely prohibitive and partly because faculty are unlikely to trade valued intrinsic motivations of doing this work for extrinsic rewards (Csikszentmihalyi, 1997). While the circumstances that prompt and make manifest these latent strains may differ among institutions, we think it likely that these latent tensions are not confined to liberal arts colleges but may surface wherever UR is conducted.

In the face of all these costs and strains, practical support from departmental colleagues made faculty's work as research advisors possible. They described colleagues who gave scientific advice, made time to address student questions, and stepped in to support students while they went to a meeting. Colleagues who did not work with summer students contributed by undertaking a greater share of other departmental tasks. Untenured faculty also acknowledged understanding and support from senior colleagues. Even more valued were tolerance and respect for faculty who chose to do UR and those who did not. The significance of collegial support may be difficult to quantify, but it is clearly important to the survival and success of undergraduate research.

The Benefits of Doing Research with Undergraduates

Advisors cited three main types of benefits (section C of Table 9.1), more than half of which were couched as intrinsic pleasures, satisfactions, and growth experiences, in contrast with costs that were largely concrete, explicit, and extrinsic. It is notable that observations about career-related benefits that ensued from productive research work nearly balanced in number the reported costs to research productivity. Moreover, advisors' commitment to the education, mentoring, and preparation of future scientists through authentic research permeates their descriptions of both costs and benefits.

Career-Related Benefits

Although they acknowledged that they could sometimes work faster and more fruitfully alone, advisors nonetheless described how students had contributed to good results that yielded publications. Many students had proved to be effective researchers who produced "reams of data" and had made UR projects successful: "What do I get out of doing this? I get to work with some damn smart people. And I can't do and know everything. I have research that's progressing on three fronts. If I was going to be involved in all the detail and do all the modeling, I could only work on one. But because I get such smart students, I can rely on them to get things done."

Advisors cited the high caliber and trustworthiness of their "mini-colleagues." "There's no way I can get done what I need without them," said one. Several advisors described students as "keeping them on track," finding that the discipline of organizing students' work helped them to manage their own time efficiently. Their young researchers were "good problem solvers" who learned with energy and speed. One advisor enthused, "I still can't believe what a good job they did. They just took minimal information from me and just ran with it. . . . And I still can't believe how much data they got and what nice analyses they did."

Advisors also offered examples of students' creativity. Their language about partnership and collegiality did not appear to be hyperbole, but was grounded in cumulative experience of solid student contributions to their work over time: "I've often had students that have been extremely innovative and creative in their own approaches. They've contributed much more to the project than just being a pair of hands. They've raised questions and had intriguing ways to approach a particular problem. I always think of the research for the students and myself as a partnership." With such students, UR experiences were a matter of mutual benefit: "I need them, but they learn from me. So it's good for both of us."

Some advisors described presenting and publishing as benefits of their work with student researchers. Publications came in spurts once sufficient results had accumulated and advisors found time to write them up: "The work of last summer's students is all going to be published. We're at a point where some of the students have beat their heads against the wall, working on techniques which now work, and we can test them on a whole bunch of different things. I think it's probably been eight years of just trying different things, but now we're set to go."

In the longer term, students' results helped some faculty to secure further research funding and contributed to successful tenure bids by others. Finally, some advisors reported that their research students had enhanced their professional reputation as researchers in their own right but also as producers of competent graduate students: "Very selfishly speaking, I love seeing the ones who go off to graduate schools where I have colleagues. And they tell me, 'Oh, so-and-so is great! You guys really train 'em well.' I love that."

Satisfaction in Students' Gains

A second group of benefits referenced advisors' satisfactions from seeing their students grow in all of the ways we have described: "thinking for themselves, making good choices . . . and gaining confidence in their role as research collaborators." "But to see the pride and excitement that these students take in their work," noted one advisor, "and what they've been able to do in a relatively short time—I mean, it's justification enough."

Advisors derived professional satisfaction from knowing that they had helped students find the right career direction for themselves, given them a chance to "try research on for size," helped them settle graduate school decisions, and prepared them well for graduate work. They were pleased when current and former students succeeded as scientists and felt that they had helped to build the next generation of their profession:

> *I was sitting in a room at CalTech about a year ago, watching one of my former students give a seminar. Sitting next to me was my advisor when I was an undergraduate; on the other side was my Ph.D. advisor, who was my student's advisor as well. It's that connection, you know—being in the room and watching the generational transfer, that's what it's all about for me. I mean, that made me feel like everything I've ever done is worth it. When these kids get up on their feet and talk about what they've done and when they deal with the questions and deflect the arrows, then I know I've done it right.*

Intrinsic Benefits

Finally, advisors noted a range of "internal rewards" that arose from their UR work. Chief among these were the pleasures of working with students: an increasing collegiality, the camaraderie of their everyday interactions—"they make my day almost every day"—and the opportunity for one-on-one teaching by which to pass on their own skills and knowledge: "It's the nicest kind of teaching, where you've got a small number of students in a personal setting, where you really feel that you can do things that you can't do otherwise. I think it's the most enjoyable kind of teaching."

Advisors found individual mentoring intrinsically rewarding. They treasured long-term relationships with former students who had become colleagues and friends and being "a part of" their students' lives. "I've got a whole folder full of e-mails from previous students that keep in touch with me from wherever they are now," said one, "And I wouldn't trade that e-mail folder for anything." Another described her experience upon giving a presentation at a disciplinary meeting: "At the end, I looked out into the audience, and all of the students that I had trained in this field were there. They were cheering, and afterward, they came and gave me hugs. Later at dinner with the other speakers, someone from Harvard said, 'Well, I don't think my students would ever do that.' It was the feeling that I had been a useful part of their lives that was really quite satisfying."

Some advisors described their work with students as "intellectually stimulating." It was exciting when "better science" resulted from student insights:

> *There's always a chance that a student who has not necessarily been soaked in a lot of this stuff that you've been thinking about for so long will come up with a new way of looking at it.*

• • •

> *I could perhaps do the research faster and I might get more papers written on my own, but I wouldn't discover nearly as much. My depth of understanding would not be nearly as strong—and it'd be worse science. So what I get out of it is personal satisfaction and intellectual challenge.*

One advisor described watching students succeed as "discovery by proxy": "There's as much joy in discovering the solution to a problem through a student as it is by yourself. In fact, the most satisfying moments are when you send a student off with a hard problem, and not only does she come back with the problem done, but has come up with a more elegant solution. It's rare, I admit. But when it happens, it's immensely rewarding."

While many such observations expressed the satisfactions of working with students, they also begin to hint at other benefits of their summer research. Faculty described how doing science served them as teachers: keeping them "intellectually sharp" and professionally connected in their field, maintaining their enthusiasm, refreshing their supply of teaching examples, and helping to attract strong students to their departments. "I want my faculty to be proficient and competent . . . and not just to vicariously report the success of others," said one administrator. "I'm not gonna win the Nobel Prize, but I feel pretty good about what I do," said an advisor. "We really are researchers, you know; teacher-scholars. We aren't just teachers," said another. All of these comments link research to faculty's identity as scientists. For these faculty, doing science—not just telling about it—was essential for maintaining their status and identity, just as doing science enabled the same process to begin for their students.

Finally, faculty's research was tied to their sense of self. One advisor noted, "Most people are drawn into research out of genuine interest. It's too hard a row to hoe, to stick with it for very long if you don't like it somewhere deep down." Indeed, many advisors described their personal pleasure in doing lab work and analyzing data themselves. This "deep-down" enjoyment and curiosity drove their participation in research, as evident in the following quotations:

> *There's no end of things that I can do that will be of interest and of value to the field. I just wanna keep doing the research, you know.*

. . .

> *Chemistry is amazing. . . . It's just more fun than you could even imagine, having the chance to do science full time in the summer.*

. . .

> *Any one of us could spend the summer going fishing. But we don't. . . . I think part of it is 'cause research is just kinda what we do, you know. We can't help going into the lab.*

Thus, our theme of "real science" comes full circle: research advisors sought to provide students with authentic research experiences, because they believed that these were effective learning experiences, invaluable to students' self-discovery, professional preparation, and maturation into adults. At the same time, they relished their own experience of "real science" for the parallel benefits of learning, growth, and the thrill of discovery that it provided them: "I'm no Watson or Crick, but to discover something one day that no one else knew is an experience everyone should have." These comments show how advisors linked their own intrinsic pleasure in doing science to their work with students:

> *Those benefits that I think the students can, and I hope will, get—those are the same things that drive us. [You have] a question, and you're trying to find the answer. It's very stimulating to think, "Let's go in the lab and see if we can get that."*

. . .

> *"I do it because I enjoy science, I enjoy being in the lab, and I enjoy trying to solve some of these problems. And I hope some of that enthusiasm gets thrown over.*

. . .

For me, doing science in laboratories is so exciting. I love it, it's thrilling, I want them to see that. I don't care what discipline they go into, I don't care if they don't even do a Ph.D. program, but I do want them to see that many people find it the most exciting thing they can do. . . . That research is exciting, research is fun, people do it not because they want to be famous but because they love it. That's what makes me happy, is when they start to see that it can be very exciting. [emphasis in original]

Conclusion

The portrait of undergraduate research that emerges from our study shows an organically evolved endeavor that simultaneously serves several, inherently competing objectives. Advisors tolerated but also sought to resolve the difficulties raised by these tensions in order to preserve the essential, authentic character of UR: its effectiveness in science education, its role in the future of their discipline, and its contributions to their own research. Advisors enjoyed aspects of their work with students despite the challenges of providing authentic research opportunities summer after summer, and despite struggles with unresolved issues in academic science that affected their ability to continue this work and invite students into their profession. During periods of stress, advisors' participation was sustained by their high level of moral commitment to UR work, intellectual curiosity, joy in doing science, and a strong identity as both researchers and teachers. Thus, UR remains in this portrait a two-faced entity, serving both students and faculty and concerned at heart with both teaching and research. One advisor expressed the strength of her commitment in this way: "If ever the administration decided they didn't want to support undergraduate research any more, then I would quickly look for another place to go."

Chapter 10

Summary, Implications, and Issues for the Future

TO BEGIN THIS book, we asked, What is undergraduate research (UR)? In describing the outcomes of this research for students, over time and in comparison with other college experiences, and in elucidating the processes by which UR provides these benefits and is sustained, we have offered a more complete answer than previously available. In this final chapter, we discuss some themes that cut across the components of our analysis, and raise some questions about the implications and use of these findings. We also note questions that remain to be answered by research studies and by thoughtful, evaluated experimentation by practitioners in the field.

How Do We Know What We Know? The Nature of Evidence and Interpretation

We have framed, categorized, and labeled interviewees' accounts to show common patterns across the variable details of actual UR experiences. Qualitative researchers seek to distill patterns of intention, practice, and experience from descriptions of real events and thereby make extant what is implicit in these descriptions. For example, the categories of student gains (Chapters Three to Five) are analytical constructs offered to make sense of data in ways that are consistent with students' accounts and bolstered by advisors' explanations of their observations and learning objectives. Some categories are dual in nature, such as personal/professional gains, and "thinking and working like a scientist," which encompasses both intellectual understanding and the increased ability to apply such understanding to research problems. "Becoming a scientist" is a construct that expresses the process of professional socialization, with its optimal dual outcomes that mark students' shifts into both the identity and status of scientist. Other studies have found similar patterns and given them similar names, but this is the first study to offer evidence from both students and faculty for a comprehensive set of six types of gain.

Our most complex gains construct is a metaphorical pyramid that suggests students' progression in developing higher-order thinking skills. At the end of summer research, the pyramid had a wide base and a narrow peak. Most students had gained the ability to apply their scientific knowledge to research problems, but only small numbers saw themselves as able to think creatively about research design or to comprehend how scientific knowledge is created. Two years later, when the interviewees had entered careers or graduate school, the pyramid depicting their higher-order thinking skills had become nearly square. Many alumni now reported that they had learned from UR how to design investigations and how scientific knowledge was constructed from this process.

Informants in an interview study rarely abstract the common patterns that define their activity; seldom does someone give an abstract explanation of why things operate in certain ways. While we make use of informants' explanatory insights, it is largely the analyst's job to figure out the patterns and explanations from respondents' detailed commentary and examples. For example, no one actually explained to us how formal and informal processes of student selection work in tandem (Chapter Seven), although they may seem obvious to advisors when mirrored back in this generalized way. Our account is entirely distilled from the raw data.

However, we found an unusual departure from this general rule in the case of advisors' teaching strategies. Research advisors were quite conscious about their teaching objectives, methods, and outcomes; these were a matter of wide consensus, and advisors had no difficulty in articulating and illustrating them. Labels such as "cheerleading" and "mentoring" are their shorthand for certain methods. We have added further labels to refer to objectives and outcomes that advisors described but did not consistently name, such as the term "markers" as an analytical gloss on an assessment practice that was widely used but not formalized.

Generalizability of the Findings to Other UR Settings

Related to "how do we know" is the question of generalizability: To what extent are our findings relevant outside the sites where the data were collected? The four colleges in our research study were selected as best-case scenarios where we could explore a relatively homogeneous, common, and well-honed model of UR in action. As noted in Chapter One, the study sought to answer the question, "What is possible?" in well-implemented UR experiences within an important model, rather than the broader question of what actually takes place under variable, real-world conditions. In the strong and positive student outcomes that we observe, these study sites do indeed represent best cases—among many others nationwide. Indeed, there is no reason to believe that such outcomes are rare. Among our comparison group and in our evaluation studies, most students whose UR experience took place at a university report the same strong student gains described by students at the liberal arts colleges and in SOARS. A few students, however, report lower gains, feel less satisfied with their UR experience, and draw negative conclusions about pursuing further research or a scientific career. These cases are infrequent and have been hard to characterize, but they remind us that there is nothing automatic about UR's educational value.

Based on the evidence, we view it as quite possible to achieve similar positive outcomes from UR experiences of similar duration and intensity in a variety of institutional settings, but it is by no means guaranteed. Students' gains clearly depend in large part on the thoughtful work of their research advisors to provide an individual research experience that is also an optimal learning opportunity. However, there is much we do not know—for example, about the gains accrued from research experiences of shorter duration or about the impact of differences in students' preparation, background, and interests on the quality of their UR experience. Understanding how and why student gains may vary among groups of undergraduates and across various UR types and venues is one topic for further study. Even less is known about the outcomes of summer research for other populations, such as K–12 teachers and gifted high school students, to whom research opportunities have been offered with a variety of objectives. The outcomes reported here may provide a useful starting place for studies of these groups but should not be extrapolated wholesale to them.

The apparent robustness of student outcomes across UR venues is understandable if research advisors' intensive teaching approaches are also widespread. However, we know little, as yet, about the nature and variation of UR advising practice across different types of institutions and models. SOARS researchers reported many of the same practices as did faculty at the four colleges, but their methods were not documented in detail. In our work on UR at research universities, we find that UR advising often works much the same as it does at the colleges (Chapters Seven and Eight); in other cases, UR advising is less than optimally effective. Where the quality of advising may be variable, structured UR programs can augment students' development through cocurricular programming that complements their scientific work.

This also raises questions of how best to design UR programs and prepare UR advisors for their work. For those developing structured UR programs, especially for students from underrepresented groups, Chapters Two and Six offer an entry to the larger literature from which can be borrowed many strategies (see also Boyd & Wesemann, 2009). It seems particularly important that developers of structured programs and individual advisors be aware of UR's potential to create both synergy and tension between their scholarly and educational goals, and consider ways to cope with these tensions in the short and long terms. For faculty new to UR, Chapters Seven and Eight in particular offer an embedded how-to manual that complements the practical resources already available in the literature by supplying an evidence-based rationale for these teaching practices. Advisor training may most fruitfully target graduate students and postdocs who work with undergraduates in their research groups (Pfund, Pribbenow, Branchaw, Lauffer, & Handelsman, 2006). For young scientists eager to prepare for a faculty career that may include supervising student researchers, the double advantages of professional development of this type may encourage their participation.

Efforts in advisor professional development may also offer opportunities to study whether and how advisors' approaches evolve, and with what results. Recent research in our group suggests that aspects of authenticity, adequate balance of support and challenge, and mismatched expectations on both students' and advisors' sides may most often be at issue when UR "goes wrong." There is clearly more work to do to both clarify and optimize the processes that typify UR under different models and in different settings. Such work should also attend to the issue of faculty costs and benefits in these settings, as we elaborate below.

Finally, we have said little about how these findings apply to UR in other disciplines. Our data reveal surprisingly few differences in the outcomes and nature of UR in different fields, but our subsamples in some disciplines were small, including engineering, mathematics, computer science, and psychology. We argue that further research and development on UR in the arts, humanities, social sciences, and other fields should pay particular attention to how authenticity can be incorporated as a guiding principle for both scholarly aims and pedagogical methods.

The Deep Roots of Authenticity as a Central Organizing Principle

Authenticity is central to undergraduate research because it is necessary for both students and their research advisors. Students' gains arise directly from the intellectual and technical requirements of real research projects and from the opportunities and challenges that crop up along the way. Advisors begin with a research question that is real because its answer is unknown but of interest to them and their discipline; they have a vested interest in its answer. They refine the scope of that question and devise approaches to it that offer a right-sized project to a novice researcher with a limited time frame, then purposefully exploit its teachable moments.

In the talents and traits for which advisors select students, in their approaches to nurturing and amplifying these, in their measures of students' progress, and in the overall markers by which they assess whether a student has ultimately adopted the identity and status of a scientist, engineer, or mathematician, research advisors are constantly framing and judging their own and students' work by the standards of their discipline. They offer students the opportunity to "do what scientists do," then watch to see how they respond. Advisors' standards for what counts as real science are based both in their disciplines and on their objectives for students, and these standards are vigorously defended: unless the research experience is real in its nature and consequences, it does not offer adequate tests of aptitude and engagement. Advisors claim the sole right to make these determinations, but they understand what novices can handle in their introduction to the standards and hazards of the profession, and thus carefully moderate the extent to which undergraduates experience alone the unmitigated rigors of authentic research. Doing real science thus permeates advisors' approaches and students' experiences within the educational functions of UR.

Doing real science is also critical for advisors: it is the underlying reason that they pursue scholarly work. The colleges in our study encourage and support scholarly work in a form that also includes undergraduates; for many faculty at these schools, this is also the most feasible way to accomplish their laboratory and field work. At these institutions, UR holds the same place as scholarship conducted elsewhere in other forms: it provides faculty with professional rewards and recognition, keeps them intellectually vital and connected to their disciplinary community, and sustains their own status and identity as scientists. Like any other scholarship, undergraduate research is governed by high faculty autonomy in setting their own intellectual direction and deciding how to pursue it.

Research advisors spoke eloquently about the importance of authenticity in their UR practice and students spoke, less eloquently but equally often, of UR as being "real." In contrast, the closely related concept of apprenticeship is nearly taken for granted—perhaps because advisors have themselves learned to do science by apprenticeship through STEM Ph.D. programs, as well as, for many, through undergraduate research. Barab and Hay (2001) offer this passage that links authenticity to apprenticeship but distinguishes apprenticeship as an "even more real" kind of authenticity:

> *While an investigation is . . . focused on actively engaging learners in authentic scientific inquiry, apprenticeship goes one step further and situates this investigation in the context of . . . a particular scientist's research agenda. Here, the apprentice is under an expert's tutelage, using the scientist's lab and equipment, doing the science that contributes to the scientist's work, and doing the science in which the scientist (and potentially the apprentice) has a vested interest. This experience allows the learner to gain insights into the communal nature of science and may facilitate the learner's adoption of ways of perceiving and interacting with the world that are consistent with those of real scientists. [p. 71]*

Summer research serves as a preprofessional apprenticeship for the sciences because like many other occupations, it offers novices a distinctive process of professional education, skills training, and socialization into norms, attitudes, and behaviors regarded as essential for practice. As the accounts of both the craft masters—the research advisors—and the apprentices themselves show, early, hands-on, authentic experience allows novices to settle the essential question of whether this work is a good fit with their interests and temperament before they commit to further, strenuous courses of study. In any occupation that includes both skilled physical work and intellectual engagement, apprentices need to understand what they are getting into and find out whether they like it, while members of the craft in turn need some evidence of apprentices' aptitude before investing further in their training. As they progress, students undergo transitions in identity and status, also typical of apprenticeship experiences. Their work is not just "like" real; it is real.

Certain aspects of UR that recur throughout these chapters are also not accidental: they appear repeatedly because they are authentic aspects of the profession as well as useful learning resources. Peers offer practical help, moral support, and sounding boards for ideas—each a helpful function for UR students' learning that also accurately reflects a collegial and collaborative practice common to the STEM fields. Professional presentation offers students the opportunity to develop skills of communication and critique, deepen understanding, and build confidence and ownership; it is also essential to how scientists refine and disseminate their findings. Thus the legitimacy conferred by presenting at an off-campus conference becomes especially meaningful because it has been hard earned. Making mistakes—and recovering from them—may deliver memorable lessons and test a student's temperament; both are inevitable activities in the laboratory, field, or computer room.

Finally, the term *authentic* seems fitting in describing the intensive relationship of research student and advisor. Both students and advisors note the development of collegial partnerships that differ markedly from classroom hierarchies. These arise in part from proximity: spending many hours together in the close quarters of the laboratory does not preserve formalities. Intimacy also arises from mutual disclosure of ideas and emotional responses. In their struggle to work out and articulate their ideas, and in their open emotional responses to the challenges that research forces them to confront, students make themselves vulnerable to their advisors. In return, advisors share aspects of their professional and, more notably, emotional and personal lives in ways they do not in their classes. Perhaps this mutual vulnerability seems fair to both groups: it is a sign of trust, as each exposes aspects of his or her authentic self. Perhaps too, students and their research advisors share an experience of simple joy: "Whereas there are many good reasons for doing undergraduate research, students and faculty finally do it because it is fun. Research is an integral part of what any chemist or chemistry professor does to warrant the title, and one does not enter a profession or succeed in it without knowing that its pursuits give pleasure and satisfaction" (Luther Erickson, quoted in Mohrig & Wubbels, 1984)

The Role of Student Metacognition

All of our UR participants—faculty, students, and alumni—expressed an awareness of the processes by which UR-derived gains were generated. We have largely explained these processes through the eyes of advisors, but students too spoke of how their gains came about. They noticed how their advisors had prompted or encouraged particular experiences of self-development, as evident, for example, as they learned to present, discuss, and critique their work. Their explanations of the learning process thus complement their advisors' accounts of teaching, and the reflective character of their accounts is striking. Alumni go further in describing the genesis and significance of certain gains. For example, they shared a process of reflection that brought them to their current levels of insight into the nature of scientific knowledge.

In exploring the main sources of student gains, we have recognized several key contributors to these gains. Research advisors made the most pervasive and complex contributions, but important and mutually beneficial roles are also played by student peer groups, departments, institutions, and leaders, as discussed in Chapters Six, Seven, and Nine. The last source—students' contributions to their own process of growth— is more obliquely laid out in Chapters Three through Five. That is, student gains do not fall like rain on passive recipients, but emerge from an interactive and reflective process in which students are active, thinking, self-reflective collaborators.

While some gains emerged as sudden revelations, or only when compounded by later experience in research and in life, often students were very aware of the changes that they were undergoing. Students contributed to their own gains by reflecting on the intellectual and emotional processes in which they were engaged and discussing them with their advisors and peers—for example, when struggling (at their advisor's insistence) to find their own ways through a research problem. They were aware of their own frustrations, and sometimes resistance, at being pressed to make this effort. However, they also acknowledged that this mental wrestling had fostered the confidence to tackle new and complex problems. Reflecting on the meaning and consequences of these key experiences, students reached their own understanding of why a research-based career was, or was not, right for them. Likewise, how alumni thought about and mentally built on their initial gains from UR helped them to transfer some of these gains to later scientific work and life in general.

That students understand and can describe much about their own processes of growth shows that they play an active role in that growth. Advisors' regular practice of talking their apprentices through research problems modeled for students the intellectual importance of thinking out loud with others and provided emotional rehearsal of the professional practice of laying tentative ideas out for scrutiny rather than striving to perfect them in private. Thus, by cultivating metacognitive practices, advisors' methods for teaching good science also teach methods for good learning. Making explicit to students the intellectual work at hand and fostering reflection in teacher-learner and peer group conversations are recognized in the research literature on learning as key to growth (Bransford, Brown, & Cocking, 1999; Pintrich, 2002). This is one more way in which students become more sophisticated learners in doing UR and in which advisors' methods represent teaching at a high level.

Implications for Assessment and Evaluation

For UR considered as scholarly work, assessment is done through disciplinary peer review and publication of the research. But when UR is considered as education, the need arises for methods and metrics for student assessment. Advisors already use a subtle, profound, and widely understood set of indicators to gauge student progress toward specific learning objectives and in making complex, cumulative transitions. What they have not yet done is to translate this experiential wisdom into practical assessment tools. Individual advisors seem confident that they can accurately judge the progress of their own students; they routinely do so in writing recommendation letters. However, it is not clear how best to compare these internally calibrated assessments with those of other faculty advisors for other students. Departments and UR programs appear to avoid formalizing the assessment task by handing it over to outside specialists or by having a dean or program director conduct student exit interviews.

The current gap between informal and formal UR assessment practices may be bridged in part by a new survey instrument for student assessment that is grounded in our study findings and in the alignment of published studies presented in Chapter Two. This instrument, the Undergraduate Research Student Self-Assessment (URSSA), focuses on student gains from UR and the experiences that provide these gains (Ethnography & Evaluation Research, n.d.). It also includes items to measure student satisfaction with aspects of their UR program and gather demographic data. Intended for use in both formative and summative evaluation, URSSA is available online at no cost, for administration to students by UR program directors or evaluators. URSSA has been developed and tested by our group, in collaboration with Tim Weston, and refined based on pilot data from over five hundred students in a varied sample of institutions (Hunter, Weston, Laursen, & Thiry, 2009). Since 2009 it has been housed, along with other learning assessment instruments, on the

Web platform for the Student Assessment of their Learning Gains (http://salgsite.org). The SALG was originally designed by Elaine Seymour and Susan Lottridge to meet the needs of faculty who had adopted innovative teaching methods and materials, but aims to encourage wider use of formative learning assessment by all faculty by extending the range of instruments, survey questions, and teaching and learning settings to which learning gains instruments may be applied.

In common with the other SALG instruments, URSSA offers a central core of questions that focus on student gains, in this case from UR. Departmental and program directors of UR can then select and edit survey items from a template, add questions tailored to their own programs, administer the survey to students, and save it for future use. Numerical results can be reviewed as statistical summaries and graphs or raw data downloaded for further analysis. As is clear from this study, students' own accounts are a valuable source of information for evaluating UR efforts, but we acknowledge limitations to student self-report, especially in their ability to assess gains that are a new type for them in comparison to prior course and work experiences. When using tools like URSSA, it is also important to protect student anonymity and trust on both sides of the intensive student-advisor relationship. Thus, URSSA is intended to serve as part of a comprehensive evaluation design that gathers information about student outcomes from multiple sources and addresses outcomes not only for students but for faculty, their departments, and their institutions.

Implications for Expanding Opportunities for Undergraduate Research

The evidence is ample that UR is a powerful educational experience that prepares students for and enables them to explore and confirm their interest in STEM higher education and professions—a "high-impact educational practice" (Kuh, 2008) for improving undergraduate learning and success. Institutional leaders have come to view UR as an asset that attracts potential students and their parents and distinguishes an institution from its competitors. The argument for enlisting UR in the national effort to diversify the STEM workforce is well grounded, and there is some evidence that student demand for such experiences is also rising. For all these reasons, it may seem self-evident to offer UR to undergraduates in greater numbers and in a wider array of institutions. We discuss this issue at two levels: the potential to expand or add UR at any given institution and the relationship of UR to broader efforts at improving undergraduate STEM education.

Our data offer several indications that incorporating UR apprenticeships into an institutional curriculum is a difficult proposition. First, the origins and practice of UR as a scholarly endeavor of faculty mean that it is not easily governed from above. At undergraduate institutions, research advisors and administrators concur that intensive, faculty-led summer research is conducted largely independent of the institution in which it is located. Advisors work with their apprentices as teachers, but colleges do not typically recognize this work as part of advisors' teaching duties. During the summer, science faculty shift their attention away from college-defined educational goals to those defined by their own scholarly agendas, disciplines, and commitments. Only when their institutions take an interest in requisitioning their services as teachers of research methods do faculty protest their lack of compensation for what amounts to full-time summer teaching. As independent, autonomous scholars and as guardians of the standards of their discipline, faculty do not readily surrender control over the nature and organization of summer research. In a very real sense, during the summer, research advisors work not for the college but for themselves. At research institutions, this is likely to be even more strongly the case.

Second, the costs of doing authentic research with students every summer are high. In addition to the monetary costs, many strains are inherent because faculty needs for research productivity may compete with education and professional development goals for students. Indeed, UR is just one of many educational practices that are good for students but hard on faculty. These strains cannot be resolved except by temporary accommodation, and managing them is in itself stressful, as advisors juggle the time and effort between UR work and competing professional and personal priorities. Some strains may be ameliorated by careful (or lucky) student selection, but as efforts are made to extend UR to a wider range of students, including those with poorer preparation, they have the potential to confound careful efforts to distribute both good and risky students fairly. UR is sustained by the faculty's passion for their research and their moral commitment to educating their research students. Even so, many advisors report periods of burnout and withdrawal, and departments worry about their collective capacity to keep this work going. And as advisors noted, not all students want to do research; forcing them to do so can be a miserable experience for all involved. Thus, in schools like our four study sites, the number of UR opportunities for students might be marginally extended in disciplines with lower levels of faculty participation, but not in departments where almost every member is already engaged and accommodating as many students as she or he can reasonably handle.

At schools with little or no UR involvement, there is clearly greater potential for net growth in student opportunities. This was the idea behind initiatives such as STEM-ENGINES, a consortium of ten community colleges in the Chicago area that formed to provide UR opportunities to a diverse and eager group of students (Higgins, 2008). As Higgins notes, the UR offerings of these colleges are "driven by faculty members with a passion for both their students' success and a desire to re-connect with their primary discipline" (p. 2), just as at the liberal arts colleges in our study. From experiments like this one, initiated as a deliberate effort to explore the possibilities of UR at community colleges, we may hope to learn more about the balance of benefits and costs in establishing and sustaining a new UR tradition (Sachs, 2008).

Still, serious philosophical and practical questions must be addressed before any attempt to import UR into colleges where it has not previously been established. These include fundamental questions about the role of research in an institution's mission. Husic (2003) describes such challenges for public comprehensive universities, which grew from "teachers' colleges" and whose cultures continue to strongly value teaching. As she notes, local political forces that emphasize easily quantifiable measures of accountability to state legislatures and boards of education can hinder moves to make research a larger portion of the faculty role. Similarly, many community colleges define their educational and service mission in terms of an open-door policy to all students, however underprepared they are. They attract faculty members who are deeply committed to teaching—and, increasingly, work part time—some of whom may see a research expectation as "bogging down" their teaching mission (Clark, 1989, p. 6). These are challenges because, as we have argued, embedding UR in faculty scholarship is essential to offer all the advantages of authenticity. A commitment to apprentice-model UR thus could require deep changes in the institutional commitment and perception of scholarly work that generate conflict elsewhere.

A different type of challenge exists at research universities. There the institutional mission and infrastructure already support research, and the number of students who might be accommodated is large. However, the tension between UR's educational role for students and faculty's needs for research productivity is even greater. In our evaluation studies of UR at research universities, advisors report the same intrinsic rewards as do those at the liberal arts colleges, but their discussion of costs is often dominated by publish-or-perish pressures for faculty and the need for steady progress on research by graduate students and postdocs who often serve as UR advisors. Young faculty especially are often eager to take on undergraduates, both to hand down their own positive UR experiences and to staff their new labs with low-cost, readily recruited help—but as new advisors, they are still learning to juggle their educational and research goals. Untenured faculty also run the most palpable risk: they and others often tell us that UR work is not valued within existing rewards structures at their institutions. Given the growing variety of successful UR programs that do exist, it is evident that all these challenges are not insurmountable, but neither are they issues to be taken lightly.

Implications for Broadening Participation in STEM

The preceding discussion raises a further question: If there is not limitless potential for expanding UR opportunities, to whom should the opportunities be offered? One easy answer is that, given its professional socialization benefits, UR should be offered first to the best and brightest students who will pursue professional careers in STEM research. However, advisors repeatedly noted their incomplete success in predicting who these might be. Faculty told of "diamonds in the rough," students with lesser academic records who showed unexpected aptitude, insight, and diligence in the lab, and contrasting tales of academically high-achieving students who could not cope with the frustrations of research. Students themselves saw many gains from UR as highly transferable to "life in general," and future teachers and physicians reported new perspectives on research that benefited them as professionals (Laursen et al., 2006). Thus, we argue that pursuit of UR should remain largely a matter of student interest and choice, with care taken to ensure that all students know about the option. The good outcomes of UR may be equally diminished by too much elitism in selecting participants, as by coercion of students who do not have the desire or of advisors to accept all comers without some choice in the matter.

However, when there is competition for student places, choices must be made. Some would argue that the greatest benefit lies in offering UR positions to younger students who can draw on the resulting skills and knowledge throughout more of their college careers. There is some truth to this view, as well as some caveats to ponder. Evidence to date indicates that the benefit of early entry UR is not from doing UR at a younger age, but from the longer engagement that an early start makes possible. In several studies, we have observed greater growth and stronger gains, especially in the higher-order intellectual gains, among students with multiyear UR experience. With longer experience, students have more time to become independent, achieve meaningful results, and draw the profound gains that ensue from presenting and publishing findings, at the same time as their successes also bolster their advisor's scholarly program. Starting research earlier—especially for students not otherwise exposed to the possibilities offered by STEM professions and graduate study—may be argued to have a potentially greater impact on students' career choices, although we know of little evidence on this point.

However, students also need to be developmentally ready to realize UR's benefits. In comparing structured UR programs for novice and experienced students (Thiry & Laursen, 2009), we saw distinct developmental differences in the nature of students' gains, suggesting that some gains clearly precede others. Novice students learned how to carry out experiments, but experienced students made more progress on learning to design them. Novices learned about their discipline, while older students learned how to apply what they knew. And novices gained confidence by being around scientists, while more senior students gained confidence in being scientists themselves. In another study, both first-year students and their advisors reported more difficulties with UR than did the older students—students were aware of being underprepared and frustrated by not yet being able to contribute (Hunter, Thiry, & Crane, 2009). Thus there are trade-offs to consider in determining when is the best time for a UR experience.

Second, early entry offers an additional set of risks for faculty. Beginners bring lower levels of knowledge, experience, and skills to the laboratory, slowing research progress and raising the risk of broken equipment, lost samples, and preventable errors. Thus, faculty incur real risks to their productivity in working with these students (Chapters Seven and Nine). Moreover, it can be challenging to devise projects that are fully authentic yet accessible to beginning STEM students. Indeed, in one study, first-year college students more often reported poor UR experiences than did their junior and senior peers. Faculty interviews illuminated this issue: because the students were eager but underprepared to fully engage in the science, faculty started them off slowly; rather than appreciating this scaffolded learning opportunity, freshmen felt bored (Hunter, Thiry, & Crane, 2009). Issues like these may thus raise the risk of turning students off to further research. Early-entry students who do stay on in the lab may be among faculty's most productive, but this net return on an advisor's training investment is realized only if the student stays with the initial project rather than seeking new opportunities elsewhere. Students who occupy a UR place for several years may also limit the availability of UR opportunities for others. Thus, with respect to longer UR experience, the benefit for an individual student is clearly greater, but the number of students who benefit may be lower. If a student starts early but does not continue, the cost to faculty is increased without any real payoff. We argue that efforts to promote early entry into UR are likely to fail unless the costs to faculty in taking on novices are also addressed, perhaps by making it possible for them to leverage a novice into an experienced hand—and ideally without also restricting UR spaces for others or overburdening faculty. Clearly the overall cost-benefit balance sheet for early entry models is complex, and more study of these models, as they are tried, is well warranted.

These issues also arise in considering UR's relation to the goal of broadening participation in STEM education and careers by people from groups historically underrepresented in these fields. Access to UR has been lower for these students, especially ethnic minorities and first-generation college students, as well as older, transfer, and part-time students (Kuh, 2008). In order to provide opportunities to these students, UR programs will need to reach out to a wider range of students and schools and modify selection processes to value not just past achievement but future potential. Advisors will need to learn how to work effectively with students of different cultures and abilities. Expanding opportunities may also incur some added costs, such as advisor training and laboratory accommodations to meet the research needs of students with disabilities.

The personal payoff of UR opportunities for these students may be substantial, even transformative, as may the societal payoff in diversifying the STEM fields—but as with early entry, several kinds of risk are also heightened. If some students come to UR academically less prepared, faculty risk higher training costs and lower productivity as they do for younger students. Moreover, compared to students of high socioeconomic status who have already been exposed to possibilities for advanced STEM education and careers, students from more diverse backgrounds may be more likely to leave a research experience with many important gains but deciding that research is not a good fit to their interests (Chapters Four and Five). Thus UR programs that admit more "risky" students will need to find new measures of success—and their funders will need to accept these measures—where documenting graduate school application and entry will not suffice to indicate positive impacts of UR on students' career paths. Given the strains we have already documented, we fear that efforts to broaden UR participation will not succeed if they rely solely on faculty's moral commitment and goodwill, without also finding pragmatic ways to balance the risks to their scholarly productivity and program success that are inherent in offering this educational opportunity to a wider array of students.

Emerging Issues

Our research findings do not touch on all of the issues of current interest to undergraduate research practitioners and directors. For example, in 2008, prompted by concerns about research integrity, federal agencies began requiring institutions to have a plan for training students supported by federal funds in the responsible and ethical conduct of research. This requirement has prompted a surge of interest and accompanying creativity in how to offer meaningful training on research ethics to young researchers. New evaluation and research studies will be required to document the outcomes and impact of such training on students and on the disciplines in the short and long terms.

Another development not reflected in our data set is the growth of international UR opportunities. Such cross-cultural experiences undoubtedly generate a host of benefits and challenges for students that may both combine and expand on the benefits of UR and of foreign study alone. These outcomes must be studied in order first to document them and then to enable meaningful assessment of student outcomes across multiple program models.

Potential Contributions of Undergraduate Research to STEM Classroom Reform

Many voices have called for improved undergraduate STEM education by incorporating research-grounded teaching approaches that result in deeper and more lasting student learning (Chapter One). Yet the uptake of these approaches appears to have stalled. As Seymour (2007, p. 4) argues:

> *Notwithstanding major financial investment, organization of reform activities by networks of engaged faculty, and the accumulation of knowledge, resources, know-how, and skills in the reform community, the diffusion and uptake of research-grounded teaching practice remains*

*limited. It is confined to pockets of activity in particular departments,
disciplinary networks, participants in the few large coalitions that still
have funding, and small institutions (notably liberal arts colleges)
that have a history of commitment to excellence in teaching. In short,
research-grounded teaching methods have not yet been adopted by the
majority of faculty in STEM departments in universities and colleges.*

A similar conclusion is reached by Walczyk, Ramsay, and Zha (2007).
Only about 20 percent of students at 123 research-intensive universities
surveyed were found to have opportunities for active learning or real-
world problem solving in their introductory science courses (Boyer
Commission, 2002). Similarly low proportions of students experience
"high-impact" practices according to Kuh (2008; Lederman, 2008).
DeHaan (2005) too concludes that for the moment, the STEM education
reform effort has stalled.

Thus, it is interesting, and perhaps no coincidence, that funding agencies
have given more attention to UR at the same time that the momentum for
improvement of STEM undergraduate teaching and learning has waned.
The gains in student learning from UR appear solid, and the quality of
faculty practice appears generally high. Thus, sponsoring undergraduate
research as a way to enhance STEM undergraduate education may seem an
appealing option while everyone figures out how to scale up good teaching
practices to the point where they make a difference.

But UR is no magic bullet; there are obvious limitations to the notion
that UR can be a spearhead for a new campaign of STEM education
improvement. We have already discussed the possibilities and limitations
of expanding authentic UR apprenticeships to new institutions. Other
efforts seek to replicate what are assumed to be core UR experiences or
to design UR-like experiences that can more easily be franchised. These
activities may have been hampered by lack of data about precisely what
elements of undergraduate research make it effective as an education in and
about science, but it also seems clear that other factors will limit the
authenticity of research experiences constrained to a classroom setting and
time frame. As discussed in Chapter Nine, efforts at redesigning UR can
also fan into flames a set of latent strains that science faculty normally
manage if they are left to direct UR according to their own standards.

UR is also argued as a way to leverage greater uptake of active,
interactive, and discovery-based teaching and learning methods. For
example, Wood (2003) asserts that the emphasis should not be "on making
every student into a researcher but, rather, on graduating students, in all

disciplines, with the mindset of researchers" (p. 113). Like others, he sees that this can be accomplished through greater understanding and faculty use across the curriculum of inquiry-based teaching and learning, which he defines as "any process in which problems or questions are posed—by the students themselves, by their instructor, by their textbook, or by the professional literature—and students attempt to solve or answer them during class time" (p. 114).

Inquiry-based approaches seem most fruitful for teaching what we have called "thinking and working like a scientist"—how to design and carry out an investigation, how to apply one's knowledge in doing so, and how this process enables humans to create and revise scientific knowledge. As Chapters Three and Five emphasize, research does help students develop a more sophisticated understanding of the nature of science, but it takes a long time for such understanding to become explicit and general. This suggests that the design and implementation of classroom experiences to build this understanding should take into account both the difficulty of these ideas, and the need to sequence them appropriately, when establishing and scaffolding student learning objectives. It is interesting to consider how more, and earlier, inquiry experiences at the undergraduate level could further enhance UR students' growth in these areas. It may also be that for net impact, moneys now invested in UR would be better spent on classroom inquiry.

While we heartily endorse inquiry-based classroom approaches, we offer two cautions, one pragmatic and one conceptual. First, even in our sample of colleges with an overt commitment to teaching, there is a perplexing disconnect between advisors' summer teaching methods emphasizing authentic problem solving and their reversion to traditional lecture and laboratory sessions during the academic year. UR students commented on the differences between their experiences in summer research and courses (Chapter Three). Comparison students (Chapter Four) also noticed what they were missing by not participating in UR and pointed to the limitations of course work compared with what they saw from their peers' UR experiences or in their own apprenticeship experiences of other types. Some STEM faculty in these and other colleges have been pioneers in practicing and promoting research-grounded methods that foster student learning, but there seems to be no automatic transfer to classroom teaching of methods that are seen as essential in summer research.

Second, classroom-based, "research-like" or "research-supportive" approaches should be crisply distinguished from undergraduate research apprenticeships as we have characterized them. These approaches lie along a spectrum: classroom-based approaches may well prepare students for UR; their outcomes may presage those of UR; and useful strategies may be derived by adapting approaches used by UR advisors or by helping faculty to apply strategies they already use in their laboratories. But for clarity in defining and applying classroom approaches, inquiry-based teaching that incorporates research-like elements should not be conflated with UR itself. In particular, we propose that the traditions, outcomes, and cultural understandings of UR as faculty scholarship play an essential and defining role in differentiating UR from other inquiry-based learning experiences. Much important work remains to be done to establish the benefits of inquiry-based learning experiences at the undergraduate level and define the conditions that enable them to succeed, understand their relation to the benefits offered by UR, learn how to stage and scaffold student experiences so that they cumulatively build toward a "research mind-set," and understand how to better encourage and support faculty and institutions in undertaking these approaches. It is equally important to respect the scholarly meaning of UR for faculty and not to treat it simply as yet another hammer in their pedagogical toolkit.

If the scholarly origins and traditions of UR make it unique along the spectrum of inquiry pedagogies, then a final type of authenticity becomes salient. Classroom inquiry parallels the scientific process, engaging students in discovering knowledge that is new to them. In apprenticeship-model undergraduate research, students are engaged in seeking knowledge that is new not just to themselves but to the world. Independent of whether students are successful in obtaining publishable results, UR is authentic both because the knowledge they seek is new and because it is important to their advisor and to an external community in their discipline. Students are "doing the science that contributes to the scientist's work, and doing the science in which the scientist has a vested interest" (Barab & Hay, 2001, p. 71).

A mathematics faculty member offered this personal account of working with a summer student on an open problem posed by a well-known mathematical researcher: "I banged my head on parts of it, and he banged his head, and we were able to pull things together. Now we have a paper that's gonna appear in a very nice journal." He and many research advisors will agree with our interviewee who said that leading undergraduate research is a "great and important job to have."

Appendix A

Interview Samples

SELECTION OF INTERVIEW samples is crucial to the design of any qualitative research study. Sample groups are chosen that can provide information that bears on the research questions—in this case, undergraduate research participants are one obvious choice—and within those groups, a broad range of perspectives is sought. The choice of an appropriate comparison group for UR participants is less self-evident; here we sought comparative perspectives from people whose experiences partially overlap but are partially distinct from those of the UR participants.

In this appendix, we provide details of the interview samples. Figure A.1 shows an overview of the study samples for the four-college study, including their numbers and timing. Table A.1 shows the distribution of interviewees in each sample by gender, race/ethnicity, and discipline. To preserve the anonymity of respondents, we do not identify their institutions or indicate multiple demographic characteristics simultaneously. Each sample included multiple respondents from all four colleges—Grinnell College, Harvey Mudd College, Hope College, and Wellesley College—such that the sample as a whole was not strongly biased toward any one college. When analyzing for gender differences in both student and advisor samples, we examined the data from the coeducational colleges separately, as well as the full data set, to ensure that the findings were not affected by the inclusion of Wellesley, an all-women's college.

The sample of students participating in undergraduate research (UR) was composed of seventy-six students who were science majors and participated in summer UR during summer 2000 as rising seniors, about to enter their senior year. Most were students attending the four colleges that were the study sites, but twelve students were visitors from other campuses who did not have UR opportunities on their home campuses and were participating in Research Experiences for Undergraduates programs at these colleges. The UR participants were interviewed three times: near the end or soon after the summer UR experience, at the end of their senior year, and about two years after graduation. Students who worked

FIGURE A.1

Overview of Interview Study Design and Sampling

	UR participants	**UR nonparticipants**
Students	Rising seniors from STEM departments who conducted research in summer 2000 (including 12 from other institutions, supported on REU or similar site grants)	Students from the same departments who: • Chose not to do UR until senior year ("late" research) • Chose not to participate in UR • Had other experiences: internships, clinic, "alternative" UR sites off campus • Applied for, but did not get a UR position
	Interviewed three times: o As rising seniors, soon after their UR experience (76) o As graduating seniors (69) o As alumni: 2–3 years past graduation, working or in graduate school (56)	Interviewed twice: o As graduating seniors (62) o As alumni: 2–3 years past graduation, working or in graduate school (25)
	201 UR student interviews, total	*87 comparative student interviews, total*
Research advisors	• 55 faculty with whom the UR student participants were working • 12 administrators including college presidents, deans, department chairs, UR or REU program directors	13 faculty who: • No longer did research with undergraduates • Were taking time out from research with undergraduates
	80 advisor interviews, total	
	368 interviews in all	

in the same research group were interviewed in focus groups; students who worked alone were interviewed alone. Findings from the senior-year interviews, denoted "interim" in Figure A.1, largely duplicated the student interview data and are not discussed in detail in the book. Follow-up interviews with members of the UR student sample were conducted with fifty-six of the original seventy-six interviewees; some original interviewees could not be reached, and some declined to participate as alumni.

A student characteristic of interest, whether they had single or multiple UR experiences, could be determined for many members of the sample from interview data. When the seventy-six UR students were

TABLE A.1

Distribution of Interviewees by Gender, Race/Ethnicity, and Discipline

Demographic Category	UR Students	UR Alumni	Advisors	Comparison Students	Comparison Alumni
Total	76	56	80	62	25
Gender					
Women	33	23	32	34	16
Men	43	33	48	28	9
Race/ethnicity (self-reported)					
White	67	50	76	56	22
White, of Middle Eastern descent	2	1	1	1	
Hispanic	3	1		1	
Asian American	2	2	3		1
African American	1	1		3	1
International	1	1			
Unknown				1	1
Discipline[a]					
Biology[b]	25	20	25	21	8
Chemistry[b]	21	14	25	4	2
Physics	10	9	11	6	3
Mathematics and computer science[c]	8	4	10	16	5
Engineering	6	3	4	4	
Psychology	6	6	4	11	7
Education[d]			1		

[a]When students reported double academic majors, we have identified them by their STEM major. No student reported two STEM majors. Among UR students, the STEM major was primary, as they had pursued UR in their STEM field. Among comparison students, the STEM major was sometimes a secondary interest. Non-STEM majors reported by double-majoring students included education, anthropology, and women's studies; other students discussed significant academic interests besides their STEM major but did not report these interests as part of their formal academic record. We did not record academic minors if they were offered. One college offered a science education program, and several science students who pursued UR were in this program.

[b]Biochemistry was sometimes offered as a separate track within a biology or chemistry program, and sometimes as a joint major between two departments. Based on the field of students' UR experience and the organization of the biochemistry program at their school, we have assigned them to either biology or chemistry in the table. Comparison students who reported a biochemistry major were included as part of the chemistry totals.

[c]Some colleges had separate mathematics and computer science departments, while others had joint math/computer science departments. For simplicity, we have combined both fields in this table.

[d]Some students had double majors that included education, but they were coded for this table by their STEM major.

interviewed, twenty had participated in UR on their home campus prior to the rising senior summer. Fifteen described prior UR experience off campus, but it was not always clear whether this was apprenticeship-based UR or an internship. Eighteen students specified that they had no UR experience prior to the rising senior summer, and twenty-three did not specify. Because of the way experience data were recorded, it is likely that these students had no prior experience. Among fifty-six UR alumni, thirty-three described their total UR experience as more than one summer, including both those who pursued further academic year research after the rising senior summer and those who had begun earlier. Fourteen alumni reported more than two full years (including academic year and summer) of UR experience. We cannot separate on- and off-campus experiences for alumni.

The comparison sample included sixty-two students who could offer information that would enable us to explore whether the gains from UR were unique or could be achieved through other educational experiences. This group represented the same departments and the same senior class as the UR student sample, but they were identified by their departments as not participating in UR in summer 2000. Some of these students chose not to pursue UR, while some applied but did not obtain a summer UR position on their home campus. Some undertook an alternative form of UR, conducting research off-campus at another university or laboratory, and some undertook late UR as seniors during the regular academic year. Finally, some undertook internships or the clinic experience offered at one study site. As discussed in Chapter Four, these alternative experiences, along with students' courses and general college experiences, provided a rich view of other potential sources of gains that the UR students received from doing UR. The comparison students were interviewed twice: at the end of their senior year, in order to allow for gains, if any, to emerge from their entire undergraduate experience, and again about two years later. For the alumni interviews, twenty-five of the original sixty-two respondents were reached and agreed to participate. Because of this low response rate, the alumni data should not be assumed to represent the entire sample.

The advisor sample included eighty faculty and administrators who currently or formerly had worked with UR students in their research. Fifty-five faculty were the research advisors of the same UR students we interviewed, designated "active" advisors. In addition, thirteen faculty had previously led UR but had temporarily or permanently discontinued their work with student researchers. These inactive advisors provided an experienced perspective on UR but also discussed their reasons for discontinuing

UR work. Twelve administrators were department chairs, deans, provosts, and UR program directors and also were or had been UR advisors. They provided information on UR in a broader institutional context as well as on their own UR experiences. Because of the overlapping experiences of the active and inactive UR advisors, we have not separated these samples in Table A.1. We attempted to include in the interview sample STEM faculty who had never led UR with students; however, such faculty were rare on these campuses, and those invited declined to be interviewed.

Appendix B
Research Design and Methodology

CHAPTER ONE OUTLINES the rationale and design of the four-college study of undergraduate research (UR) that is the focus of this book, written with readers in mind who are not social scientists or education researchers. Here we provide additional background and full details on our methods of data collection and analysis. Although the specific details refer to the four-college study, similar approaches were used in conducting the evaluation study of Significant Opportunities in Atmospheric Research and Science (SOARS) discussed in Chapter Six.

The qualitative four-college study was designed to address fundamental questions about the benefits (and costs) of undergraduate engagement in faculty-mentored research undertaken outside of class work. Longitudinal and comparative, the study explores the immediate and long-term benefits to students of participation in UR as perceived by both advisors and students (Hunter, Laursen & Seymour, 2007, 2008; Laursen et al., 2006; Seymour, Hunter, Laursen, & DeAntoni, 2004); how these benefits are achieved; the benefits and costs to advisors from their own engagement in UR; and whether the benefits of UR for students can be achieved in other contexts (Thiry, Laursen, & Hunter, 2010). The data from this study represent a large and diverse set of comparative and longitudinal interviews with student and faculty research participants and nonparticipants. Indeed, the total sample of 367 interviews is unusually large for an intensive interview study. The SOARS sample is separately discussed in Chapter Six; with over two hundred participants, it is also quite large.

Our methods of data collection and analysis are ethnographic, rooted in theoretical work and methodological traditions from sociology, anthropology, and social psychology (Berger & Luckman, 1967; Blumer, 1969; Garfinkel, 1967; Mead, 1934). Classically, qualitative studies such as ethnographies precede survey or experimental work, particularly where existing knowledge is limited, because these methods of research can uncover and explore issues that shape informants' thinking and actions.

Thus we use in-depth, semistructured interviews to better understand complex behaviors, interactions, and social processes that are relatively uninvestigated (Fontana & Frey, 1994). These interview methods enable researchers to explore specific themes identified in research questions, yet also allow interviewers to spontaneously follow up on interviewees' comments. In this way, new issues invariably arise from the interview session.

Development of the Interview Protocols

Interview protocols with student research participants focused on the nature, value, and career consequences of UR experiences and the methods by which these were achieved. The full protocols are provided in Appendix C; their design and use are summarized here.

To develop the interview protocols, we classified the range of benefits claimed in the literature (see Chapter Two) and constructed a "gains" checklist to discuss with all participants "what faculty think students may gain from undergraduate research." During the interview, UR students were asked to describe the gains from their research experience (or by other means). If, toward the end of the interview, a student had not mentioned a gain identified on our list, the student was queried as to whether he or she could claim to have gained the benefit and was invited to add further comment. Students also mentioned gains they had made that were not included in the list. With slight alterations in the protocol, we invited comments on the same list of possible gains from students who had not experienced UR and solicited information about the sources of their gains (or lack thereof). All students were asked to expand on their answers and to highlight the gains most significant to them.

In the longitudinal set of interviews, alumni were asked to reflect back on their research experiences as undergraduates and comment on the relative importance of their research-derived gains for their current career or educational endeavors, for the careers they planned, and for other aspects of their lives. In these interviews, alumni were asked to offer a retrospective summary of the origins of their career plans and the role that UR and other factors had played in shaping them and to comment on the longer-term effects of their UR experiences—especially the consequences of UR for their career choices and progress, including their current educational or professional engagement. Comparison alumni were also invited to comment on the importance of their gains from other experiences and on the longer-term effects of these alternative experiences on their career paths and long-term career goals.

The advisor interview protocol was developed from the same research literature that informed the student interview protocols. However, there was—and still is—little research that addresses advisors' work with student researchers. The advisor interview protocol focused on understanding the context of UR at the colleges and within departments, advisors' perceptions of what students gain from the research experience, the costs and benefits to advisors of directing UR students, and advisors' methods of working with students, including project and student selection. Because the majority of comparison faculty had directed UR in the past, we followed the same interview protocol for the comparison group as for the active advisors, asking additional questions about why they had chosen to change their level of participation in UR. One interviewer conducted the interviews with students and faculty; two interviewers conducted the follow-up interviews with alumni. Protocols are in Appendix C.

All interview protocols, and the study design overall, were submitted for review and approved by the University of Colorado's Institutional Review Board to ensure that the study met high ethical, professional, and legal standards for research involving human subjects. Interviewees read and signed an informed consent agreement that described the study and their rights as research participants to anonymity, confidentiality, and other protections of the information they provided. They could decline to answer any questions, stop the interview if desired, or decline to be tape-recorded.

Methods of Data Transcription, Coding, and Qualitative Analysis

Student interviews took between 60 and 90 minutes; some faculty interviews ran as long as 180 minutes. Both UR and comparison students, and all groups of faculty and administrators, were interviewed in person at campus site visits conducted in 2000–2001. Faculty were interviewed individually, and students were interviewed either individually or in focus groups of students who worked with the same UR advisor. Both student and comparison alumni were interviewed by telephone in 2003-2004. Taped interviews and focus groups were transcribed verbatim into a word-processing program and submitted to *The Ethnograph* (Seidel, 1998), a software program for qualitative data analysis. For the four-college study, the total data set of 367 interviews represents over thirteen thousand pages of text data.

To analyze the data, each transcript was searched for information bearing on the research questions. In this type of analysis, text segments referencing issues of different type are tagged by code names. Codes are not preconceived but empirical: each new code references a discrete idea not previously raised. Interviewees also offer information in spontaneous narratives and examples, and they may make several points in the same passage, each of which is separately coded. As transcripts are coded, both the codes and their associated passages are entered into *The Ethnograph*, creating a data set for each interview group (eight, in this study; see Appendix A). Code words and their definitions are concurrently collected in a codebook. Groups of codes that cluster around particular themes are assigned and grouped by "domains" (Spradley, 1980). A taxonomic analysis reveals subcategories within the larger domains. Because an idea that is encapsulated by a code may relate to more than one theme, code words may be assigned to multiple domains. Thus, a branching and interconnected structure of codes and domains emerges from the text data, which at any point in time represents the state of the analysis.

As information is commonly embedded in speakers' accounts of their experience rather than offered in abstract statements, transcripts can be checked for internal consistency— that is, by comparing the opinions or explanations offered by informants, their descriptions of events, and the reflections and feelings these evoke. In ongoing discussions, members of our research group continually reviewed the types of observations arising from the data sets to assess and refine category definitions and to ensure inter-rater reliability and content validity. In addition, the validity of the qualitative findings is strengthened by the independent emergence across multiple data sets of certain themes, such as the types of student gains. Triangulation between student and advisor data sets allows sharpening of the themes and detection of similarities and differences in perspectives, as in the example of "becoming a scientist" discussed in Chapter Three (Bowden & Marton, 1998; Strauss, 1987). In the case of alumni interviews, we conducted member checks with alumni so that they could offer commentary on our findings to date from the student interviews.

Analysis and Presentation of Quantitative Information Derived from the Text Data

The clustered codes and domains and their relationships define the primary themes of analysis, yielding both broad structure and fine nuance. In addition, quantitative information can be derived from the text data. The frequency of use can be counted for codes across a data set, and for important subsets (for example, by gender), using conservative counting conventions that are designed to avoid overestimating the weight of particular opinions. For example, each code is counted only once within a given interview, even if the respondent noted that idea repeatedly. Counting conventions for focus groups are similarly conservative when multiple speakers agree with a point that has been made. Together these frequencies describe the relative weighting of issues in participants' collective report. The number of observations is generally much larger than the number of speakers, and thus is a measure of the depth of broad topics. For instance, a particular student may report gains in each of several different subcategories of "thinking and working like a scientist" (Chapter Three). The number of speakers is a better measure of the distribution of views on a topic, such as advisors' preference for one or another set of criteria in student selection (Chapter Seven).

Because they are drawn from targeted, intentional samples rather than from random samples, these frequencies are not subjected to tests for statistical significance. They hypothesize the strength of particular variables and their relationships that may later be tested by random sample surveys or by other means. For example, survey items in the online Undergraduate Research Student Self-Assessment discussed in Chapter Ten are based on the student gains analysis from this qualitative study. The findings in this study are unusually strong because of near-complete participation by members of each group under study.

To compare weight of opinion on topics within a data set, the raw frequency counts are often reported as simple percentages of the total. Comparison across data sets (or between subsets) poses other challenges. Weights of opinion in data sets with different numbers of interviewees are most easily compared using per capita observations, the number of observations per person. Per capita observations underlie the sources of analysis presented in Chapter Four, where we examined the relative importance of several educational experiences as sources of gains, as well as the several types of gains. Within each positive or negative/mixed gains category, the proportion of student comments derived from that particular source is weighted by the number of students participating in each type of educational experience. These per capita observations are then expressed as a percentage of all per capita observations in that category. For example, eighty-seven positive observations about "thinking and working like a scientist" were reported as deriving from late research experiences by the sixteen students who had these experiences, yielding 5.4 gains statements per person. Across all experience groups, the total of observations about "thinking and working like a scientist" was 19.9 total gains statements per person. The weighted percentage for late research as a source of this gain, as shown in Figure 4.1, is thus 27 percent, or 5.4 statements per person from late research students out of 19.9 from all sources. If all sources contributed equally, the weighted percentages would be equal at 16.7 percent each; thus, late research is a relatively more important source of student gains in thinking and working like a scientist.

Interview groups also differ in the amount and complexity of information they offer. For example, we commonly observe in our work that faculty offer more observations per capita than do students. Interview circumstances also affect the number of observations. In this study, there were more per capita observations from UR alumni than from the same group as students. There may be many reasons for this increase: the later protocols are informed by earlier findings, and interviewers could thus probe in later interviews some gains in detail that in the first round had emerged only spontaneously. One-on-one telephone interviews with alumni may have been more relaxed, held at a time of the interviewee's choosing rather than scheduled into a busy student's workday. Moreover, at the time the last interviews were conducted, interviewees had developed interest in and familiarity with the study. Finally, there is always variation because interviewers differ and because open-ended interviews are conducted as freely flowing conversations responsive to the individual being interviewed, not as rigid telephone surveys.

To account for these differences, the relative weight of opinion among different groups is most easily compared by weighting observations by both the number of interviewees and the total number of observations in the set being analyzed. We use the latter approach in discussing the changes in emphasis on gains from UR over time, discussed in Chapter Five. Because we are interested in change in emphasis over time, we use a ratio of alumni to student per capita observations. Because we also want to compare the change in emphasis between UR and comparison groups, we scale both ratios to the ratio of total observations on student gains. This takes into account the different size of the total data sets and thus enables direct comparison of the ratios, as in Figure 5.1.

For convenience, we call this weighted ratio the "emphasis factor" and take it as a measure of the change in emphasis on a given topic across interview samples of different size and degrees of complexity:

$$\text{Emphasis factor} = \frac{\text{Ratio of per capita observations in subcategory (alumni : students)}}{\text{Ratio of per capita observations on all gains (alumni : students)}}$$

Thus values of the emphasis factor greater than 1 reflect increases and values below 1 reflect decreases in emphasis on a given topic (see Figure 5.1). To identify noteworthy changes, we use the very conservative assumption that changes of a factor of 2 in the emphasis factor are meaningful changes not solely due to the variations discussed above, while changes of less than a factor of 2 may be explainable by such variation. We also examine the number of observations that go into the numerator and denominator of the emphasis factor. We use the conservative approach of ignoring large or small emphasis factors that are based on fewer than eight observations in any of the counts.

Some examples may clarify our uses of frequency counts. In this study, the total numbers of per capita observations about student gains from UR range from sixteen to forty in different data sets, reflecting the large number of gains reported across the samples. Broken out by category, the average number of per capita observations for the UR student sample is 1.2 (career preparation) to 4.1 (personal/professional gains). When comparing the UR student and comparison student samples, per capita observations help to account for the different sample sizes of seventy-six UR students and sixty-two comparison students. For the UR group, the total number of per capita gains statements increased by a factor of 2.5 from student to alumni interviews; for the comparative sample, the overall increase was a factor of 1.4. The emphasis factor normalizes both ratios to 1 so that differences in emphasis appear as increases or decreases from 1, taking into account these differences in per capita observations.

Appendix C
Interview Protocols

THE INTERVIEW PROTOCOLS for each group in the study are presented here as a reference and a resource for other investigators. They have been compiled so that parallels across the groups are evident. Student gains from undergraduate research (UR) and other experiences were probed with all of the interview groups; these questions were based on the gains checklist, which was derived from the literature as discussed in Chapter One and Appendix B. Student interviews were conducted in a parallel form for UR participating and nonparticipating (comparison) students; variations in how questions were asked for the different student groups and subgroups of comparison students are noted in the protocol. The alumni interviews also note small differences for different groups. Interviews with inactive UR advisors and administrators were similar to the advisor interviews; again, minor differences are noted in context. The following notation was used to indicate these variations:

- UR: Were placed with a UR position
- Comparison Group
  - ALT: Chose an alternative to UR
  - LATE: Began UR late in senior year
  - CHOSE NOT: Chose not to do UR
  - DENIED: Not accepted into UR program

The student interview protocol and variations are included in the following section. The advisor protocol follows after that.

Checklist for Student Gains: Used as a Reference in All Interviews

Tell me about some of the changes you can see in your (or in the students') understanding, skills, confidence, or attitudes, etc. (students) since your first undergraduate research experience. (Ask first without probing; then ask for gains by category.)

- Development of collegial relationships with faculty/peers/others

- Sense of "community" of researchers? Possible effects:
  - Sustained or increased interest in the discipline/career
  - Bonding with faculty (and, thereby, the discipline/career path)
  - Increased persistence in major/career direction
- Increased understanding of research/science
  - What research is
  - The research process
  - How scientists think: "habits of mind"
  - How scientists work on real problems
  - What science is: authentic experience/real science
  - How scientific knowledge is built
- Intellectual gains
  - Knowledge (subject/cross-disciplinary)
  - More complete/concrete understanding of field
  - Critical thinking/problem solving
  - Approaches to research problems
  - Hands-on/experiential learning (makes course work more meaningful/relevant)
  - Opportunity to apply theory in practice
- Increased skills
  - Research and lab techniques
  - Conducting literature reviews
  - Working collaboratively
  - Communication (writing, presentation, argument)
- Changes in approach to learning
  - Shift from passive to active learners
  - Greater personal responsibility
  - Learning to work independently
  - Other
- Personal/professional gains
  - Increased self-confidence in ability to do research
  - Self-esteem
  - Benefits of establishing a mentoring relationship
  - Working collaboratively (peers/faculty)
  - Prestige of having done research as an undergraduate
- Career direction
  - Clarification, confirmation, choice of a career path (including graduate school)
  - New knowledge about possible career options
  - Engagement of students of color in the sciences

- Enhanced career preparation

  - Greater readiness for more demanding research/careers in the sciences
  - Professional socialization: understanding how the profession works/ professional conduct/how you enter it
  - Opportunities for networking
  - Strengthen qualifications/chances of entry to graduate/professional school of choice, job options
  - Real work experience
  - Networking opportunities
  - Eases transition to graduate/professional school or work

Interview Protocol for Students

Establish

- Discipline
- Year in school (this campus or elsewhere?)
- Prior UR experience (when begun? How much total experience?)
- Which faculty working with this summer?
- Working alone/with other undergraduates but regular contact with other students?

For comparison students: Identify their other experiences (alternative or late research, internship, clinic, etc.) and ask these questions about those experiences:

- Participation
  - How are students made aware of the research opportunities open to them?
  - How they are selected? (How strong is the competition for places?)
  - What is the selection process? (Nomination required? By whom? On what criteria is are the selection made?) (Ask off-campus students: How did you come to select this institution as a place to do summer research?)
- Motivation
  - What has motivated you to participate (or not to do so)?
    - Career linked? Educational reasons? Work skills?
    - How important is a stipend? How much do you get? Adequate for needs? Source?
    - Do you get research supplies money? Amount? How requested/ source?

- Nonparticipation
  - Do you know any students who applied and were not accepted?
  - Do students who do not participate in UR lose out in some ways? (short/long term, career choices/chances/skills)
- Matching
  - How were you matched to particular research mentors, projects, and project groups?
    - By assignment? Chose/design own project? Related to objectives of research group?
    - List of suggested projects? Mutual selection process (chose project, then interviewed with several faculty to find good fit)?
    - How importance is getting a good match to quality of the experience, your satisfaction, success of the research project?
- Student gains (Work from list. For non-UR participants, frame in terms of "things faculty think students may gain from undergraduate education")
  - What have you learned that you would not have learned without UR/ALT experience(s)?
- How learning happens
  - What kinds of experience have you had that helped you to understand (ask each separately)
    - What science is
    - How science is done
    - How knowledge in your discipline is built
  - How has your mentor structured the UR experience so that you could learn from it?
- Dealing with normal research issues
  - What have you learned about the difficulties of doing real research?
    - Listen for: frustration, slow progress, blind alleys, complexity, ambiguity, things going wrong with experiments, equipment breakdown/failure
    - Time management issues/how much time it takes (conflict with advisor?)
  - Transfer of research knowledge and skills
    - Is any of what you have learned (about research) transferable to another discipline?
    - Could you work with researchers in another field?
    - Would the research skills that you used be the same as/different from theirs?

- Faculty mentoring
  - Tell me about the importance of your relationship with your faculty mentor in what you get out of the UR experience.
    - Why does it matter?
    - How does it work? (Did your mentor structure your experience so you would learn certain things?)
    - Are there problems? (Listen for: lack of supervision/direction, conflict re advisor's expectations about time required)
    - Does faculty UR involvement seem to affect the way that they teach?
    - Advice to your mentor/mentors in general?
- Sources of student satisfaction
  - What has contributed to your level of satisfaction (or dissatisfaction) with your research experience? Listen for: amount/quality of contact with faculty advisor. Match of UR project with student interest.
- Targeted groups
  - Are there particular advantages for a woman (or student of color) in getting research experience as an undergraduate?
  - Would you recommend that other women/students of color do summer research? Why?
  - Has the experience been different in any way than it would have been if you were a white male student? (Check for any positive or negative experiences.)

Interview Protocol: Advisors of Research Students

Establish discipline, years in department/as a faculty member; tenure (and/or promoted) status. For inactive advisors: Refer to past experience.

- Departmental engagement with UR
  - Ask chair (and other faculty as they are able to answer)
    - How long has your department/faculty in your department been offering UR experiences to undergraduates?
    - How does your department organize its UR programs?
    - How many students (at what levels) are served each summer (each year)?
    - What determines the kind of programs that you offer? (curriculum structure, educational priorities, money and resources)
- Departmental support
  - What would you say was the standing/importance of undergraduate research programs within your department? (check for recognition and rewards)

- How are they supported? (institution/funders)

Ask all faculty:

- How long have you been offering undergraduates a research experience? (this department/other institutions) How/why did you begin to do this?
- Did you have research experience(s) as an undergraduate?
- How many students do you have this summer? Working alone and/or in small groups? How many students over time?
- Student funding
    - Do they have stipends? How much?
    - Importance of student stipends? (Adequate?)
    - How acquired?
    - Do students have research supplies money? How acquired?
- Participation
    - How do students become participants (and others not)?
    - How do students learn about research opportunities?
    - What do you think motivates students to participate? (Career linked? Educational reasons? Work skills?)
    - Do you have any sense of why some students choose not to participate?
    - How are they selected? If by faculty: What are you looking for in a prospective research student? How strong is the competition for places? Nomination required? By whom? On what criteria is the selection made?
- Matching
    - How do particular students become matched with you?
    - How do students come to be working on particular projects? (You select? They propose/select from options/negotiate?)
- Authentic experiences
    - What are you looking for in a "good project" for entering seniors?
    - Are there some essential elements that make an undergraduate research experience "good" or "authentic"?
    - Listen for: Experiences that can change students' views of what science is/student discoveries about the nature of science, dealing with the nature of research (frustration, slow progress, changes of direction in research questions and design in light of data)
    - What are the projects that your current research student(s) is/are working on?

- Is this/are they (a) good project(s) in your terms? (Explain)
- How do you get your students to work at an appropriate theoretical level and level of complexity in lab work? Is this a problem area? How resolved?

- Essential features of research (across disciplines)
  - Are there patterns in the types of research projects that your students have done/are doing, or in the kinds of research questions that they address? (A typical project?)
  - Are some of these elements common across different fields? Are there things that you want students to learn that are particular to your discipline?

- Student gains
  - What do you most want students to gain? (Listen for items on checklist. Add others mentioned.)
  - What are the longer-term consequences you predict for students with UR experience? (career or personal)
  - What is "lost" (if anything) by students who do not participate, and with what consequences—including their career choices and performance?
  - Are there particular advantages for a woman (or students of color, or other less-represented groups in the sciences) in getting research experience as an undergraduate?

- "Success"
  - What do you like to see in a student and their work that tells you that their research experience has been successful?
  - How do you evaluate their work/progress? How do you convey this to your student(s)?
  - How "successful" (in these terms) are most of your students?
  - What are the most difficult aspects of learning the research process for students? Causes?

- Structuring the experience (teaching research science)
  - How do you structure/set up the research experience so that students can learn the things that you think are important?
  - What helps students to understand how science is done/how knowledge in the discipline is constructed?
  - Are some/all of these things that you can teach?
  - Opportunities for students to present their own work? How done? Value? Learning to argue a case/field questions?

- Collaborative work
  - Do the students work collaboratively with you (with other students, anyone else)?
  - What's the importance of these experiences?
- Mentoring
  - Tell me something about your role as a research advisor/mentor. (Check what term is used in this department.)
  - What does it mean (in practical terms) to be a good research mentor?
  - How much time does it take? How often do you and your student(s) meet?
  - Do you have ongoing research, academic, or personal relationships with your research apprentices after the summer program is over?
  - What proportion of them work with you on research projects more than once? (When do these relationships typically start?)
  - Do you help your research students in their academic program or career development in particular ways? (encourage/assist with graduate or professional school entry/contacts)
  - Do they ask your advice about career options?
- Faculty gains
  - How important to your professional career is your research engagement with undergraduates?
  - Tell me something about the professional or personal gains that that you have discovered in working with undergraduate researcher and that encourage you to continue doing this. (Don't prompt, but listen for):
    - Helps to stay current in the field
    - Intellectual growth/stimulation
    - Increases energy/enthusiasm
    - Sustains my research agenda
    - Undergraduates make good research assistants
    - Students offer new perspectives, innovative approaches, create new knowledge
    - Great projects/great students—success stories, level of scholarship, publications/presentations? (Summer students or those who continue to work on a project with their advisor/mentor during the academic year?)
    - Their achievements reflect back on me—prestige/reputation (colleagues and students)
    - Departmental rewards
    - Increased pride/confidence

- Creates networking opportunities (discipline, graduate schools, industry)
- Improved interaction with students
- Development as a teacher/researcher
- Improves my teaching
- Faculty costs/losses
  - Are there any losses to you in offering UR experiences to students? Listen for:
    - Time issues: takes away from own research work/mentoring takes a lot of time/time for preparation, grading work/heavy teaching load (no grad students to take up the slack)
    - Risk: UR teaching not valued by department
    - Costs: funded work requires valid/timely results reporting/cost of maintaining equipment, support staff
    - Students: lack high school prep/motivation or maturity/lack enough time or difficulties in prioritizing or assessing time commitment needed/fear of failure, confidence lacking
- Departmental/institutional gains
  - What are the benefits to departments or to the institution overall from engagement in UR programs? (Listen for changes in climate, building of "learning communities")
  - What drives/sustains it?
- Departmental support
  - (If not asked at outset) Is your work with student researchers recognized/rewarded by your department/institution? How? (summer stipend?)
  - Are there any pressures to participate? (Check for untenured faculty)
  - Are there any (other) obstacles to getting faculty to participate?
- The future
  - Will you be participating as a research mentor next summer and/or during the academic year?
  - What recommendations do you have for improving the program in your department or institution?

Interview Protocol: Administrators Involved in UR Programs

History and role of UR within the institution

- How long has this institution been offering research experiences to undergraduates?
- How long have you been involved (Explain: in what capacity/ies?)

- What does the institution see as the goals of its undergraduate research program?
- What are the benefits to departments or to the institution overall from engagement in UR programs? (Listen for changes in climate, building of "learning communities")
- How is UR (variously) funded across the campus?
- Relationships with graduate schools, employers, industry related to UR programs?
- Participation
  - Do all departments participate?
  - What different kinds of UR experience are offered? (Timing during undergraduate career?)
  - Are students required to participate (some/all departments)?
  - (How) Are departments and their faculty encouraged to participate? (Is this expected of faculty? Rewards/recognition? Workload adjustments?)
  - What support does institution give to (participating) departments to maintain their UR programs? (money, faculty time, clerical/administrative, library, computer, grant writing)
    - How much grant writing—individual faculty/departmental/institutional—is specifically aimed at supporting UR programs?
  - Are there any factors that discourage faculty participation? (How does the institution respond to this?)
  - How do students become participants (and others not)?
    - How is undergraduate research promoted?
    - How do students learn about research opportunities?
    - Are some student groups targeted? Who? How?
- Selection and matching
  - Where relevant:
    - How are students selected?
    - How strong is the competition for places? Nomination required? By whom?
    - On what criteria is selection made?
  - As far as you are aware, how are matches made between particular students and faculty mentors?
- Student gains
  - What do you see as the "gains" from undergraduate research experience:
    - Students (individuals, sections within the student population—women, students of color, disabled students, first generation undergraduates)

- Faculty
- Departments
- The institution
- Industry/employers
- Societal benefits: teachers, citizens, policymakers?
- Where relevant
  - What is "lost" (if anything) by students who do not participate?
  - With what consequences?
- Quality
  - How do you judge the quality of the programs offered?
  - Are there some qualities that make undergraduate research experiences "good" or "authentic"? (Which of these are most important?)
- Success
  - What does the institution count as "success" in its undergraduate research programs?
  - How "successful" are your UR programs?
  - By what measures (over what time)? (Types of data gathered?)
  - Findings? Reports/publication of results?
    - Engagement of targeted groups—women, students of color, with disabilities, first generation in college
    - Participation in STEM disciplines
    - Persistence in majors
    - Clarification, confirmation, choice of career paths—graduate/professional school
    - Other? (Probe)
- Issues/problems
  - Some studies report problem areas: institutionalizing programs beyond funding, faculty or departmental support issues. Have you experienced any such difficulties here? (Listen for: inadequate funding, initial funding running out, unpredictability of faculty availability, departmental rewards/disincentives for faculty participation)
- The future
  - What more would you like to see done with the UR programs that you have? How would you improve them or extend them? (Ask why.)

Combined Interview Protocol for Alumni (UR and Comparison)

Follow-up on career decisions and their sources:

- What have you been doing since you graduated/doing now? (Listen for and explore "taking time off.")
- How and when did you decide to do this/these?

- Has your thinking about your career changed since we last talked? (Listen for shifts in intention to go to grad school; changes in field)
- Tell me something about how your work is going.
- Do you like what you're doing? (If not already covered: What are your plans from here?)
- What factors have been at play in your decision making?
- Who have you talked to about possible career options over time?
- Who or what have been the most important influences on your career thinking?
- Role of UR/alternative experiences in career thinking/decisions
  - Review for me, what originally prompted you to:
    - UR: Undertake a UR placement?
    - ALT: Choose an alternative to UR at your school?
    - LATE: Wait until senior year to do UR?
    - CHOSE NOT: Choose not do UR?
    - CHOSE NOT AND DENIED: Did you find an alternative placement? What was that? (If YES, ask all the ALT questions FOR THIS PERSON from here)
    - ALL INTERVIEWEES: To what extent was your choice career related?
    - UR, LATE, ALT: What role did your UR experiences (ALT: "alternative placement") play in developing your career plans?
  - Did you reach any conclusions about research or the academic life as possible careers because of your UR (or ALT) experiences?
- Mentors and other influences on career thinking
  - Did you have someone (whether faculty or others) who acted as a mentor to you?
  - How did that relationship come about?
  - Did you have the opportunity to work closely with a mentor in a situation where you could:
    - Observe her or his working life?
    - Discuss career possibilities with her or him?
  - How important was this/these relationship(s) in developing and implementing your career plans?
  - Have any of your summer experiences (UR or other) shaped your ideas about what you do (or do not) want from your own working life?

- Gender/balance issues (prompt if not raised)
  - When you were thinking about career options, did you think much about the balance between personal and professional life that particular careers might entail?
  - Have you had experiences since graduation that prompt you to think about life/work balance issues?
  - Have you adjusted any of your plans in light of these considerations?
  - On balance, what would you say have been the most important factors in shaping your career ideas?
- Ownership of project
  - UR and LATE: Have you kept in touch with your research advisor since you graduated?
    - Have you followed up in any way on the research that your group was working on? (listen for: in touch with later research students, outcomes of the work, contacts with advisor or their network)
    - Did you help other students to take over your project?
    - Did you have an opportunity to write or publish an article, present at conferences?
  - ALT: Have you kept in touch with anyone from the last placement/internship that you did since you graduated?
    - If so: What has been the value to you of that ongoing contact?
- Career/graduate school preparation
  - Did you make any contacts through your faculty's networks that helped your early career?
  - UR, LATE, and ALT: Was UR (or ALT) experience viewed as a plus by employer, grad school?
    - Did UR (OR ALT) experiences help you to prepare for the world you are now in? How?
  - ALL INTERVIEWEES: How easy or hard did you find it to make the transition into the workplace/graduate school?
- Retrospective evaluation of benefits
  - UR, LATE, ALT: Looking back, what has continued to be useful to you from your UR (ALT) experiences?
  - Many faculty tell us that students don't always realize how much they have gained from doing UR (SUMMER EXPERIENCES OFF CAMPUS) until after they have been away from it for a while:
    - Do some of the things you gained seem more important/useful now than they did at the time?

Responses to first-round findings on student benefits:

- In our analysis of the first round of interviews done at the end of your last summer as an undergraduate, we found six major types of benefits described by UR participants. We sent a description of them to you by e-mail and asked you to print them.
  - UR, LATE, ALT: Would you take a look at each group with me and comment on the importance of each of these types of benefits to you? Do any of these things seem more important to you now than when you were an undergraduate?
  - CHOSE NOT OR DENIED: Would you take a look at them with me and comment on whether and how you gained any of these as an undergraduate? Do any of these things seem more important to you now than when you were an undergraduate?
- Personal/professional gains
  - Increased confidence to do research/contribute to science/feeling like a scientist
  - Probe for how that happened. Listen for: being taken seriously by mentor/others; attending conferences, meeting, talking with "real scientists"; confidence in presenting/defending oral argument
  - Importance of relationship with faculty advisor/other faculty
  - Collegiality: peers/faculty
  - Ongoing communication with faculty advisor/peers?
  - Networking with other scientists/professional contacts?
- "Thinking and working like a scientist":
  - Making use of your critical thinking and problem-solving skills to address real research questions. (Appreciation of UR as a real world, hands-on research experience?)
  - Understanding how to approach research design: generating research questions and framing them for investigation; developing a research design
  - Developing a more valid conception of science (understanding of what science is/is not; its open-ended character; incorporates multiple perspectives; what is a "fact"; the role of "experts")
  - Understanding how scientific knowledge is built
  - Understanding the process of research: frustration, setbacks, failure
  - Deepening your understanding/knowledge of particular aspects of science
  - Relevance of science to real life/work; seeing the application of theory to real-world problems

- Gains in skills
  - Communication: Oral skills (presentation and argument), writing
  - Technical (lab, computer)
  - Work organization
  - Reading complex material
  - How to get information
  - Clarification/confirmation of career plans
- We have already talked somewhat about the next two kinds of benefits. (If not already covered/discussed:)
  - Role of UR in career/graduate school decision: clarification, confirmation, introduction to new area/discipline?
  - Did UR increase probability of going to graduate school? Increase interest in a research career?
  - Increased interest in field of study, generally?
  - UR experience enabled decision that "research is not for me"
- Career preparation
  - Is there anything more that you would like to say about how any aspect of your undergraduate life contributed either to your career direction or preparation? (If not already covered/discussed:)
    - UR as a "real-world work experience"?
    - Opportunity to network, gain professional introductions through mentors, attending conferences?
    - Enhanced résumé?
    - Learning to work collaboratively?
- Changes in learning
  - Learning to work independently
  - Intrinsic interest to learn
- Transferable gains
  - There are particular aspects of these benefits that students felt were applicable to other areas of work and life. We also sent you this short list. Could you comment on what you gained (from UR or from any other undergraduate source) in any of these ways:
    - Dealing with frustrations, tedium, setbacks, "failure"
    - Growth in ability to analyze, approach problems
    - Taking decisions about what to do next
    - Taking ownership of projects you are working on
    - Being responsible for your own work
- Skills learned
  - Are there any other gains from your UR or from other undergraduate experiences that you see as transferable to other contexts?

- Do you see any other changes in yourself that came about as a result of doing research or other aspects of your undergraduate experience?
- Since you graduated, have you changed in the ways you think about yourself, your work, and your future? (Listen for indicators of "self-authorship": maturity, self-directed activity, own definitions of success versus influence of external sources; also any gender issues raised.)
- LATE ONLY: Do you feel you lost out or perhaps gained by doing your UR experience later than most?
- CHOSE NOT and DENIED: Do you feel there have been any longer-term impacts of not having done UR?

- Elements in the UR process
  - UR AND LATE ONLY: We are interested in the ways in which these benefits of doing UR came about. Looking back, can you see ways in which the UR experience was set up and done that made some of these good things happen? (listen for particular structure/ elements, faculty, research group, department, financial factors)

- Advice
  - UR AND LATE ONLY: Clearly your schools, and others like them, gave you and other students some things of value that continue to be valuable to you. Did anything detract from the experience? Do you have any advice to offer them that would make a good experience even better?
  - Are there any other aspects of the undergraduate research experience we haven't discussed that you think are important and would like to add?

Appendix D
Detailed Frequency Counts for Observations of Student Gains

AS DISCUSSED IN Appendix B, frequency counts for groups of related codes are a useful indicator of the relative weight of opinion among topics and for comparing weights of opinion among different interview groups. Chapters Three through Five present analyses based in part on frequency counts for student gains categories and subcategories (see Tables 3.1 and 4.2 and Figure 5.1). For completeness, we include in Table D.1 a complete table showing the finely grained frequency counts that are the basis of these analyses, across all the interview groups. The table includes positive gains observations only, as negative and mixed observations were significant in number only for the comparison group (Chapter Four).

Because the codes and categories were initially developed from the UR student data set, "comparable" gains categories are those identified in that initial analysis for which similar observations, coded using the same set of codes, were reported by other interview groups (alumni, advisors, and/or comparison groups). Where new code categories emerged from these other data sets, for which no comparable observations were present in the UR student sample, these are designated as "noncomparable." In some cases, observations are noncomparable because a gain observed by others was simply not reported by the UR students. A good example is advisors' observations that senior research students gained confidence from their role in mentoring more junior researchers in their group; student researchers did not have a perspective that enabled them to see this. In other cases, observations are similar in content but are still strictly noncomparable because of differences in perspective based on situation, timing, or certainty. For example, advisors could report the past experience of coauthoring a paper with their research students, but UR students could only report their expectation that they might do so in the future.

The designations of comparable and noncomparable gains categories are relevant in practice because they differentiate which groups of gains are used in different analyses. Chapter Three focuses on student gains reported by UR students and faculty, and Chapter Four does the same for comparison students. Arguments in those chapters about the relative importance of different gains to respondents as a group, or about differing importance placed on certain gains by different respondent groups, rely on the counts across all gains subcategories, both comparable and noncomparable. In contrast, Chapter Five reports changes in emphasis by alumni relative to students, with reference to a ratio that we call the emphasis factor. Because zero counts can skew ratio calculations, only the comparable gains categories were used in the emphasis analysis.

Overall, 85 to 95 percent of gains observations were comparable for each group. Within the six main categories, the proportion of comparable gains is also generally high. Noncomparable code categories that emerge for alumni reflect gains from UR that were perceived by alumni with time, in several categories that reflect deepened understanding of science and their profession among alumni, as discussed in Chapter Five. The large number of noncomparable gains observations in the category of enhanced career preparation is due to the fact that both alumni and advisors could report concrete career preparation gains, which had not yet come into play for students.

One group of codes was included in two of the main categories. "Feeling like a scientist" is listed as a personal/professional gain because students expressed this gain primarily in terms of their own emotional experience of growth in confidence and self-assurance. As discussed in Chapters Three and Eight, advisors recognized this as students' adoption of the identity and status of a scientist, a marker of their joining the profession; thus, these codes also reflect "becoming a scientist."

Frequency Counts for Positive Observations on Student Gains from Undergraduate Research by All Interview Groups

Observed Category	Comparable Across Categories (Y/N)	UR Students	UR Alumni	Advisors	Comparison Students	Comparison Alumni
Number of interviews		76	56	80	62	25
Total, comparable observations		1,149	2,067	1,885	1,563	864
Total, noncomparable observations		70	254	266	86	100
Total, all observations		1,219	2,321	2,151	1,649	964
Total percentage of gains observations that are comparable across sample categories		94%	89%	88%	95%	90%
Personal/professional gains						
Increases in confidence to do research or contribute to science	Y	145	90	133	107	63
Establishing a collegial relationship with faculty; recognition of faculty advisors' positive influence on students	Y	51	203	102	55	59
Establishing peer or professional collegiality (with other UR students)	Y	29	98	55	29	26
Feeling like a scientist	Y	85	52	46	28	10
Comparable observations, personal/professional gains		310	443	336	219	158
Gains in maturity or self-discovery	N	0	59	27	0	36
Belonging to a "community of learners"	N	0	20	18	0	12
Seeing who/what a "real scientist" is/does; seeing faculty as "real people" at work	N	0	13	24	0	0
Gains in confidence due to mentoring role of more senior UR students of more junior UR students	N	0	0	15	0	0
Noncomparable observations, personal/professional gains		0	92	84	0	48
All observations, personal/professional gains		310	535	420	219	206

(Continued)

TABLE D.1   (Continued)

Observed Category	Comparable Across Categories (Y/N)	UR Students	UR Alumni	Advisors	Comparison Students	Comparison Alumni
Percentage of personal/professional gains observations that are comparable		100%	83%	80%	100%	77%
Thinking and working like a scientist						
Increased knowledge; understanding in depth; understanding theory or concepts; making connections between or within sciences; solidifying knowledge	Y	46	51	66	82	48
Increased appreciation of the relevance of course work to understanding science	Y	30	30	12	24	7
Gain in critical thinking and problem-solving skills related to research—using critical thinking and problem-solving skills in an authentic research experience; analyzing data within theoretical or conceptual frameworks	Y	66	73	130	122	42
Improved critical thinking and problem solving generally, not linked to UR	Y	6	0	0	159	16
Understanding science research through hands-on, authentic experience	Y	70	154	219	31	37
Understanding how to pose and investigate research questions, develop or refine a research design	Y	26	36	10	38	15
Understanding the nature of scientific knowledge: its open-endedness, the nature of scientific "fact," science as "fallible," how scientific knowledge is built	Y	10	47	90	12	18
Comparable observations, thinking and working like a scientist		254	391	527	468	183

Consolidating and deepening knowledge through presentation and teaching	N	40	0	0	0	0
Noncomparable observations, thinking and working like a scientist		40	0	0	0	0
All observations, thinking and working like a scientist		294	391	527	468	183
Percentage of observations on thinking and working like a scientist that are comparable		86%	100%	100%	100%	100%
Becoming a scientist						
Understanding how scientists practice their profession; awareness of attitudes, behaviors, and norms required of professional practice	Y	7	128	62	11	29
Demonstrated gains in attitudes and behaviors needed to become a scientist; "takes ownership" of project; "intellectual engagement," creative and independent approach to decision making	Y	38	127	236	79	99
Increased understanding of the nature of research work—that research is messy, riddled with problems/setbacks; can be tedious, boring and slow	Y	20	74	106	38	37
Beginning to see self as a scientist	Y	85	52	46	28	10
Comparable observations, becoming a scientist		150	381	450	156	175
All observations, becoming a scientist		150	381	450	156	175
Percentage of observations on becoming a scientist that are comparable		100%	100%	100%	100%	100%
Gains in skills						
Improvement of presentation skills or ability to defend oral argument	Y	77	134	65	92	31
Computer skills	Y	20	61	14	11	18
Lab or field skills; instrumentation, measurement, technical skills	Y	48	44	55	25	16
Work organization skills; time management, note taking	Y	23	42	8	69	24

(Continued)

TABLE D.1 (Continued)

Observed Category	Comparable Across Categories (Y/N)	UR Students	UR Alumni	Advisors	Comparison Students	Comparison Alumni
Improvement of writing skills	Y	14	36	14	99	51
Collaborative working skills	Y	10	34	6	70	16
Reading comprehension and critiquing skills	Y	18	31	7	9	23
Information searching and retrieval	Y	4	21	0	6	16
Comparable observations, gains in skills		214	403	169	381	195
General communication and writing skills	N	0	2	5	26	4
Noncomparable observations, gains in skills		0	2	5	26	4
All observations, gains in skills		214	405	174	407	199
Percentage of observations on gains in skills that are comparable		100%	100%	97%	94%	98%
Enhanced preparation for career and graduate school						
Provides "real-world work experience" (students); good graduate school/job preparation (faculty)	Y	38	113	28	131	28
Enhances résumé: good for graduate/medical school prospects	Y	19	54	18	33	18
Offers opportunity to network with faculty, peers, other scientists	Y	33	40	9	28	22
Comparable observations, enhanced preparation for career and graduate school		90	207	55	192	68
Faculty have provided career advice or information, guided students' career plans/decisions; faculty have facilitated student placement or provided letters of recommendation	N	0	112	44	46	38
Student has presented at a conference (UR symposium or professional conference)	N	0	33	53	7	5

Student has coauthored/published an article based on UR work	N	0	9	52	3	5
Students have coauthored papers presented at conferences/abstracts submitted to conferences; students' contribution cited	N	0	0	9	0	0
Students have won academic awards/received grants linked to UR participation	N	0	0	15	0	0
Student plans to present at a conference	N	9	0	0	0	0
Student plans to attend a conference	N	9	0	0	0	0
Student plans to coauthor an article to be published	N	5	0	0	0	0
Good for current education: good preparation for senior thesis course work	N	5	0	0	0	0
Working collaboratively enhances career or graduate school preparation	N	1	0	0	0	0
Enhances career generally	N	1	0	0	0	0
Provides exposure to new opportunities or experiences	N	0	3	0	4	0
Noncomparable observations, enhanced preparation for career and graduate school		30	157	173	60	48
All observations, enhanced preparation for career and graduate school		120	364	228	252	116
Percentage of observations on enhanced preparation for career and graduate school that are comparable		75%	57%	24%	76%	59%

Clarification and confirmation of career and educational goals

Clarified or confirmed student's interest in field of study; aided student in deciding which area of study to pursue; provided concrete recognition of fit between own interests and particular fields of study	Y	47	120	69	73	25

(Continued)

TABLE D.1   (Continued)

Observed Category	Comparable Across Categories (Y/N)	UR Students	UR Alumni	Advisors	Comparison Students	Comparison Alumni
Increased student's interest or enthusiasm for field of study	Y	16	45	199	39	19
Experience clarified that a research career is not what student wants	Y	7	26	37	14	3
Introduced student to new field of study	Y	10	12	12	3	7
Clarified or confirmed level of interest in graduate school or increased likelihood of going to graduate school	Y	51	39	31	18	31
Comparable observations, clarification and confirmation of career and educational goals		131	242	348	147	85
Introduced idea of graduate school or research career	N	0	3	4	0	0
Noncomparable observations, clarification and confirmation of career and educational goals		0	3	4	0	0
All observations, clarification and confirmation of career and educational goals		131	245	352	147	85
Percentage of observations on clarification and confirmation of career and educational goals that are comparable		100%	99%	99%	100%	100%

References

Abraham, N. B. (2001, September). Academic excellence—The meeting and the sourcebook. *Council on Undergraduate Research Quarterly*, 11–15.

Adelman, C. (2006). *The toolbox revisited: Paths to degree completion from high school through college*. Washington, DC: U.S. Department of Education.

Adhikari, A., Givant, S., & Nolan, D. (1997). The Mills College Summer Mathematics Institute. In D. Nolan (Ed.), *Women in mathematics: Scaling the heights* (pp. 97–104). Washington, DC: Mathematical Association of America.

Adhikari, N., & Nolan, D. (2002). "But what good came of it at last?": How to assess the value of undergraduate research. *Notices of the AMS, 49*(10), 1252–1257.

Ainley, P., & Rainbird, H. (Eds.). (1999). *Apprenticeship: Towards a new paradigm of learning*. London: Kogan Page.

Alexander, B. B., Foertsch, J. A., & Daffinrud, S. (1998, July). *The Spend a Summer with a Scientist Program: An evaluation of program outcomes and the essential elements of success*. Madison: University of Wisconsin, LEAD Center.

Alexander, B. B., Lyons, L., Pasch, J. E., & Patterson, J. (1996, June). *Team approach in the first research experience for undergraduates in botany/zoology 152: Evaluation report*. Madison: University of Wisconsin, LEAD Center.

Allen, W. R. (1992). The color of success: African-American college student outcomes at predominately white and historically black colleges and universities. *Harvard Educational Review, 62*, 26–44.

American Council of Learned Societies. (2007, May). *Student learning and faculty research: Connecting teaching and scholarship* (White paper). Teagle Foundation, American Council of Learned Societies. Retrieved June 11, 2009, from www.teaglefoundation.org/learning/publications.aspx.

American Society for Biochemistry and Molecular Biology. (2008, Fall). *Biochemistry/molecular biology and liberal education: A report to the Teagle Foundation*. Bethesda, MD: Author.

Anderson, E. L., & Kim, D. (2006). *Increasing the success of minority students in science and technology*. Washington, DC: American Council on Education.

Arnold, K. D. (1993). The fulfillment of promise: Minority valedictorians and salutatorians. *Review of Higher Education, 16*(3), 257–283.

Asera, R., & Treisman, U. (1995). Routes to mathematics for African-American, Latino and Native American students in the 1990s: The educational trajectories of Summer Mathematics Institute participants. *CBMS Issues in Mathematics Education, 5*, 127–151.

Astin, A. W. (1977). *Four critical years*. San Francisco: Jossey-Bass.

Astin, A. W. (1982). *Minorities in American higher education: Recent trends, current prospects and recommendations*. San Francisco: Jossey-Bass.

Astin, A. W. (1992). *What matters in college? Four critical years revisited*. San Francisco: Jossey-Bass.

Astin, A. W., & Astin, H. S. (1992). *Undergraduate science education: The impact of different college environments on the educational pipeline in the sciences*. Los Angeles: University of California, Graduate School of Education, Higher Education Research Institute.

Auerbach, J. L., Gordon, J., May, G., & Davis, C. (2007, June). *A comprehensive examination of the impact of the summer undergraduate research program on minority enrollment in graduate school*. Paper presented at the American Society for Engineering Education Annual Conference and Exposition, Honolulu, HI.

Ball, D. B., Wood, M., Lindsley, C., Mollard, P., Buzard, D. J., Vivian, R., et al. (2004). Research, teaching, and professional development at a comprehensive university. *Journal of Chemical Education, 81*(12), 1796–1800.

Barab, S. A., & Hay, K. E. (2001). Doing science at the elbows of experts: Issues related to the Science Apprenticeship Camp. *Journal of Research in Science Teaching, 38*(1), 70–102.

Barlow, A.E.L., & Villarejo, M. (2004). Making a difference for minorities: Evaluation of an educational enrichment program. *Journal of Research in Science Teaching, 41*(9), 861–881.

Bauer, K. W., & Bennett, J. S. (2003). Alumni perceptions used to assess undergraduate research experience. *Journal of Higher Education, 74*, 210–230.

Baxter Magolda, M. B. (1999). *Creating contexts for learning and self-authorship: Constructive-developmental pedagogy*. Nashville, TN: Vanderbilt University Press.

Baxter Magolda, M. B. (2004). Evolution of a constructivist conceptualization of epistemological reflection. *Educational Psychologist, 39*(1), 31–42.

Berger, P. (1963). *Invitation to sociology: A humanistic perspective*. New York: Doubleday.

Berger, P. L., & Luckman, T. (1967). *The social construction of reality: A treatise in the sociology of knowledge.* London: Penguin Press.

Bhushan, A. (2007, November 28). Number of undergrads in research rising. *Yale Daily News.* Retrieved July 28, 2008, from www.yaledailynews.com/articles/view/22567.

Biggs, H. (2006, March). *Undergraduate research as capstone: Marking trends and developing strategies* [PowerPoint slides]. Presentation at Bridging Research and Teaching Workshop—Capstone Experiences: Transitioning Students Beyond College, Pew Midstates Science and Mathematics Consortium, Chicago. Retrieved July 28, 2008, from http://pewscimath.hope.edu/activities_.htm.

Blau, P. M. (1974). *On the nature of organizations.* Hoboken, NJ: Wiley.

Blumer, H. (1969). *Symbolic interactionism: Perspective and method.* Upper Saddle River, NJ: Prentice Hall.

Bowden, J., & Marton, F. (1998). *The University of Learning: Beyond quality and competence in higher education.* London: Kogan Page.

Boyd, M., & Wesemann, J. (Eds.). (2009). *Broadening participation in undergraduate research: Fostering excellence and enhancing the impact.* Washington, DC: Council on Undergraduate Research.

Boyer Commission on Educating Undergraduates in the Research University. (1998). *Reinventing undergraduate education: A blueprint for America's research universities.* Stony Brook, NY: Stony Brook University.

Boyer Commission on Educating Undergraduates in the Research University. (2002). *Reinventing undergraduate education: Three years after the Boyer Report.* Stony Brook, NY: Stony Brook University.

Boyle, P., & Boice, B. (1998). Systematic mentoring for new faculty teachers and graduate teaching assistants. *Innovative Higher Education, 22*(3), 157–179.

Bransford, J. D., Brown, A. L., & Cocking, R. R. (Eds.). (1999). *How people learn: Brain, mind, experience, and school.* Washington, DC: National Academies Press.

Brown, D. R. (2006). Undertaking chemical research at a community college. *Journal of Chemical Education, 83*(7), 970–972.

Brown, S. V. (2000). The preparation of minorities for academic careers in science and engineering. In G. Campbell, R. Dense, & C. Morrison (Eds.), *Access denied: Race, ethnicity, and the scientific enterprise* (pp. 239–268). New York: Oxford University Press.

Building Engineering & Science Talent. (2004). *A bridge for all: Higher education design principles to broaden participation in science, technology, engineering and mathematics.* San Diego, CA: Author. Retrieved September 28, 2008, from www.bestworkforce.org/PDFdocs/BEST_BridgeforAll_HighEdDesignPrincipals.pdf.

Bunnett, J. F. (1984). The education of butchers and bakers and public policy makers. *Journal of Chemical Education, 61*(6), 509–510.

Campbell, G. (1996). Bridging the ethnic and gender gaps in engineering. *NACME Research Letter, 6,* 1–10.

Campbell, T. A., & Campbell, D. E. (1997). Faculty/student mentor program: Effects on academic performance and retention. *Research in Higher Education, 38*(6), 727–741.

Carmichael, J. W., Labat, D. D., Huter, J. T., Privett, J. A., & Sevenair, J. P. (1993). Minorities in the biological sciences: The Xavier success story and some implications. *Bioscience, 43*(8), 564–570.

Carnegie Foundation for the Advancement of Teaching. (2007). *The Carnegie Classification of Institutions of Higher Education.* Stanford, CA: Author. Retrieved November 11, 2008, from www.carnegiefoundation.org/classifications/.

Catsambis, S. (1995). Gender, race, ethnicity, and science education in the middle grades. *Journal of Research in Science Teaching, 32*(3), 243–257.

Chubin, D. E., & Malcom, S. M. (2008, October 6). Making a case for diversity in STEM fields. *Inside Higher Ed.* Retrieved October 8, 2008, from www .insidehighered.com/views/2008/10/06/chubin.

Chubin, D. E., May, G. S., & Babco, E. L. (2005). Diversifying the engineering workforce. *Journal of Engineering Education, 94*(1), 73–86.

Clark, B. R. (1989). The academic life: Small worlds, different worlds. *Educational Researcher, 18*(5), 4–8.

Clewell, B. C., de Cohen, C. C., Deterding, N., & Tsui, L. (2006). *Final report on the evaluation of the National Science Foundation, Louis Stokes Alliances for Minority Participation Program.* Washington, DC: Urban Institute. Retrieved November 7, 2008, from www.urban.org/publications/411301.html.

Coates, C., Liston, C., Thiry, H., & Laursen, S. (2005, October). *Evaluation of the summer undergraduate research program in biological science at the University of Colorado and comparative analysis of summer and academic year programs, 2002–03 and 2003–04.* Boulder: Ethnography & Evaluation Research, Center to Advance Research and Teaching in the Social Sciences, University of Colorado.

Cohen, N. H., & Galbraith, M. W. (1995). Mentoring in the learning society. In M. W. Galbraith & N. H. Cohen (Eds.), *Mentoring: New strategies and challenges* (pp. 5–14). New Directions for Adult and Continuing Education, no. 66. San Francisco: Jossey-Bass.

Colbeck, C. L., & Drago, R. (2005). Accept, avoid, resist: Faculty members' responses to bias against caregiving . . . and how departments can help. *Change, 37*(6), 10–17.

Cole, D. (2007). Do interracial interactions matter? An examination of student-faculty contact and intellectual self-concept. *Journal of Higher Education, 78*(3), 249–281.

Cole, J. R., & Zuckerman, H. (1987). Marriage, motherhood and research performance in science. *Scientific American, 256*(2), 119–125.

Colon, F. (2009, July). *The view from NSF.* Presentation to NSF REU Chemistry PIs' meeting, San Antonio, TX.

Committee on Equal Opportunities in Science and Engineering. (2004). *Broadening participation in America's science and engineering workforce: The 1994–2003 decennial and 2004 biennial reports to Congress.* Retrieved July 22, 2005, from www.nsf.gov/od/oia/activities/ceose/.

Committee on Maximizing the Potential of Women in Academic Science and Engineering, Committee on Science, Engineering, and Public Policy, National Academy of Sciences, National Academy of Engineering, & Institute of Medicine. (2006). *Biological, social, and organizational components of success for women in academic science and engineering: Report of a workshop.* Washington, DC: National Academies Press.

Committee on Maximizing the Potential of Women in Academic Science and Engineering, Committee on Science, Engineering, and Public Policy, National Academy of Sciences, National Academy of Engineering, & Institute of Medicine. (2007). *Beyond bias and barriers: Fulfilling the potential of women in academic science and engineering.* Washington, DC: National Academies Press.

Council on Undergraduate Research. (2006). *CUR timeline.* Retrieved August 14, 2009, from www.cur.org/timeline.html.

Council on Undergraduate Research. (n.d.). *Frequently asked questions: What is the definition of undergraduate research?* Retrieved November 6, 2008, from www.cur.org/faq.html.

Craig, N. C. (1999). The joys and trials of doing research with undergraduates. *Journal of Chemical Education, 76*(5), 595–597.

Crampton, S. B. (2001). Questions from the past for the future. In M. Doyle (Ed.), *Academic excellence: The sourcebook. A study of the role of research in the natural sciences at undergraduate institutions* (pp. 59–63). Tucson, AZ: Research Corporation.

Crim, E. J., Jr. (1998, November). *Aversive racism on campus: Explaining mechanisms of isolation for students and staff of color on campus.* Paper presented at the meeting of the Association for the Study of Higher Education, Miami, FL.

Csikszentmihalyi, M. (1997). Intrinsic motivation and effective teaching: A flow analysis. In J. L. Bess (Ed.), *Teaching well and liking it: Motivating faculty to teach effectively* (pp. 72–89). Baltimore: Johns Hopkins University Press.

Darling-Hammond, L. (2000). Teacher quality and student achievement: A review of state policy evidence. *Education Policy Analysis Archives, 8*(1). Retrieved November 19, 2009, from http://epaa.asu.edu/epaa/v8n1/.

DeAntoni, T., Pedersen-Gallegos, L., Hunter, A.-B., Marschke, R., Seymour, E., & Wiese, D. (2001, March). *The Los Alamos National Laboratory Student Internship*

Program: A formative evaluation: Report to Los Alamos National Laboratory. Boulder: Ethnography & Evaluation Research, Center to Advance Research and Teaching in the Social Sciences, University of Colorado.

DeHaan, R. L. (2005). The impending revolution in undergraduate science education. *Journal of Science Education and Technology, 14*(2), 253–269.

De Welde, K., & Laursen, S. L. (2008). The "ideal type" advisor: How advisors help STEM graduate students find their "scientific feet." *Open Education Journal, 1,* 49–61.

Doyle, M. P. (Ed.). (2000). *Academic excellence: The role of research in the physical sciences at undergraduate institutions.* Tucson, AZ: Research Corporation.

Drinker, C. K. (1912). Undergraduate research work in medical schools. *Science, 36*(935), 729–738.

Eccles, J. S., Barber, B. L., Stone, M., & Hunt, J. (2003). Extracurricular activities and adolescent development. *Journal of Social Issues, 59,* 865–889.

Elliott, R., Strenta, A. C., Adair, R., Matier, M., & Scott, J. (1996). The role of ethnicity in choosing and leaving science in highly selective institutions. *Research in Higher Education, 37*(6), 681–709.

Ethnography & Evaluation Research. (n.d.). *Undergraduate Research Student-Self-Assessment (URSSA).* Retrieved October 1, 2009, from www.colorado.edu/eer/research/undergradfaqs.html.

Etzkowitz, H. (2000). Why are minority and women scientists still treated so badly? In G. Campbell Jr., R. Denes, & C. Morrison (Eds.), *Access denied: Race, ethnicity, and the scientific enterprise* (pp. 295–306). New York: Oxford University Press.

Exploring the concept of undergraduate research centers: A report on the NSF workshop. (2003). Retrieved November 8, 2008, from http://urc.arizona.edu/.

Feagin, J. R., & Sikes, M. P. (1994). *Living with racism: The black middle-class experience.* Boston: Beacon Press.

Ferrante, J. (2005). *Sociology: A global perspective* (6th ed.). Belmont, CA: Wadsworth.

Fisher, B. J., & Hartmann, D. J. (1995). The impact of race on the social experience of college students at a predominately white university. *Journal of Black Studies, 26*(2), 117–133.

Fitzsimmons, S. J., Carlson, K., Kerpelman, L. C., & Stoner, D. (1990). *A preliminary evaluation of the Research Experiences for Undergraduates (REU) Program of the National Science Foundation.* Washington, DC: ABT Associates.

Foertsch, J. A., Alexander, B. B., & Penberthy, D. L. (1997, June). *Evaluation of the UW–Madison's summer undergraduate research programs: Final report.* Madison: University of Wisconsin, LEAD Center.

Fontana, A., & Frey, J. (1994). Interviewing: The art of science. In N. Denzin & Y. Lincoln (Eds.), *The handbook of qualitative research* (pp. 361–376). Thousand Oaks, CA: Sage.

Ford, D., & Harris, J. J., III. (1997). A study of the racial identity and achievement of black males and females. *Roeper Review, 20*(2), 105–110.

Fullilove, R. E., & Treisman, P. U. (1990). Mathematics achievement among African American undergraduates at the University of California, Berkeley: An evaluation of the mathematics workshop program. *Journal of Negro Education, 59*(3), 463–478.

Gaglione, O. G. (2005). Underground existence of research in chemistry in two-year college programs. *Journal of Chemical Education, 82*(11), 1613–1614.

Gándara, P., with Maxwell-Jolly, J. (1999). *Priming the pump: Strategies for increasing the achievement of underrepresented minority undergraduates.* New York: College Entrance Examination Board.

Garfinkel, H. (1967). *Studies in ethnomethodology.* Upper Saddle River, NJ: Prentice Hall.

Gavin, R. (2000). The role of research at undergraduate institutions: Why is it necessary to defend it? In M. Doyle (Ed.), *Academic excellence: The role of research in the physical sciences at undergraduate institutions* (pp. 9–17). Tucson, AZ: Research Corporation.

Gentile, J. (2001). Faculty: Our greatest investment. In M. Doyle (Ed.), *Academic excellence: The sourcebook. A study of the role of research in the natural sciences at undergraduate institutions* (pp. 64–69). Tucson, AZ: Research Corporation.

Glazer, E. M., & Hannafin, M. J. (2006). The collaborative apprenticeship model: Situated professional development within school settings. *Teaching and Teacher Education, 22*(2), 179–193.

Good, J. M., Halpin, G., & Halpin, G. (2000). A promising prospect for minority retention: Students becoming peer mentors. *Journal of Negro Education, 69*(4), 375–383.

Grant, L., Kennelly, I., & Ward, K. B. (2000). Revisiting the gender, marriage, and parenthood puzzle in scientific careers. Building inclusive science: Connecting women's studies and women in science and engineering [Special issue]. *Women's Studies Quarterly, 28*(1&2), 62–85.

Greater Expectations National Panel. (2002). *Greater expectations: A new vision for learning as a nation goes to college: A national panel report.* Washington, DC: Association of American Colleges and Universities. Retrieved September 12, 2007, from www.greaterexpectations.org.

Greene, M. L., Way, N., & Pahl, K. (2006). Trajectories of perceived adult and peer discrimination among black, Latino, and Asian American adolescents: Patterns and psychological correlates. *Developmental Psychology, 42*(2), 218–238.

Greenwood, E. (1972). Attributes of a profession. In R. Pavalko (Ed.), *Sociological perspectives on occupations*. Itasca, IL: Peacock.

Hakim, T. (2000). *How to develop and administer institutional undergraduate research programs*. Washington, DC: Council on Undergraduate Research.

Handelsman, J., Ebert-May, D., Beichner, R., Bruns, P., Chang, A., DeHaan, R. L., et al. (2004). Scientific teaching. *Science, 304*(5670), 521–522.

Handelsman, J., Pfund, C., Lauffer, S. M., & Pribbenow, C. M. (2005). *Entering mentoring: A seminar to train a new generation of scientists*. Madison: University of Wisconsin Press.

Hansch, C., & Smith, R. N. (1984). Research and its support in the undergraduate chemistry department. *Journal of Chemical Education, 61*(6), 517–519.

Hathaway, R., Nagda, B., & Gregerman, S. (2002). The relationship of undergraduate research participation to graduate and professional educational pursuit: An empirical study. *Journal of College Student Development, 43*(5), 614–631.

Healey, M., & Jenkins, A. (2009). *Developing undergraduate research and inquiry*. York, UK: Higher Education Academy.

Helm, P. (1971). Manifest and latent functions. *Philosophical Quarterly, 21*(82), 51–60.

Henderson, C. (2005). The challenges of instructional change under the best of circumstances: A case study of one college physics instructor. *American Journal of Physics, 73*(8), 778–786.

Henderson, C., & Dancy, M. H. (2008). Physics faculty and educational researchers: Divergent expectations as barriers to the diffusion of innovations. *American Journal of Physics, 76*(1), 79–91.

Henry, C. M. (2005). Undergrad research makes a difference: Studies look at the impact of undergraduate research on retention and student outcomes. *Chemical and Engineering News, 83*(17), 37–38.

Higgins, T. B. (2008). What works—A PKAL essay. STEM-ENGINES: NSF Undergraduate Research Collaborative (URC). In *Volume IV: What works, what matters, what lasts*. Washington, DC: Project Kaleidoscope. Retrieved December 8, 2008, from www.pkal.org/documents/ResearchRichHaroldWashington.cfm.

Hochschild, A. (1971). Inside the clockwork of male careers. In F. Howe (Ed.), *Women and the power to change*. New York: McGraw-Hill.

Hodson, D. (1992). In search of a meaningful relationship: An exploration of some issues relating to integration in science and science education. *International Journal of Science Education, 14*(5), 541–562.

Hotchkiss, J. L., Moore, R. E., & Pitts, M. M. (2006). Freshman learning communities, college performance, and retention. *Education Economics, 14*(2), 197–210.

Hunter, A.-B., Laursen, S. L., & Seymour, E. (2007). Becoming a scientist: The role of undergraduate research in students' cognitive, personal and professional development. *Science Education, 91*(1), 36–74.

Hunter, A.-B., Laursen, S. L., & Seymour, E. (2008). Benefits of participating in undergraduate research in science: Comparing student and faculty perceptions. In R. Taraban & R. L. Blanton (Eds.), *Creating effective undergraduate research programs in science: The transformation from student to scientist* (pp. 135–171). New York: Teachers College Press.

Hunter, A.-B., Thiry, H., & Crane, R. (2009). *Student outcomes from the LA-STEM Research Scholars Summer Bridge Program. An evaluation of the LA-STEM Research Scholars Program at the Louisiana State University, 2007–2008: Qualitative results.* Boulder: Ethnography & Evaluation Research, Center to Advance Research and Teaching in the Social Sciences, University of Colorado.

Hunter, A.-B., Weston, T. J., Laursen, S. L., & Thiry, H. (2009). URSSA: Evaluating student gains from undergraduate research in science education. *Council on Undergraduate Research Quarterly, 29*(3), 15–19.

Husic, D. W. (2003). *Politics and higher education: Barriers to undergraduate research opportunities at public comprehensive institutions.* White paper written for CUR Undergraduate Research Summit, Lewiston, ME, August 2–4. Retrieved November 7, 2008, from http://abacus.bates.edu/acad/depts/chemistry/twenzel/white_papers.html.

Ishitani, T. T. (2006). Studying attrition and degree completion behavior among first-generation college students in the United States. *Journal of Higher Education, 77*(5), 861–885.

Jonides, J., and others. (1992, August). *Evaluation of minority retention programs: The Undergraduate Research Opportunities Program at the University of Michigan.* Paper presented at the meeting of the American Psychological Association, Washington, DC.

Kardash, C. M. (2000). Evaluation of an undergraduate research experience: Perceptions of undergraduate interns and their faculty mentors. *Journal of Educational Psychology, 92*(1), 191–201.

Karukstis, K. K., & Elgren, T. E. (Eds.). (2007). *Developing and sustaining a research-supportive curriculum: A compendium of successful practices.* Washington, DC: Council on Undergraduate Research.

Katkin, W. (2003). The Boyer Commission Report and its impact on undergraduate research. In J. Kinkead (Ed.), *Valuing and supporting undergraduate research* (pp. 19–38). New Directions for Teaching and Learning, no. 93. San Francisco: Jossey-Bass.

Kenny, S. S. (2003). New challenges in a post-Boyer world. *American Scientist, 91*(2), 103–105.

Kinkead, J. (2003). Learning through inquiry: An overview of undergraduate research. In J. Kinkead (Ed.), *Valuing and supporting undergraduate research* (pp. 5–17). New Directions for Teaching and Learning, no. 93. San Francisco: Jossey-Bass.

Kremer, J. F., & Bringle, R. G. (1990). The effects of an intensive research experience on the careers of talented undergraduates. *Journal of Research and Development in Education, 24*(1), 1–5.

Kuh, G. D. (2008). *High-impact educational practices: What they are, who has access to them, and why they matter.* Washington, DC: Association of American Colleges and Universities.

Laursen, S. L. (2006). Getting unstuck: Strategies for escaping the science standards straitjacket. *Astronomy Education Review, 5*(1), 162–177.

Laursen, S. L., Hunter, A.-B., Seymour, E., DeAntoni, T., De Welde, K., & Thiry, H. (2006). Undergraduate research in science: Not just for scientists any more. In J. J. Mintzes & W. Leonard (Eds.), *Handbook of college science teaching* (pp. 55–66). Arlington, VA: NSTA Press.

Laursen, S. L., Thiry, H., & Liston, C. (2005). *Evaluation of the Science Squad Program for the Biological Sciences Initiative at the University of Colorado at Boulder: II. Influence of Squad participation on members' career paths.* Boulder: Ethnography & Evaluation Research, Center to Advance Research and Teaching in the Social Sciences, University of Colorado.

Lederman, D. (2008, October 6). Putting what works to better use. *Inside Higher Ed.* Retrieved December 6, 2008, from www.insidehighered.com/news/2008/10/06/aacu.

Lee, W. Y. (1999). Striving toward effective retention: The effect of race on mentoring African American students. *Peabody Journal of Education, 74,* 27–43.

Lewis, C. W., Ginsberg, R., Davies, T., & Smith, K. (2004). The experience of African American Ph.D. students at a predominately white Carnegie I-research institution. *College Student Journal, 38,* 231–246.

Lichter, R. L. (2000). "Research is important, but . . ." In M. Doyle (Ed.), *Academic excellence: The role of research in the physical sciences at undergraduate institutions* (pp. 41–53). Tucson, AZ: Research Corporation.

Lohfink, M. M., & Paulsen, M. B. (2005). Comparing the determinants of persistence for first-generation and continuing-generation students. *Journal of College Student Development, 46*(4), 409–428.

Long, J. S. (1987). Problems and prospects for research on sex differences. In L. S. Dix (Ed.), *Women: Their underrepresentation and career differentials in science and engineering* (pp. 157–169). Washington, DC: National Academies Press.

Lopatto, D. (2004). Survey of Undergraduate Research Experiences (SURE): First findings. *Cell Biology Education, 3*(4), 270–277.

Lopatto, D. (2007). Undergraduate research experiences support science career decisions and active learning. *CBE Life Sciences Education, 6*(4), 297–306.

Lopatto, D. (2008). Exploring the benefits of undergraduate research: The SURE survey. In R. Taraban & R. L. Blanton (Eds.), *Creating effective undergraduate research programs in science* (pp. 112–132). New York: Teachers College Press.

Lovitts, B. E. (2001). *Leaving the ivory tower*. Lanham, MD: Rowman & Littlefield.

Massachusetts Institute of Technology. (2000, February 4). *Trend-setting undergraduate research program turns 30*. Cambridge, MA: MIT News Office. Retrieved July 28, 2008, from http://web.mit.edu/newsoffice/2000/urop30.html.

Massachusetts Institute of Technology. (n.d.). *Biography of Margaret MacVicar*. Retrieved June 11, 2009, from http://web.mit.edu/provost/macvicar/biography.html.

Maton, K., & Hrabowski, F. (2004). Increasing the number of African American PhDs in the sciences and engineering: A strengths-based approach. *American Psychologist, 59*(6), 547–556.

Maton, K., Hrabowski, F., & Schmitt, C. (2000). African American college students excelling in the sciences: College and postcollege outcomes in the Meyerhoff Scholars Program. *Journal of Research in Science Teaching, 37*(7), 629–654.

May, G. S., & Chubin, D. E. (2003). A retrospective on undergraduate success for underrepresented minority students. *Journal of Engineering Education, 92*(1), 1–13.

McMillan, E., & Pauling, L. (1927). An x-ray study of the alloys of lead and thallium. *Journal of the American Chemical Society, 49*(3), 666–669.

Mead, G. H. (1934). *Mind, self, and society: From the standpoint of a social behaviorist*. Chicago: University of Chicago Press.

Melton, G., Pedersen-Gallegos, L., & Donohue, R., II, with Hunter, A.-B. (2005). *SOARS: A research-with-evaluation study of a multi-year research and mentoring program for underrepresented students in science* (Report to SOARS). Boulder: Ethnography & Evaluation Research, Center to Advance Research and Teaching in the Social Sciences, University of Colorado.

Merkel, C. A. (2001). *Undergraduate research at six research universities: A pilot study for the Association of American Universities*. Pasadena: California Institute of Technology.

Merkel, C. A. (2003). Undergraduate research at the research universities. In J. Kinkead (Ed.), *Valuing and supporting undergraduate research* (pp. 39–53). New Directions for Teaching and Learning, no. 93. San Francisco: Jossey-Bass.

Merkel, C. A., & Baker, S. M. (2002). *How to mentor undergraduate researchers*. Washington, DC: Council on Undergraduate Research.

Merton, R. K. (1968). *Social theory and social structure*. New York: Free Press.

Mervis, J. (2001a). Student research: What is it good for? *Science, 293*(5535), 1614–1615.

Mervis, J. (2001b). Undergraduate research: Liberal arts schools pass science check-up. *Science, 293*(5528), 193.

Mohrig, J. R., & Wubbels, G. G. (1984). Undergraduate research as chemical education: Report of a symposium. *Journal of Chemical Education, 61*(6), 507–508.

Monroe, K., Ozyurt, S., Wrigley, T., & Alexander, A. (2008). Gender equality in academia: Bad news from the trenches, and some possible solutions. *Perspectives on Politics, 6*(2), 215–233.

Morley, K. M. (2003). Fitting in by race/ethnicity: The social and academic integration of diverse students at a large, predominately white university. *Journal of College Student Retention, 5*(2), 147–174.

Murguia, E., Padilla, R. V., & Pavel, M. (1991). Ethnicity and the concept of social integration in Tinto's model of institutional departure. *Journal of College Student Development, 32*(5), 433–439.

Nagda, B. A., Gregerman, S. R., Jonides, J., von Hippel, W., & Lerner, J. S. (1998). Undergraduate student-faculty research partnerships affect student retention. *Review of Higher Education, 22*(1), 55–72.

National Academy of Sciences, National Academy of Engineering, & Institute of Medicine. (1997). *Adviser, teacher, role model, friend: On being a mentor to students in science and engineering.* Washington, DC: National Academies Press.

National Research Council. (1996). *National Science Education Standards.* Washington, DC: National Academies Press.

National Research Council. (1999). *Transforming undergraduate education in science, mathematics, engineering and technology.* Washington, DC: National Academies Press.

National Research Council. (2000). *Inquiry and the National Science Education Standards: A guide for teaching and learning.* Washington, DC: National Academies Press.

National Research Council. (2005). *Assessment of NIH minority research and training programs: Phase 3.* Washington, DC: National Academies Press. Retrieved September 28, 2008, from www.nap.edu/catalog.php?record_id=11329.

National Research Council. (2007). *Rising above the gathering storm: Energizing and employing America for a brighter economic future.* Washington, DC: National Academies Press.

National Science Board. (2008). Science and engineering labor force. In *Science and Engineering Indicators: 2008.* Retrieved November 8, 2008, from www.nsf.gov/statistics/seind08/c3/c3h.htm.

National Science Foundation. (1996). *Shaping the future: New expectations for undergraduate education in science, mathematics, engineering, and technology.* Washington, DC: U.S. Government Printing Office.

National Science Foundation. (2002). *Women, minorities and persons with disabilities in science and engineering.* Text Table 4.1. Retrieved March 19, 2009, from www .nsf.gov/statistics/nsf03312/c4/tt04–01.htm.

National Science Foundation. (2007a). *Report of the Committee of Visitors, Division of Chemistry, National Science Foundation, February 7–9, 2007.* Retrieved November 15, 2007, from www.nsf.gov/mps/advisory/covdocs/CHEcov_07.pdf.

National Science Foundation. (n.d.). *A timeline of NSF history.* Retrieved August 14, 2009, from www.nsf.gov/about/history/timeline80s.jsp#1980s.

National Science Foundation, Division of Science Resources Statistics. (2007b). *Women, minorities, and persons with disabilities in science and engineering.* Retrieved December 11, 2008, from www.nsf.gov/statistics/wmpd.

Neckers, D. C. (2000). Reminiscences and recommendations on undergraduate research. In M. Doyle (Ed.), *Academic excellence: The role of research in the physical sciences at undergraduate institutions* (pp. 57–77). Tucson, AZ: Research Corporation.

Nettles, M. T., & Millet, C. M. (1999). *The human capital liabilities of underrepresented minorities in pursuit of science, mathematics, and engineering doctoral degrees.* Stanford, CA: Stanford University, School of Education, National Center for Postsecondary Improvement.

Netwatch: Net news: Undergraduate research journals take root on Web. (1998). *Science, 282*(5396), 1951.

Nuhfer, E., & Pavelich, M. (2001). Levels of thinking and educational outcomes. *National Teaching and Learning Forum, 11*(1), 9–11.

Olson, S., & Fagen, A. P. (2007). *Understanding interventions that encourage minorities to pursue research careers: Summary of a workshop.* Washington, DC: National Academies Press. Retrieved November 19, 2009, from www.nap.edu/catalog/12022.html.

Orwell, G. (1945). *Animal farm.* London: Penguin Books.

Osborne, J. W. (1995). Academics, self-esteem, and race: A look at the underlying hypothesis of the disidentification hypothesis. *Personality and Social Psychology Bulletin, 21*(5), 449–455.

Osborne, J. W., & Walker, C. (2006). Stereotype threat, identification with academics, and withdrawal from school: Why the most successful students of colour might be most likely to withdraw. *Educational Psychology, 26*(4), 563–577.

Page, S. E. (2007). *The difference: How the power of diversity creates better groups, firms, schools and societies.* Princeton, NJ: Princeton University Press.

Pandya, R. E., Henderson, S., Anthes, R. A., & Johnson, R. M. (2007). BEST practices for broadening participation in the geosciences: Strategies from the UCAR Significant Opportunities in Atmospheric Research and Science (SOARS) Program. *Journal of Geoscience Education, 55*(6), 500–506.

Parsons, T., & Smelser, N. J. (1956). *Economy and society*. New York: Free Press.

Pascarella, E. T., & Terenzini, P. T. (1991). *How college affects students: Findings and insights from twenty years of research*. San Francisco: Jossey-Bass.

Pascarella, E., & Terenzini, P. (2005). *How college affects students: A third decade of research* (Vol. 2). San Francisco: Jossey-Bass.

Paulsen, M. B., & St. John, E. P. (2002). Social class and college costs: Examining the financial nexus between college choice and persistence. *Journal of Higher Education, 73*(2), 189–236.

Perry, W. G., Jr. (1998). *Forms of ethical and intellectual development in the college years: A scheme*. San Francisco: Jossey-Bass.

Pfund, C., Pribbenow, C. M., Branchaw, J., Lauffer, S. M., & Handelsman, J. (2006). Professional skills: The merits of training mentors. *Science, 311*(5760), 473–474.

Pintrich, P. R. (2002). The role of metacognitive knowledge in learning, teaching, and assessing. *Theory into Practice, 41*(4), 219–225.

Pladziewicz, J. R. (1984). Factors important to the maintenance of undergraduate research programs. *Journal of Chemical Education, 61*(6), 515–516.

Preston, A. E. (2004). *Leaving science: Occupational exit from scientific careers*. New York: Russell Sage Foundation.

Prince, M. J., Felder, R. M., & Brent, R. (2007). Does faculty research improve undergraduate teaching? An analysis of existing and potential synergies. *Journal of Engineering Education, 96*(4), 283–294.

Project Kaleidoscope. (2006). *Report on Reports II: Recommendations for urgent action. Transforming America's scientific and technological infrastructure*. Washington, DC: Project Kaleidoscope. Retrieved November 8, 2008, from www.pkal.org/documents/ReportOnReportsII.cfm.

Rauckhorst, W. H., Czaja, J. A., & Baxter Magolda, M. (2001, July). *Measuring the impact of the undergraduate research experience on student intellectual development*. Paper presented at Project Kaleidoscope Summer Institute, Snowbird, UT.

Research Corporation. (2001). *Academic excellence: The sourcebook. A study of the role of research in the natural sciences at undergraduate institutions*. Tucson, AZ: Author.

Rosenbloom, S. R., & Way, N. (2004). Experiences of discrimination among African American, Asian American, and Latino adolescents in an urban high school. *Youth and Society, 35*(4), 420–451.

Rosser, S. V. (2001). Balancing: Survey of fiscal year 1997, 1998 and 1999 POWRE awardees. *Journal of Women and Minorities in Science and Engineering, 7*(1), 9–18.

Russell, S. H. (2005, November). *Evaluation of NSF support for undergraduate research opportunities: Survey of STEM graduates, draft final report*. Menlo Park, CA: SRI

International. Retrieved September 28, 2008, from www.sri.com/policy/csted/reports/university/documents/STEM%20report%20Nov%207%2005.pdf.

Russell, S. H., with Hancock, M. P., & McCullough, J. (2006). *Evaluation of NSF support for undergraduate research opportunities: Follow-up survey of undergraduate NSF program participants, draft final report.* Arlington, VA: SRI International.

Russell, S. H., Hancock, M. P., & McCullough, J. (2007). The pipeline: Benefits of undergraduate research experiences. *Science, 316*(5824), 548–549.

Ryder, J., Leach, J., & Driver, R. (1999). Undergraduate science students' images of science. *Journal of Research in Science Teaching, 36*(2), 331–346.

Sachs, P. (2008, October 7). City colleges students dive into scientific research. *Chi-Town Daily News.* Retrieved December 8, 2008, from www.chitowndailynews.org/Chicago_news/City_colleges_students_dive_into_scientific_research,17236.

Seidel, J. V. (1998). *The Ethnograph: A program for the computer assisted analysis of text-based data (version 5.0)* [Computer software]. Thousand Oaks, CA: Qualis Research/Scolari Sage Publications Software.

Seidman, E., Allen, L., Aber, J. L., Mitchell, C., & Feinman, J. (1994). The impact of school transitions in early adolescence on the self-system and social context of poor urban youth. *Child Development, 65*(2), 507–522.

Sellers, R. M., Caldwell, C. H., Schmeelk-Cone, K. H., & Zimmerman, M. A. (2003). Racial identity, racial discrimination, perceived stress, and psychological distress among African American young adults. *Journal of Health and Social Behavior, 44*(3), 302–317.

Service, R. F. (2002). New lure for young talent: Extreme research. *Science, 297*(5587), 1633–1634.

Seymour, E. (2002). Tracking the processes of change in U.S. undergraduate education in science, mathematics, engineering, and technology. *Science Education, 86*(1), 79–105.

Seymour, E. (2007, April). *The US experience of reform in science, technology, engineering, and mathematics (STEM) undergraduate education.* Paper presented at Policies and Practices for Academic Enquiry: An International Colloquium, Winchester, UK. Retrieved December 1, 2008, from http://portal-live.solent.ac.uk/university/rtconference/2007/resources/elaine_seymour.pdf.

Seymour, E., & Hewitt, N. M. (1997). *Talking about leaving: Why undergraduates leave the sciences.* Boulder, CO: Westview Press.

Seymour, E., Hunter, A.-B., Laursen, S., & DeAntoni, T. (2004). Establishing the benefits of research experiences for undergraduates: First findings from a three-year study. *Science Education, 88*(4), 493–534.

Shotten, H. J., Oosawhe, E.S.L., & Rosa, C. (2007). Stories of success: Experiences of American Indian students in a peer-mentoring retention program. *Review of Higher Education, 31*(1), 81–107.

Singngam, F. (2007, February 9). Undergrad research rising trend at UConn. *Daily Campus* [online edition]. Retrieved July 28, 2008, from http://media.www .dailycampus.com/media/storage/paper340/news/2007/02/09/News/ Undergrad.Research.Rising.Trend.At.Uconn-2709760.shtml.

Sirin, S. R. (2005). Socioeconomic status and academic achievement: A meta-analytic review of research. *Review of Educational Research, 75*(3), 417–453.

SOARS: Significant Opportunities in Atmospheric Research and Science. (2008, September 9). Retrieved December 1, 2008, from www.soars.ucar.edu/ index.php.

Sonnert, G., Fox, M. F., & Adkins, K. (2007). Undergraduate women in science and engineering: Effects of faculty, fields, and institutions over time. *Social Science Quarterly, 88*(5), 1333–1356.

Spencer, J. N., & Yoder, C. H. (1981). A survey of undergraduate research over the past decade. *Journal of Chemical Education, 58*(10), 780–786.

Spradley, J. P. (1980). *Participant observation.* New York: Holt.

Starr, I., Jr., Stokes, J., Jr., & West, L. B. (1919). The progress of undergraduate research in medical schools. *Science, 50*(1291), 308–311.

Steele, C. M. (1997). A threat in the air: How stereotypes shape intellectual identity and performance. *American Psychologist, 52*(6), 613–629.

Strauss, A. (1987). *Qualitative analysis for social scientists.* Cambridge: Cambridge University Press.

Sullivan, W. M., Colby, A., Welch Wegner, J., Bond, L., & Shulman, L. S. (2007). *Educating lawyers: Preparation for the profession of law.* San Francisco: Jossey-Bass.

Summers, M. F., & Hrabowski, F. A., III. (2006). Preparing minority scientists and engineers. *Science, 311*(5769), 1870–1871.

Tai, R. H., Sadler, P. M., & Mintzes, J. J. (2006). Factors influencing college science success. *Journal of College Science Teaching, 36*(1), 52–56.

Tapia, R., & Lanius, C. (2000, May). *Underrepresented minority achievement and course taking: The kindergarten-graduate continuum.* Paper presented at NISE Forum: Diversity and Equity Issues in Mathematics and Science Education, Detroit, MI. Retrieved October 17, 2008, from http://ceee.rice.edu/publications.html.

Taylor, E., & Antony, J. S. (2000). Stereotype threat reduction and wise schooling: Towards the successful socialization of African American doctoral students in education. *Journal of Negro Education, 69*(3), 184–198.

Thiry, H., & Laursen, S. L. (2009). *Evaluation of the undergraduate research programs of the Biological Sciences Initiative: Students' intellectual, personal and professional outcomes from participation in research.* Boulder: Ethnography & Evaluation Research, Center to Advance Research and Teaching in the Social Sciences, University of Colorado.

Thiry, H., Laursen, S. L., & Hunter, A.-B. (2010). Where do students become scientists? A comparative study of research and other sources of personal and professional gains for STEM undergraduates. *Journal of Higher Education.*

Thiry, H., Laursen, S. L., & Liston, C. (2007). (De)valuing teaching in the academy: Why are underrepresented graduate students overrepresented in teaching and outreach? *Journal of Women and Minorities in Science and Engineering, 13*(4), 391–419.

Tinto, V. (1975). Dropouts from higher education: A theoretical synthesis of recent research. *Review of Educational Research, 45*(1), 89–125.

Tinto, V. (1987). *Leaving college: Rethinking the causes and cures of student attrition.* Chicago: University of Chicago Press.

Tinto, V. (1993). *Leaving college: Rethinking the causes and cures of student attrition* (2nd ed.). Chicago: University of Chicago Press.

Tobias, S. (1990). *They're not dumb, they're different: Stalking the second tier.* Tucson, AZ: Research Corporation.

Tobochnik, J. (2001). The importance of undergraduate research. *American Journal of Physics, 69*(9), 933.

Treisman, U. (1992). Studying students studying calculus: A look at the lives of minority mathematics students in college. *College Mathematics Journal, 23*(5), 362–372.

Trzupek, L. S., & Knight, L. B., Jr. (2000). Chemical bonding between students and faculty: The chemistry program at Furman University. In M. Doyle (Ed.), *Academic excellence: The role of research in the physical sciences at undergraduate institutions* (pp. 101–129). Tucson, AZ: Research Corporation.

Tsui, L. (2007, Fall). Effective strategies to increase diversity in STEM fields: A review of the research literature. *Journal of Negro Education, 76*(1), 555–581.

U.S. Census Bureau. (2004, August 26). *Income stable, poverty up, numbers of Americans with and without health insurance rise, Census Bureau reports* [Press release]. Retrieved November 19, 2009, from www.census.gov/Press-Release/www/releases/archives/income_wealth/002484.html.

U.S. Census Bureau. (2007). *Educational attainment in the United States: 2007: Detailed tables.* Retrieved October 17, 2008, from www.census.gov/population/www/socdemo/education/cps2007.html.

U.S. Department of Education, National Center for Education Statistics. (2000). *Entry and persistence of women and minorities in college science and engineering education.* Washington, DC: Author.

Walczyk, J. J., Ramsay, L., & Zha, P. (2007). Obstacles to instructional innovation according to college science and mathematics faculty. *Journal of Research in Science Teaching, 44*(1), 85–106.

Walters, N. B. (1997, November). *Retaining aspiring scholars: Recruitment and retention of students of color in graduate and professional science degree programs.* Paper presented at the meeting of the Association for the Study of Higher Education, Albuquerque, NM.

Ward, C., Bennett, J. S., & Bauer, K. W. (2002). *Content analysis of undergraduate research student evaluations.* Retrieved March 2005, from www.udel.edu/RAIRE.

Ward, K., & Wolf-Wendel, L. (2004). Academic motherhood: Managing complex roles in research universities. *Review of Higher Education, 27*(2), 233–257.

Wells, R. (2008). The effects of social and cultural capital on student persistence: Are community colleges more meritocratic? *Community College Review, 36,* 25–46.

Wenzel, T. (2003, August). *Definition of undergraduate research.* Retrieved November 7, 2008, from www.bates.edu/x50818.xml.

Wieman, C. (2007). Why not try a scientific approach to science education? *Change, 39*(5), 9–15.

Wilson, R. (2000). Barriers to minority success in college science, mathematics, and engineering programs. In G. Campbell Jr., R. Denes, & C. Morrison (Eds.), *Access denied: Race, ethnicity, and the scientific enterprise.* New York: Oxford University Press.

Windham, T. L., Stevermer, A. J., & Anthes, R. A. (2004). SOARS: An overview of the program and its first 8 years. *Bulletin of the American Meteorological Society, 85*(1), 42–47.

Wong, C. A., Eccles, J. S., & Sameroff, A. (2003). The influence of ethnic discrimination and ethnic identification on African American adolescents' school and socioemotional adjustment. *Journal of Personality, 71*(6), 1197–1232.

Wood, W. B. (2003). Inquiry-based undergraduate teaching in the life sciences at large research universities: A perspective on the Boyer Commission Report. *Cell Biology Education, 2*(2), 112–116.

Wunsch, M. A. (1994). Developing mentoring programs: Major themes and issues. In M. A. Wunsch (Ed.), *Mentoring revisited: Making an impact on individuals and institutions* (pp. 27–34). New Directions for Teaching and Learning, no. 57. San Francisco: Jossey-Bass.

Zydney, A. L., Bennett, J. S., Shahid, A., & Bauer, K. W. (2002a). Faculty perspectives regarding the undergraduate research experience in science and engineering. *Journal of Engineering Education, 91*(3), 291–297.

Zydney, A. L., Bennett, J. S., Shahid, A., & Bauer, K. W. (2002b). Impact of undergraduate research experience in engineering. *Journal of Engineering Education, 91*(2), 151–157.

Index